P9-CEY-123

Betty Crocker®

One-Dish Family Favorites

Betty Crocker®

One-Dish Family Favorites

CASSEROLES, SKILLET MEALS,
STIR-FRIES, AND MORE
EASY, EVERYDAY DINNERS

General Mills, Inc.
Betty Crocker Kitchens

Director, Book and Online Publishing: Kim Walter

Manager, Book Publishing: Lois L. Tlusty

Editor: Heidi Losleben

Recipe Development and Testing: Betty Crocker Kitchens

Food Stylists: Betty Crocker Kitchens

Photography: General Mills Photo Studios and Mitch Mandel, Rodale Images (pages 62, 68, 74, 110, 138, 168, 175, 196, 198, and front and back covers)

Cover photo: Easy Cheesy Manicotti (page 197)

Cover design: Tara Long

Book design: Richard Oriolo and Tara Long

Notice

Mention of specific companies, organizations, or authorities in this book does not imply endorsement by the publisher, nor does mention of specific companies, organizations, or authorities imply that they endorse this book.

Internet addresses and telephone numbers given in this book were accurate at the time it went to press.

© 2006 by General Mills, Minneapolis, Minnesota

All rights reserved. No part of this publication may be reproduced or transmitted in any form or by any means, electronic or mechanical, including photocopying, recording, or any other information storage and retrieval system, without the written permission of the publisher.

Printed in the United States of America
Rodale Inc. makes every effort to use acid-free ♾, recycled paper ♻.

Published by arrangement with Wiley Publishing, Inc., Hoboken, New Jersey

Library of Congress Cataloging-in-Publication Data

Crocker, Betty.
Betty Crocker one-dish family favorites : casseroles, skillet meals, stir-fries, and more easy, everyday dinners.
p. cm.
Includes index.
ISBN-13 978–1–59486–503–9 hardcover
ISBN-10 1–59486–503–5 hardcover
1. One-dish meals. I. Title. II. Title: One-dish family favorites.
TX840.O53C76 2006
641.8'2—dc22 2006014111

6 8 10 9 7 5 direct-mail hardcover

RODALE
LIVE YOUR WHOLE LIFE™

We inspire and enable people to improve their lives and the world around them
For more of our products visit **rodalestore.com** or call 800-848-4735

The Betty Crocker Kitchens seal guarantees success in your kitchen. Every recipe has been tested in America's Most Trusted Kitchens™ to meet our high standards of reliability, easy preparation and great taste.

FIND MORE GREAT IDEAS AND SHOP FOR NAME-BRAND HOUSEWARES AT
BettyCrocker®.com

Dear Friends,

Are you a fan of one-stop shopping? Are you ready to go head-to-head with the daily question of "What's for Dinner?" Then you'll really enjoy *Betty Crocker One-Dish Family Favorites*. Make dinner easy and inviting with this fresh look at what can go into just one dish—and come out a meal.

Inside, you'll find more than 250 recipes that give you dinner all in one dish. They are quick to fix and range from tried-and-true classics like Easy Cheesy Manicotti and Hearty Tomato Soup, to updated flavors such as Lamb and Lentil Casserole and Ham and Brie Bake. These super convenient recipes include soups; stews and chilies; skillet dishes; casseroles, gratins and pizzas; as well as slow cooker suppers, salads and grilled meals. Who could ask for more?

All the recipes use everyday, on-hand ingredients and provide big-easy taste in one dish. There's something to please just about everyone, and cleanup is a snap too. It's minimum fuss and maximum results for time-crunched home cooks.

There are also helpful sections, including Tools of the Trade, which offers tips on choosing cookware; stocking your pantry; freezing and microwaving meals; and potluck pointers. Flavor Boosters suggests ways to enhance your meal with add-ins and toppings and Lighten Up shows you how to trim fat and calories from your diet. There's a one-dish meal for (almost) every occasion such as potlucks, brunches and casual at-home gatherings.

Betty Crocker One-Dish Family Favorites is your ticket to an easy fabulous family meal.

Warmly,
Betty Crocker

Contents

Tools of the Trade 8

Flavor Boosters 12

Lighten Up 13

Freezer-Friendly Foods 14

Zap It! Reheating Foods in the Microwave 15

One-Dish Meals for (Almost) Every Occasion 16

Helpful Hints for Making and Taking Dishes to Share 18

Hearty Soups, Stews, and Chilies 21

Sizzling Skillets and Stir-Fries 69

Comforting Casseroles 139

Satisfying Slow Cooker Suppers 199

Pizzas with Pizzazz 247

Main-Dish Salads 279

One-Dish Grilling 333

Helpful Nutrition and Cooking Information 360

Metric Conversion Guide 362

Index 363

Tools of the Trade

To whip up great-tasting one-dish meals, it's important to have the right utensils on hand. Whether you're adding to an already extensive collection of pots and pans, or you're just starting to stock your kitchen cabinets, it's wise to buy good-quality cookware. You—and your family—will reap the benefits for years to come.

One-Dish Cookware Basics

Most recipes in this book call for one of the standard-size utensils specified on the following page. If you're unsure of the capacity of a dish, look for measurements on the bottom or under the handles. Or, use a measuring cup to see how many cups of water it takes to fill the dish to the brim.

DISH IT UP

	DESCRIPTION	SIZES	APPROXIMATE VOLUME	GOOD FOR
Baking Dish	A square or rectangular shallow dish that is ovenproof	8 × 8 × 2-inch 11 × 7 × 1 1/2-inch 13 × 9 × 2-inch	8 cups 6 cups 15 cups	Casseroles, lasagna
Casserole	A covered or uncovered ovenproof utensil, often round or oval in shape, in which food can be baked and served	1 1/2-quart 2-quart 3-quart	1 1/2 cups 8 cups 12 cups	Casseroles, stews, cassoulets
Dutch Oven/ Stockpot	A cast-iron pot or kettle with a close-fitting cover; some Dutch ovens have handles	4- to 14-quart	16–56 cups	Soups, stews, chilies
Saucepan	A covered or uncovered round and generally deep pan	1- to 4-quart	4–16 cups	Soups
Skillet/frying pan	A covered or uncovered shallow pan with flared or straight sides and one long handle	8-inch 10-inch 12-inch		Stir-fries, skillet dinners
Slow Cooker	An electric "casserole" with a ceramic liner; heating coils in the outer metal shell heat the liner	1- to 6-quart	4–24 cups	Soups, stews, chilies, less tender cuts of meat
Wok	A round-bottomed cooking utensil with two handles, typically made of rolled steel	Varies		Stir-fries

Don't Have It?

To get the best results, it's a good idea to stick with the cooking utensil specified in the recipe. In a pinch, use the following substitutions:

- For a 1- to 1 1/2-quart casserole, use a square baking dish, 8 × 8 × 2 inches.
- For a 2-quart casserole, use a rectangular baking dish, 11 × 7 × 1 1/2 inches.
- For a 3-quart casserole, use a rectangular baking dish, 13 × 9 × 2 inches.

Skillet Smarts

- Use a flat-bottomed pan of medium weight for even, quick heat and uniform cooking.
- If you're cooking with gas, adjust the flame to the pan size; on an electric stove, fit the heating unit to the size of the pan.
- Use the lowest setting possible to achieve the desired cooking method. Turning the heat up and down can create hot spots and cause sticking.
- Always use the skillet size called for in a recipe. Not only does it affect the cooking time, it also affects the evaporation of liquids.
- Different skillet materials have different heating properties. See the chart that follows for more information.

Common Materials of One-Dish Utensils

Although you may be tempted to buy an entire set of pots and pans at once, keep in mind that no one metal is ideal for all purposes. Look for utensils and materials that suit your personal style and the kinds of food you commonly cook. Remember, there's no rule about having all your pots and pans match!

POTS AND PANS 101

	PROS	CONS
Aluminum	Conducts heat well Moderately priced Lightweight and sturdy	Can react with acidic ingredients Finish can scratch
Anodized Aluminum	Extremely hard metal surface Low-stick Available in chip-, stain- and scratch-resistant finishes Good for freezer Can go from stovetop to oven	Finish can spot and fade in dishwasher
Cast Iron (regular)	Retains heat well Fairly inexpensive Has a nonstick finish after seasoning Doesn't react with or absorb food flavors (after seasoning)	Doesn't conduct heat well Often lends a metallic taste to foods Tends to rust
Ceramic/ Stoneware	Retains heat well Available in many styles and motifs Most can go from freezer to microwave or oven to dishwasher	May discolor over time
Copper	Conducts heat well Heavy duty Lined with tin or stainless steel to keep it from interacting with certain foods	Very expensive Not nonstick Requires polishing Needs to be relined about every 10 years
Earthen Ware	Retains heat well Hard and durable Can be washed in dishwasher	Doesn't conduct heat well Must cool slowly and completely before washing to prevent cracking
Enamelware (cast iron or stainless steel)	Durable Flameproof and ovenproof Good for freezer Can go from stovetop to oven Enameled *cast iron* conducts heat well Easy to clean Doesn't react with acids	Enamel can chip Enameled *stainless steel* does not conduct heat well Light-colored enamelware may not brown foods as easily as dark-colored and may discolor May crack if overheated
Glass	Retains heat well Economical and practical Coordinates well with other tableware Microwave and dishwasher safe Nonreactive to acids Easy to clean	Doesn't conduct heat well Can break easily with sudden temperature changes
Stainless Steel	Doesn't react with acidic or alkaline foods Corrosion resistant Extremely durable Easy to clean Doesn't easily scratch or dent	Doesn't conduct heat well Can burn food in spots

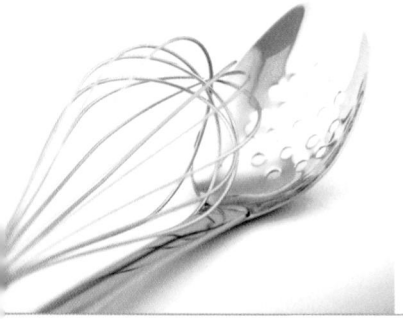

Flavor Boosters

One-dish meals are flavorful in and of themselves, but if you'd like to add more zip or zest to casseroles, skillets, soups or salads, try the following add-ins and toppings:

- Add plain or flavored feta cheese to a salad.
- Sprinkle shredded Swiss cheese over individual servings of soup.
- Intensify the flavor of vegetables by seasoning them with balsamic vinegar or soy sauce.
- Use a flavored pasta sauce instead of plain.
- Sprinkle canned French-fried onions over the top of casseroles.
- Add a dash of soy sauce to skillet and stir-fry dishes.
- Stir a tablespoon or two of pesto into a pot of soup.
- Substitute flavored mayo for plain in pasta salads.

Lighten Up

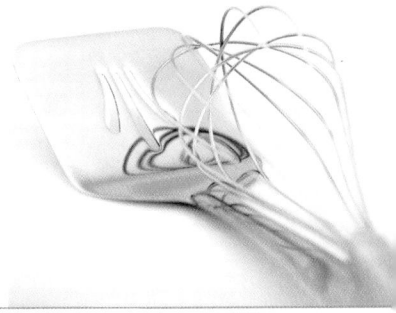

In addition to being convenient, flavorful and easy to clean up, one-dish meals can also be good for you. To trim the fat and calories from your diet:

- Grease baking dishes and skillets with cooking spray. In addition to the cans you can buy at stores, you can also buy refillable spray canisters at kitchenware shops and fill with your own olive or canola oil.
- Use fat-free or reduced-fat dairy products such as milk, buttermilk, yogurt, cottage cheese and other cheeses.
- Use egg whites or fat-free egg product (made of egg whites and flavoring) instead of whole eggs.
- Reduce the amount of meat in a recipe but keep the portion size the same by upping the amount of beans, rice, vegetables, etc.
- Reduce the amount of cheese and nuts in recipes. Try sprinkling them on top of a dish rather than mixing them in.
- Trim excess fat from meat and poultry.
- Use fat-free or reduced-sodium broths.

Freezer-Friendly Foods

One benefit of one-dish meals is that they can be made ahead and stored in the freezer. To get the best results when freezing, keep the following in mind:

- A one-dish meal that has been frozen needs to be baked slightly longer than one that is baked immediately after being made. Most need about 10 to 15 minutes longer, but it's a good idea to check the dish during baking time and adjust the time accordingly.
- Casseroles may be frozen before or after they are baked.
- Recipes with a low-fat sauce or condensed-soup base usually freeze well.
- If a recipe calls for sour cream, wait to add the sour cream after thawing and reheating the dish.
- Crisp toppings, such as nuts, crushed chips or bacon bits, should be added after the dish is thawed.
- Fresh potatoes do not freeze well. Some dairy products such as sour cream (see above), half-and-half and ricotta and cottage cheese are also not recommended for freezing.
- To make sure meats, vegetables, pastas and grains don't overcook when reheated, cook them just until tender the first time around.
- Cool foods before placing them in the freezer.
- Store foods at 0°F or colder.
- Freeze foods in sizes that are suitable for your family. Individual sizes are a good idea, as is enough for one family meal.
- Use airtight containers that are microwavable or can be go directly from the freezer to the oven.
- For best quality, use frozen casseroles within three months.

Zap It! Reheating Foods in the Microwave

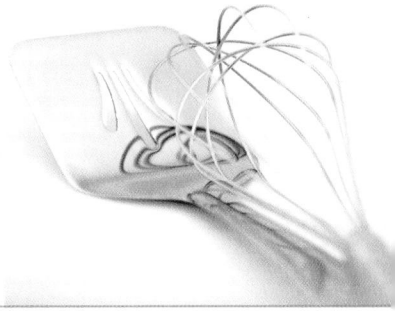

A microwave makes quick work of reheating one-dish foods. For food-safety reasons, it's recommended to bring the internal temperature to 140°F. An instant-read thermometer is helpful to determine whether the food is hot enough at its center. Do not leave a thermometer in the food while microwaving; use it to check the temperature only after reheating.

- Moist foods reheat best, and covering foods adds speed and even heating. Pizzas and other crisp or crunchy foods reheat best when heated on a browning dish or a microwave rack, so the bottom doesn't get soggy.
- Tightly cover casseroles with microwavable plastic food wrap to speed reheating. Fold back a corner or cut a few slits in the plastic wrap to vent the steam. Stir or rotate the casserole once or twice during reheating. Casseroles that can't be stirred, such as lasagna, benefit from a standing time to allow the heat to equalize throughout the food.
- Smaller, individual servings heat more quickly than full recipes because the microwaves are able to penetrate the food more deeply and heat the center more quickly.
- To avoid overcooking, casseroles containing eggs, cheese or large chunks of meat should be heated at a lower power setting.

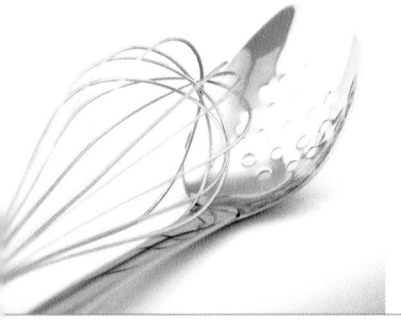

One-Dish Meals for (Almost) Every Occasion

No doubt about it: one-dish meals are varied and versatile. From easy, cheesy casseroles and slow-simmering slow cooker dishes to quick stir-fries and toss-together salads, there's a flavor and a cooking method to please just about everyone.

Kid-Friendly

The following yummy recipes feature familiar flavors kids love, from noodles and cheese to taco chips and tater nuggets.

Baked Ravioli and Meatballs, page 153
Four-Cheese Pesto Pizza, page 276
Cheeseburger Pizza, page 250
Cheesy Lasagna Soup, page 22
Cheesy Pizza Casserole, page 150
Classic Pizza, page 271
Deep-Dish Spaghetti Pie, page 151
Double-Cheese Pepperoni Pizza, page 268
Easy Taco Dinner, page 73
Hearty Tomato Soup, page 41
Sausage and Pizza Bake, page 179
Spicy Southwest Chicken Kabobs, page 339
Swiss Steak Supper, page 209
Texas Tater Casserole, page 141

Best for Brunch

Served with a cup of hot coffee, a glass of fresh OJ and a sprinkling of fresh fruit, these one-dish meals make for a virtually fuss-free brunch.

Asparagus-Dijon-Chicken Fettuccine, page 83
Breakfast Pizza, page 269
Caesar Salad with Lobster, page 323
Caribbean Shrimp Salad, page 317
Chicken and Berries Salad, page 304
Chicken-Vegetable Strata, page 162
Corn, Ham and Potato Scallop, page 222
Easy Cheese Strata, page 193
Ham and Brie Bake, page 178
Pork and Julienne Potatoes, page 112
Swiss Potato and Cheese Skillet, page 134
Ten-Minute Ham Salad, page 311
Turkey Salad with Fruit, page 309
Vegetable Strata, page 192

Good for Casual At-Home Gatherings

Hey, hey, the gang's all here so—instead of being stuck in the kitchen—why not enjoy their company with one of these easy-to-prepare, yet impressive, meals?

Beef Stroganoff, page 71
Beer and Cheese Soup, page 29
Baked Ravioli and Meatballs, page 153
Easy Bean and Kielbasa Soup, page 238
Easy Cheesy Manicotti, page 197
Easy Philly Cheesesteak Pizza, page 253
Easy Turkey Lasagna, page 175
Four-Cheese Pesto Pizza, page 276
French Onion Soup, page 240
Greek Pita Pizzas, page 275
New England Clam Chowder, page 58
Paella on the Grill, page 342
Pesto Chicken Packets, page 345
Quick Lasagna, page 143
Savory Pot Roast, page 207
Skewered Steak Dinner, page 334
Southwestern Chicken BLT Salad, page 285
Steak and Potato Soup, page 23
Steak Caesar Salad, page 280
Taco Pizza, page 249
Thai Chicken Pizzas, page 297
Turkey Chili Verde, page 215
Tuscan Panzanella Salad, page 324

Great Make-and-Take Dishes

Your schedule is packed; how are you going to find the time to make a potluck dish for the PTA meeting at 7:00? Let these make-ahead and slow cooker dishes do the work.

Dill-Turkey Chowder, page 217
Easy Bean and Kielbasa Soup, page 238
Easy Pork Chili, page 237
Greek Chicken Salad, page 294
Hearty Beef Chili, page 200
Italian Beef Stew, page 201
Ratatouille Bean Stew, page 241
Ravioli with Sausage and Peppers, page 224
Southwestern Pork Stew, page 227
Turkey Chili Verde, page 215
Turkey Tabbouleh Salad, page 305

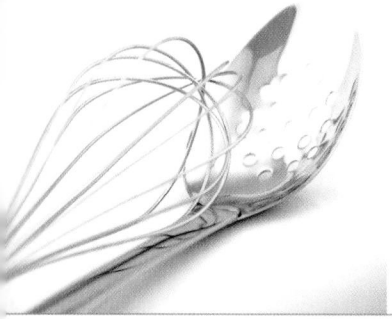

Helpful Hints for Making and Taking Dishes to Share

Whether you're toting treats to a potluck or a picnic, it's important, for food safety reasons, to keep them at a proper temperature. Insulated coolers and thermoses were invented for that very purpose. Before you transfer any food to a storage container, make sure it's either thoroughly heated or thoroughly chilled. Partially cooked foods should not be packed.

- Preheat or chill thermoses for at least 30 minutes before adding food. To preheat, pour boiling or very hot water in the thermos and replace the top. To cool a thermos, fill it with ice water and replace the top. Cool down insulated coolers by filling them with ice water or ice cubes. Close the lid and allow the cooler to chill for 45 minutes to 1 hour.
- Keep hot and cold foods separated.
- For more insulation, wrap several towels or layers of newspaper around hot food containers.
- Place frozen ice packs or bags of ice around or on top of cold foods.
- Don't peek! To keep hot foods hot and cold foods cold, try not to open thermoses and coolers until you are ready to eat.

Slow Cooker Take-Along Tips

- As mentioned above, wrapping a towel or newspaper around your container will help insulate it. There are also insulated totes designed specifically for slow cookers.
- To make sure your slow cooker stays flat in your car, place it in a box or other container. Keep in mind the floor of your car is a flat surface—the seat of your car is not.
- Attach rubber bands around the handles and lid to secure the lid when traveling.
- Serve the food within an hour, or plug in the slow cooker and set it on the Low heat (or "Keep Warm") setting to stay warm for up to 2 hours.
- Be sure to put your name or an identifiable mark somewhere on your slow cooker. Many slow cookers look alike, so it's easy to grab the wrong one.

Hearty Soups, Stews, and Chilies

Cheesy Lasagna Soup 22
Steak and Potato Soup 23
African Peanut–Chicken Soup 24
Chicken and Vegetable Bow-Tie Soup 25
Oriental Chicken Noodle Soup 26
Hearty Turkey-Barley Soup 27
Turkey-Ginger Tortellini Soup 28
Beer and Cheese Soup 29
Black Bean Soup 31
Black Bean and Salsa Noodle Soup 33
Italian Sausage and Mostaccioli Soup 34
Rich Cream of Mushroom Soup 36
Spicy Noodle Soup 37
Home-Style Potato Soup 38
Cream of Broccoli Soup 39
Ratatouille Soup 40
Hearty Tomato Soup 41
Easy Cheesy Vegetable Soup 43
Basil Rice Soup 44
Ham 'n Corn Chowder 46
Chunky Vegetable Chowder 47
Beef-Barley-Vegetable Stew 48
Quick Beef and Vegetable Stew 49
Classic Beef Stew 50
Greek Beef and Onion Stew 51
New England Baked Bean Stew 52
Chicken Stew with Potatoes 53
Zesty Autumn Pork Stew 55
Southwestern Pork and Potato Stew 56
Spicy Fish Stew 57
New England Clam Chowder 58
Oyster Stew 59
Shrimp Gumbo 60
Vegetarian Chili 61
Classic Chili 63
Buffalo Chicken Chili 64
Spicy Chicken Chili 66
White Chili 67

Cheesy Lasagna Soup

PREP 20 min COOK 20 min BROIL 2 min SERVINGS 6

- 1 pound lean ground beef
- 1 medium onion, sliced
- 2 large green bell peppers, cut into 1-inch pieces
- 2 cloves garlic, finely chopped
- 2 cups water
- 2 cans (14 1/2 ounces each) diced tomatoes in olive oil, garlic and spices, undrained
- 1 can (6 ounces) tomato paste
- 2 cups uncooked mafalda (mini-lasagna noodle) pasta or wide egg noodles (4 ounces)
- 1 tablespoon packed brown sugar
- 1 1/2 teaspoons Italian seasoning, crumbled
- 1/4 teaspoon pepper
- 1 1/2 cups Italian-style croutons
- 1 1/2 cups shredded part-skim mozzarella cheese (6 ounces)

1. Cook beef, onion, bell peppers and garlic in 4-quart Dutch oven over medium heat 8 to 10 minutes, stirring occasionally, until beef is brown and onion is tender; drain. Stir water, diced tomatoes and tomato paste into beef mixture.
2. Stir in remaining ingredients except croutons and cheese. Heat to boiling; reduce heat to low. Cover and simmer about 10 minutes, stirring occasionally, until pasta is tender.
3. Set oven control to broil. Pour hot soup into 6 ovenproof soup bowls or casseroles (do not use glass). Top each with 1/4 cup croutons. Sprinkle with cheese. Broil soup with tops 3 to 4 inches from heat 1 to 2 minutes or until cheese is melted.

1 SERVING Calories 430 (Calories from Fat 160) | Fat 18g (Saturated 8g) | Cholesterol 70mg | Sodium 910mg | Carbohydrate 40g (Dietary Fiber 5g) | Protein 27g % DAILY VALUE Vitamin A 28% | Vitamin C 64% | Calcium 28% | Iron 20% EXCHANGES 2 Starch, 2 Vegetable, 2 1/2 Medium-Fat Meat, 1 Fat CARBOHYDRATE CHOICES 2 1/2

BETTY'S TIP

Instead of using your broiler to melt the cheese, why not let the hot soup melt the cheese on its own? It cuts down on prep time, and kids will love the ooey-gooey strings of cheese that form as a result.

Steak and Potato Soup

PREP 20 min COOK 25 min SERVINGS 10

- 2-pound boneless beef sirloin steak (1 inch thick)
- 2 tablespoons vegetable oil
- 1 1/2 cups coarsely chopped onions
- 3 cloves garlic, finely chopped
- 2 pounds small red potatoes, cut into 3/4-inch pieces
- 3 cups baby-cut carrots, cut lengthwise into fourths
- 1 bag (1 pound) frozen cut green beans
- 2 tablespoons chopped fresh or 2 teaspoons dried basil leaves
- 1/2 teaspoon freshly ground black pepper
- 6 cans (14 ounces each) beef broth
- 3 tablespoons steak sauce

1. Cut beef into 1/4-inch strips; cut strips into 1-inch pieces. Heat oil in 8-quart stockpot or Dutch oven over medium-high heat. Cook and stir beef in oil 4 to 5 minutes or until brown; add onion and garlic. Cook and stir 2 minutes.
2. Stir in remaining ingredients. Heat to boiling; reduce heat to low. Cover and simmer 12 to 15 minutes, stirring occasionally, until vegetables are tender.

1 SERVING Calories 330 (Calories from Fat 90) | Fat 10g (Saturated 3g) | Cholesterol 80mg | Sodium 960mg | Carbohydrate 28g (Dietary Fiber 4g) | Protein 33g % DAILY VALUE Vitamin A 100% | Vitamin C 20% | Calcium 6% | Iron 30% EXCHANGES 1 1/2 Starch, 1 Vegetable, 4 Very Lean Meat, 1 Fat CARBOHYDRATE CHOICES 2

BETTY'S TIP

It's a snap to cut the steak into slices of even thickness if you pop it into the freezer for about 20 minutes first.

African Peanut–Chicken Soup

PREP 20 min COOK 20 min SERVINGS 6

- 1 tablespoon vegetable oil
- 1 1/4 pounds boneless, skinless chicken breasts, cut into 1-inch pieces
- 1 small onion, cut into thin wedges
- 1 clove garlic, finely chopped
- 2 medium dark–orange sweet potatoes, peeled and coarsely chopped
- 1 medium green bell pepper, chopped (1 cup)
- 2 cans (14 ounces each) chicken broth
- 1 can (11 1/2 ounces) tomato juice
- 1/2 teaspoon ground ginger
- 1/8 to 1/4 teaspoon ground red pepper (cayenne)
- 1/2 cup crunchy peanut butter

1. Heat oil in 4-quart saucepan or Dutch oven over medium-high heat. Cook and stir chicken, onion and garlic in oil 4 to 5 minutes or until chicken is no longer pink in center.
2. Stir in remaining ingredients except peanut butter. Heat to boiling; reduce heat to low. Cover and simmer 10 to 12 minutes, stirring occasionally, until vegetables are tender.
3. Stir in peanut butter. Cook over low heat, stirring constantly, until peanut butter is blended and soup is hot.

1 SERVING Calories 355 (Calories from Fat 155) | Fat 17g (Saturated 4g) | Cholesterol 50mg | Sodium 980mg | Carbohydrate 22g (Dietary Fiber 4g) | Protein 28g % DAILY VALUE Vitamin A 100% | Vitamin C 34% | Calcium 4% | Iron 10% EXCHANGES 1 1/2 Starch, 3 Lean Meat, 1 1/2 Fat CARBOHYDRATE CHOICES 1 1/2

BETTY'S TIP

For a "soup-er" special presentation, plop a mound of hot cooked rice in the middle of each bowl of soup and sprinkle chopped peanuts, flaked coconut and sliced green onions over the top.

Chicken and Vegetable Bow-Tie Soup

PREP 10 min COOK 20 min SERVINGS 6

1 teaspoon vegetable oil

1 stalk celery, thinly sliced

3 cans (14 ounces each) chicken broth

2 cups water

1 bag (1 pound) frozen broccoli, carrots and cauliflower (or other combination)

2 cups cubed cooked chicken

1 cup uncooked farfalle (bow-tie) pasta or wide egg noodles (2 ounces)

1/4 teaspoon poultry seasoning

1. Heat oil in 4-quart saucepan or Dutch oven over medium-high heat. Cook celery in oil 2 to 3 minutes, stirring frequently, until crisp-tender.
2. Add broth and water; heat to boiling. Add frozen vegetables; heat to boiling.
3. Stir in remaining ingredients; reduce heat to low. Simmer about 15 minutes, stirring occasionally, until pasta and vegetables are tender.

1 SERVING Calories 180 (Calories from Fat 55) | Fat 6g (Saturated 1g) | Cholesterol 40mg | Sodium 990mg | Carbohydrate 11g (Dietary Fiber 3g) | Protein 20g % DAILY VALUE Vitamin A 40% | Vitamin C 20% | Calcium 4% | Iron 8% EXCHANGES 1/2 Starch, 1 Vegetable, 2 1/2 Very Lean Meat, 1/2 Fat CARBOHYDRATE CHOICES 1

BETTY'S TIP

No bow-tie pasta in the pantry? Other medium-size pasta shapes, such as shells, rotini or fusilli, work too. Up the fun factor by mixing several shapes.

Oriental Chicken Noodle Soup

PREP 10 min COOK 10 min SERVINGS 4

- 3 cups water
- 1 package (3 ounces) chicken-flavor ramen noodle soup mix
- 2 cups cut-up cooked chicken
- 2 medium stalks bok choy (with leaves), cut into 1/4-inch slices
- 1 medium carrot, sliced (1/2 cup)
- 1 teaspoon sesame oil, if desired

1. Heat water to boiling in 3-quart saucepan. Break block of noodles; reserve seasoning packet. Stir noodles, chicken, bok choy and carrot into water. Heat to boiling; reduce heat to low. Simmer uncovered 3 minutes, stirring occasionally.
2. Stir in contents of seasoning packet and sesame oil.

1 SERVING Calories 205 (Calories from Fat 70) | Fat 8g (Saturated 2g) | Cholesterol 60mg | Sodium 340mg | Carbohydrate 11g (Dietary Fiber 1g) | Protein 22g % DAILY VALUE Vitamin A 62% | Vitamin C 4% | Calcium 2% | Iron 8% EXCHANGES 1/2 Starch, 1 Vegetable, 2 1/2 Lean Meat CARBOHYDRATE CHOICES 1

BETTY'S TIP

If you wind up with more bok choy than you need, use the extra to make a simple side salad. Top with a few sliced radishes and a tangy vinaigrette dressing.

Hearty Turkey-Barley Soup

PREP **5 min** COOK **35 min** SERVINGS **4**

1 pound ground turkey breast

2/3 cup uncooked quick-cooking barley

2 cans (14 ounces each) beef broth

1 can (14 1/2 ounces) diced tomatoes, undrained

1 jar (1 pound 10 ounces) tomato pasta sauce (any variety)

2 cups (from 1-pound bag) frozen sweet peas, potatoes and carrots (or other combination)

1. Cook turkey in 4-quart Dutch oven over medium heat 8 to 10 minutes, stirring occasionally, until no longer pink; drain.
2. Stir barley, broth, tomatoes and pasta sauce into turkey. Heat to boiling, stirring occasionally; reduce heat to low. Cover and simmer 15 minutes.
3. Stir in frozen vegetables. Cover and simmer about 10 minutes or until barley is tender.

1 SERVING Calories 380 (Calories from Fat 80) | Fat 9g (Saturated 2g) | Cholesterol 50mg | Sodium 1400mg | Carbohydrate 51g (Dietary Fiber 7g) | Protein 24g % DAILY VALUE Vitamin A 64% | Vitamin C 24% | Calcium 8% | Iron 16% EXCHANGES 3 Starch, 1 Vegetable, 2 Lean Meat CARBOHYDRATE CHOICES 3

BETTY'S TIP

Quick-cooking barley is aptly named. It takes only 10 to 12 minutes to cook; regular barley needs 45 to 50 minutes. This hardy grain is also packed with protein—1 cup has the same amount as an 8-ounce glass of milk.

Turkey-Ginger Tortellini Soup

PREP 15 min COOK 20 min SERVINGS 4

- 1 package (7 ounces) dried cheese-filled tortellini
- 2 1/4 cups water
- 2 tablespoons rice wine or white wine vinegar
- 2 tablespoons soy sauce
- 1 can (10 1/2 ounces) condensed chicken broth
- 1 to 2 tablespoons finely chopped fresh gingerroot or 1 to 2 teaspoons ground ginger
- 2 cups sliced bok choy (stems and leaves)
- 2 cups cut-up cooked turkey
- 2 green onions, sliced
- 1 cup enoki mushrooms (3 1/2 ounces)

1. Cook and drain tortellini as directed on package; set aside. Heat water, vinegar, soy sauce, broth and gingerroot to boiling in 3-quart saucepan; reduce heat to low.
2. Stir bok choy stems (reserve leaves), turkey and onions into saucepan. Simmer uncovered 15 minutes. Stir in bok choy leaves, mushrooms and tortellini. Simmer just until leaves are wilted.

1 SERVING Calories 235 (Calories from Fat 80) | Fat 9g (Saturated 3g) | Cholesterol 100mg | Sodium 830mg | Carbohydrate 12g (Dietary Fiber 1g) | Protein 26g % DAILY VALUE Vitamin A 28% | Vitamin C 14% | Calcium 8% | Iron 12% EXCHANGES 1/2 Starch, 1 Vegetable, 3 Lean Meat CARBOHYDRATE CHOICES 1

BETTY'S TIP

Finely chopping the fresh ginger takes a bit more time than using ginger from a can, but the extra flavor is worth it. It's hard to believe those gnarled-looking roots you see at the grocery store taste so sweet and delicious.

Beer and Cheese Soup

PREP 10 min COOK 45 min SERVINGS 5

- 2 tablespoons butter or margarine
- 1 medium onion, chopped (1/2 cup)
- 1 can or bottle (12 ounces) beer
- 1 medium carrot, finely chopped (1/2 cup)
- 1 medium stalk celery, finely chopped (1/2 cup)
- 2 cups chicken broth
- 1 teaspoon salt
- 1 teaspoon ground cumin
- 1/4 teaspoon ground nutmeg
- Dash of ground cloves
- Dash of pepper
- 1 cup sour cream
- 4 ounces Cheddar or Monterey Jack cheese, cut into 1/4-inch cubes (1 cup)

1. Melt butter in 2-quart saucepan over medium heat. Cook onion in butter, stirring occasionally, until tender. Stir beer, carrot and celery into butter. Heat to boiling; reduce heat to low. Cover and simmer 10 minutes.
2. Stir in remaining ingredients except sour cream and cheese. Heat to boiling; reduce heat to low. Cover and simmer 30 minutes; remove from heat. Stir in sour cream. Sprinkle with cheese.

1 SERVING Calories 265 (Calories from Fat 200) | Fat 22g (Saturated 13g) | Cholesterol 65mg | Sodium 1090mg | Carbohydrate 9g (Dietary Fiber 1g) | Protein 10g % DAILY VALUE Vitamin A 58% | Vitamin C 2% | Calcium 18% | Iron 2% EXCHANGES 1/2 Starch, 1/2 High-Fat Meat, 4 Fat CARBOHYDRATE CHOICES 1/2

BETTY'S TIP

Add a little crunch to this creamy soup by tossing a handful of freshly popped popcorn over each bowl before serving.

Black Bean Soup

PREP 10 min COOK 30 min SERVINGS 4

- 1 medium onion
- 1 large clove garlic
- 1 medium carrot
- 1 medium stalk celery
- Parsley sprigs
- 1 slice bacon
- 1 can (14 1/2 ounces) ready-to-serve chicken broth
- 1/2 teaspoon dried oregano leaves
- 1/2 teaspoon crushed red pepper
- 1 can (15 ounces) black beans
- 4 lemon wedges

1. Peel and chop the onion. Peel and finely chop the garlic. Peel and coarsely chop the carrot. Coarsely chop the celery.
2. Rinse springs of parsley with cool water, and pat dry with a paper towel. Chop enough parsley leaves into small pieces on a cutting board using a chef's knife to measure about 2 tablespoons, or place the leafy portion of the parsley in a small bowl or cup and snip into very small pieces with kitchen scissors. Discard the stems.
3. Cut bacon slice crosswise into 1/2-inch pieces. Cook the bacon in the saucepan over medium heat 1 minute, stirring constantly. Do not drain.
4. Add the onion and garlic to the bacon. Cook about 5 minutes, stirring frequently, until onion is tender when pierced with a fork and beginning to turn yellow. Bacon will still be soft. Remove the saucepan from the heat.
5. Stir in the chicken broth, carrot, celery, parsley, oregano and red pepper. Heat to boiling over high heat. Once mixture is boiling, reduce heat just enough so mixture bubbles gently. Cover and cook 10 minutes.
6. While broth mixture is cooking, drain the black beans in a strainer, and rinse with cool water. Measure out 1/2 cup of the beans. Place the 1/2 cup beans in a small bowl, and mash them with a fork.
7. Stir the whole beans and the mashed beans into the broth mixture. Cook about 1 minute or until beans are heated. Serve soup with lemon wedges.

1 SERVING Calories 120 (Calories from Fat 30) | Fat 3g (Saturated 1.5g) | Cholesterol 5mg | Sodium 770mg | Carbohydrate 18g (Dietary Fiber 6g) | Protein 10g % DAILY VALUE Vitamin A 50% | Vitamin C 8% | Calcium 6% | Iron 10% EXCHANGES 1 Starch, 1 Vegetable, 1 Fat CARBOHYDRATE CHOICES 1

BETTY'S TIP

Before adding the chicken broth, remove the saucepan containing the hot bacon fat and onion from the heat to prevent spattering and steam.

Black Bean and Salsa Noodle Soup

PREP **10 min** COOK **10 min** SERVINGS **6**

3 cans (14 1/2 ounces each) vegetable broth

1 jar (16 ounces) salsa

1 can (15 ounces) black beans, rinsed and drained

1 can (11 ounces) whole-kernel corn, drained

1 package (5 ounces) Japanese curly noodles or 5 ounces uncooked spaghetti

1/3 cup chopped fresh cilantro

1 tablespoon lime juice

1 teaspoon chili powder

1/4 teaspoon ground cumin

1/4 teaspoon pepper

2 tablespoons shredded Parmesan cheese

1. Heat broth to boiling in 4-quart Dutch oven. Stir in remaining ingredients except cheese; reduce heat to medium.
2. Cook 5 to 6 minutes, stirring occasionally, until noodles are tender. Sprinkle with cheese.

1 SERVING Calories 220 (Calories from Fat 20) | Fat 2g (Saturated 1g) | Cholesterol 0mg | Sodium 1660mg | Carbohydrate 48g (Dietary Fiber 8g) | Protein 10g % DAILY VALUE Vitamin A 30% | Vitamin C 14% | Calcium 12% | Iron 22% EXCHANGES 2 Starch, 2 Vegetable CARBOHYDRATE CHOICES 2 1/2

BETTY'S TIP

Store a bunch of fresh cilantro, stems down, in a glass of water and cover with a plastic bag. It will keep up to a week if you change the water every 2 or 3 days. When you're ready to use the cilantro, wash and dry with paper towels, then chop. Chopped fresh parsley can be substituted for the cilantro.

Italian Sausage and Mostaccioli Soup

PREP **10 min** COOK **25 min** SERVINGS **6**

- 1 pound turkey Italian sausage links, cut into 1-inch pieces
- 2 cups broccoli flowerets
- 1 cup uncooked mostaccioli or penne pasta (3 ounces)
- 2 1/2 cups water
- 1/2 teaspoon dried basil leaves
- 1/4 teaspoon fennel seed, crushed
- 1/4 teaspoon pepper
- 1 medium onion, chopped (1/2 cup)
- 1 clove garlic, finely chopped
- 1 can (28 ounces) roma (plum) tomatoes, undrained
- 1 can (10 1/2 ounces) condensed beef broth

1. Cook sausage in 4-quart Dutch oven over medium-high heat, stirring occasionally, until brown; drain.
2. Stir in remaining ingredients, breaking up tomatoes. Heat to boiling; reduce heat to medium-low. Cover and cook about 15 minutes, stirring occasionally, until pasta is tender.

1 SERVING Calories 310 (Calories from Fat 90) | Fat 10g (Saturated 3g) | Cholesterol 45mg | Sodium 2080mg | Carbohydrate 26g (Dietary Fiber 3g) | Protein 29g % DAILY VALUE Vitamin A 16% | Vitamin C 40% | Calcium 8% | Iron 18% EXCHANGES 1 Starch, 2 Vegetable, 3 Lean Meat CARBOHYDRATE CHOICES 2

BETTY'S TIP

Out of fennel seed? Throw in a pinch of dried tarragon leaves instead. It will add a light touch of licorice flavor to this hearty soup.

Rich Cream of Mushroom Soup

PREP **5 min** COOK **15 min** SERVINGS **6**

- 1 pound mushrooms
- 1/4 cup butter or margarine
- 3 tablespoons all-purpose flour
- 1/2 teaspoon salt
- 1 cup whipping (heavy) cream
- 1 can (14 ounces) chicken broth
- 1 tablespoon dry sherry, if desired
- Freshly ground pepper

1. Slice enough mushrooms to measure 1 cup; chop remaining mushrooms. Melt butter in 3-quart saucepan over medium heat. Cook sliced and chopped mushrooms in butter about 10 minutes, stirring occasionally, until mushrooms are golden brown.
2. Sprinkle with flour and salt. Cook, stirring constantly, until thickened. Gradually stir in whipping cream and broth; heat until hot. Stir in sherry. Sprinkle with pepper.

1 SERVING Calories 235 (Calories from Fat 190) | Fat 21g (Saturated 9g) | Cholesterol 45mg | Sodium 620mg | Carbohydrate 7g (Dietary Fiber 1g) | Protein 5g % DAILY VALUE Vitamin A 14% | Vitamin C 12% | Calcium 2% | Iron 4% EXCHANGES 1 Vegetable, 1/2 High-Fat Meat, 3 1/2 Fat CARBOHYDRATE CHOICES 1/2

BETTY'S TIP

There is no "right" kind of mushroom for this soup, so don't be afraid to experiment with different varieties to find your favorite. Crimini, portabella and shiitake are all good ones to try.

Louisiana Oyster Gumbo

PREP **10 min** COOK **24 min** SERVINGS **4**

2 tablespoons all-purpose flour

2 tablespoons olive or vegetable oil

3 large onions, coarsely chopped (3 cups)

1 medium red or green bell pepper, coarsely chopped (1 cup)

3 cups chicken broth

2 teaspoons red pepper sauce

1 1/2 teaspoons dried thyme leaves

1/3 cup all-purpose flour

1 pint shucked large oysters, undrained, or 2 cans (8 ounces each) whole oysters, undrained

Hot cooked rice, if desired

1. Heat flour and oil in Dutch oven over medium heat 5 to 10 minutes, stirring constantly, until mixture is dark brown. Stir in onion and bell pepper. Cook uncovered about 6 minutes, stirring frequently, until vegetables are tender.
2. Gradually stir in 2 1/2 cups of the broth. Stir in pepper sauce and thyme. Heat to boiling; reduce heat. Cover and simmer 3 minutes.
3. Beat remaining 1/2 cup broth and 1/3 cup flour with wire whisk. Stir into broth mixture until smooth. Heat to boiling. Stir in oysters; reduce heat. Cover and simmer about 3 minutes or until oysters are heated through. Serve gumbo over rice.

1 SERVING Calories 260 (Calories from Fat 100) | Fat 11g (Saturated 3g) | Cholesterol 60mg | Sodium 1040mg | Carbohydrate 28g (Dietary Fiber 3g) | Protein 15g % DAILY VALUE Vitamin A 20% | Vitamin C 56% | Calcium 8% | Iron 52% EXCHANGES Starch, 1 Medium-Fat Meat, 2 Vegetable, 1 Fat CARBOHYDRATE CHOICES 1

BETTY'S TIP

You'll know the flour and oil mixture is cooked to the right stage when it's the color of a penny.

Home-Style Potato Soup

PREP **10 min** COOK **20 min** SERVINGS **5**

- 1 can (14 ounces) chicken broth
- 1 pound potatoes, peeled and cut into fourths (about 3 medium)
- 1 1/2 cups milk
- 1/4 teaspoon salt
- 1/8 teaspoon pepper
- 1/8 teaspoon dried thyme leaves
- 2 medium green onions, sliced (1/4 cup)

Photo on page 20.

1. Heat broth and potatoes to boiling in 3-quart saucepan; reduce heat to low. Cover and simmer about 15 minutes or until potatoes are tender. Do not drain. Break potatoes into smaller pieces with potato masher or large fork. (Mixture should be lumpy.)
2. Stir milk, salt, pepper, thyme and onions into saucepan. Heat over medium heat, stirring occasionally, until hot. Do not let soup boil.

1 SERVING Calories 110 (Calories from Fat 20) | Fat 2g (Saturated 1g) | Cholesterol 5mg | Sodium 530mg | Carbohydrate 17g (Dietary Fiber 1g) | Protein 5g % DAILY VALUE Vitamin A 4% | Vitamin C 8% | Calcium 8% | Iron 2% EXCHANGES 1 Starch, 1/2 Fat CARBOHYDRATE CHOICES 1

Potato-Cheese Soup Make Home-Style Potato Soup as directed. When soup is finished and very hot, gradually stir in 1 1/2 cups shredded Cheddar cheese until it is melted.

BETTY'S TIP

For added flavor and color, sprinkle your favorite baked potato topping over each serving of soup. Bacon bits, shredded Cheddar cheese and additional green onions will all taste great.

Cream of Broccoli Soup

PREP 35 min **COOK** 20 min **SERVINGS** 8

- 1 1/2 pounds broccoli
- 2 cups water
- 1 large stalk celery, chopped (3/4 cup)
- 1 medium onion, chopped (1/2 cup)
- 2 tablespoons butter or margarine
- 2 tablespoons all-purpose flour
- 2 1/2 cups chicken broth
- 1/2 teaspoon salt
- 1/8 teaspoon pepper
- Dash of ground nutmeg
- 1/2 cup whipping (heavy) cream
- Shredded cheese, if desired

1. Remove flowerets from broccoli; set aside. Cut stalks into 1-inch pieces, discarding any leaves.
2. Heat water to boiling in 3-quart saucepan. Add broccoli flowerets and stalk pieces, celery and onion. Cover and heat to boiling; reduce heat to low. Simmer about 10 minutes or until broccoli is tender (do not drain).
3. Carefully place broccoli mixture in blender. Cover and blend on medium speed until smooth.
4. Melt butter in 3-quart saucepan over medium heat. Stir in flour. Cook, stirring constantly, until mixture is smooth and bubbly; remove from heat. Stir in broth. Heat to boiling, stirring constantly. Boil and stir 1 minute.
5. Stir broccoli mixture, salt, pepper and nutmeg into saucepan. Heat just to boiling. Stir in whipping cream. Heat just until hot (do not boil or soup may curdle). Serve with cheese.

1 SERVING Calories 125 (Calories from Fat 70) | Fat 8g (Saturated 5g) | Cholesterol 25mg | Sodium 520mg | Carbohydrate 8g (Dietary Fiber 2g) | Protein 5g % DAILY VALUE Vitamin A 12% | Vitamin C 42% | Calcium 4% | Iron 4% EXCHANGES 2 Vegetable, 1 1/2 Fat CARBOHYDRATE CHOICES 1/2

Cream of Cauliflower Soup Substitute 1 head cauliflower (about 2 pounds), separated into flowerets, for the broccoli. Add 1 tablespoon lemon juice with the onion in step 2.

BETTY'S TIP

Knock a few minutes off your prep time by using 3 packages (10 ounces each) of frozen chopped broccoli instead of fresh broccoli.

Ratatouille Soup

PREP 10 min COOK 15 min SERVINGS 6

- 1 tablespoon olive or vegetable oil
- 1 small onion, chopped (1/4 cup)
- 1 clove garlic, finely chopped
- 1 small eggplant (1 pound), cut into 1/2-inch cubes
- 3 medium tomatoes, coarsely chopped (2 1/4 cups)
- 1 medium zucchini, cut into 1/2-inch slices (2 cups)
- 1 small green bell pepper, chopped (1/2 cup)
- 1 can (10 1/2 ounces) condensed chicken broth
- 1 broth can water
- 1/4 teaspoon salt
- 1/4 teaspoon pepper

1. Heat oil in 4-quart Dutch oven over medium-high heat. Cook onion and garlic in oil about 3 minutes, stirring occasionally, until onion is tender.
2. Stir in remaining ingredients. Heat to boiling; reduce heat to low. Cover and simmer about 10 minutes or until vegetables are crisp-tender.

1 SERVING Calories 85 (Calories from Fat 25) | Fat 3g (Saturated 1g) | Cholesterol 0mg | Sodium 420mg | Carbohydrate 11g (Dietary Fiber 3g) | Protein 4g % DAILY VALUE Vitamin A 16% | Vitamin C 22% | Calcium 2% | Iron 4% EXCHANGES 2 Vegetable, 1/2 Fat CARBOHYDRATE CHOICES 1

BETTY'S TIP

You can throw this hearty dish together in no time when you cut up the veggies the night before.

Hearty Tomato Soup

PREP 15 min COOK 10 min SERVINGS 8

- 2 tablespoons butter or margarine
- 1 medium onion, finely chopped (1/2 cup)
- 1 clove garlic, finely chopped
- 1/2 teaspoon paprika
- 1 1/2 teaspoons chopped fresh or 1/2 teaspoon dried basil leaves
- 2 packages (3 ounces each) cream cheese, softened
- 1 1/4 cups milk
- 2 cans (10 3/4 ounces each) condensed tomato soup
- 2 cans (14 1/2 ounces each) whole tomatoes, undrained

1. Melt butter in 3-quart saucepan over medium heat. Cook onion and garlic in butter about 2 minutes, stirring occasionally, until onion is tender; remove from heat.
2. Stir paprika, basil and cream cheese into onion mixture. Gradually stir in milk and soup. Beat with hand beater or wire whisk until cheese is melted and soup is smooth.
3. Stir in tomatoes, breaking up tomatoes. Heat over medium heat, stirring frequently, until hot.

1 SERVING Calories 195 (Calories from Fat 110) | Fat 12g (Saturated 7g) | Cholesterol 35mg | Sodium 710mg | Carbohydrate 19g (Dietary Fiber 2g) | Protein 5g % DAILY VALUE Vitamin A 20% | Vitamin C 22% | Calcium 10% | Iron 8% EXCHANGES 4 Vegetable, 2 Fat CARBOHYDRATE CHOICES 1

BETTY'S TIP

This rich tomato soup tastes wonderful by itself, but pair it with a hot-from-the-griddle grilled cheese sandwich, and it's a classic comfort food combo few will be able to pass up.

Easy Cheesy Vegetable Soup

PREP **5 min** COOK **10 min** SERVINGS **4**

4 ounces reduced-fat process cheese spread loaf, cubed

3 1/2 cups fat-free (skim) milk

1/2 teaspoon chili powder

2 cups cooked brown or white rice

1 bag (1 pound) frozen cauliflower, carrots and asparagus (or other combination), thawed and drained

1. Heat cheese and milk in 3-quart saucepan over low heat, stirring occasionally, until cheese is melted.
2. Stir in chili powder. Stir in rice and vegetables; cook until hot.

1 SERVING Calories 285 (Calories from Fat 45) | Fat 5g (Saturated 5g) | Cholesterol 0mg | Sodium 600mg | Carbohydrate 43g (Dietary Fiber 4g) | Protein 17g % DAILY VALUE Vitamin A 100% | Vitamin C 18% | Calcium 46% | Iron 6% EXCHANGES 1 1/2 Starch, 1 Vegetable, 1 Milk, 1 Fat CARBOHYDRATE CHOICES 3

BETTY'S TIP

Get a head start on making this incredibly easy cheesy soup by cooking your favorite rice ahead of time. Rice can be frozen up to six months when you store it in an airtight container or resealable plastic food-storage bag.

Basil Rice Soup

PREP 10 min COOK 40 min SERVINGS 6

- 2 tablespoons olive oil
- 2 cloves garlic, finely chopped
- 2 medium stalks celery, chopped (1 cup)
- 1 medium onion, chopped (1/2 cup)
- 1 medium carrot, chopped (1/2 cup)
- 1/4 cup chopped fresh basil leaves
- 3/4 cup uncooked regular long-grain rice
- 2 medium tomatoes, chopped (1 1/2 cups)
- 1 carton (32 ounces) chicken broth (4 cups)
- 1 cup water
- 1 teaspoon salt
- 1/4 teaspoon pepper
- 1/4 cup freshly grated or shredded Romano or imported Parmesan cheese

1. Heat oil in 4-quart Dutch oven over medium-low heat. Stir in garlic, celery, onion, carrot and basil. Cover and cook 10 minutes, stirring occasionally.
2. Stir in rice and tomatoes. Cook uncovered over medium heat 5 minutes, stirring occasionally. Stir in remaining ingredients except cheese.
3. Heat to boiling; reduce heat. Cover and simmer about 20 minutes or until rice is tender. Serve with cheese.

1 SERVING Calories 185 (Calories from Fat 65) | Fat 7g (Saturated 2g) | Cholesterol 5mg | Sodium 1170mg | Carbohydrate 26g (Dietary Fiber 2g) | Protein 7g % DAILY VALUE Vitamin A 18% | Vitamin C 8% | Calcium 8% | Iron 8% EXCHANGES 1 Starch, 2 Vegetable, 1 Fat CARBOHYDRATE CHOICES 2

BETTY'S TIP

Parmesan cheese from a can works fine in this veggie-packed soup, but freshly grated Parmesan cheese will give you a richer, sharper and nuttier flavor—and add an extra special touch.

Ham 'n Corn Chowder

PREP **5 min** COOK **12 min** SERVINGS **4**

- 1 1/2 cups milk
- 1/2 cup chopped thinly sliced fully cooked ham
- 1 bag (1 pound) frozen whole kernel corn
- 1 can (10 3/4 ounces) condensed cream of celery soup
- 2 medium green onions, sliced (2 tablespoons)

1. Mix milk, ham, corn and soup in 3-quart saucepan. Heat to boiling, stirring occasionally; reduce heat to low.
2. Simmer uncovered 10 minutes, stirring occasionally. Sprinkle with onions.

1 SERVING Calories 245 (Calories from Fat 70) | Fat 8g (Saturated 3g) | Cholesterol 20mg | Sodium 860mg | Carbohydrate 32g (Dietary Fiber 3g) | Protein 11g % DAILY VALUE Vitamin A 14% | Vitamin C 6% | Calcium 16% | Iron 6% EXCHANGES 1 1/2 Starch, 1/2 Milk, 2 Fat CARBOHYDRATE CHOICES 2

BETTY'S TIP

A quick stop at your supermarket deli counter or salad bar will provide you with the ham and green onions called for in this quick-to-fix recipe.

Chunky Vegetable Chowder

PREP **15 min** COOK **15 min** SERVINGS **6**

1 tablespoon butter or margarine

2 medium bell peppers, coarsely chopped (2 cups)

8 medium green onions, sliced (1/2 cup)

3 cups water

3/4 pound new potatoes, cubed (2 1/2 cups)

1 tablespoon chopped fresh or 1 teaspoon dried thyme leaves

1/2 teaspoon salt

1 cup half-and-half

1/8 teaspoon pepper

2 cans (14 3/4 ounces each) cream-style corn

1. Melt butter in 4-quart Dutch oven over medium heat. Cook bell peppers and onions in butter 3 minutes, stirring occasionally.
2. Stir in water, potatoes, thyme and salt. Heat to boiling; reduce heat to low. Cover and simmer about 10 minutes or until potatoes are tender.
3. Stir in remaining ingredients; cook until hot (do not boil).

1 SERVING Calories 270 (Calories from Fat 70) | Fat 8g (Saturated 4g) | Cholesterol 20mg | Sodium 580mg | Carbohydrate 47g (Dietary Fiber 5g) | Protein 7g % DAILY VALUE Vitamin A 12% | Vitamin C 48% | Calcium 6% | Iron 14% EXCHANGES 3 Starch, 1/2 Fat CARBOHYDRATE CHOICES 3

BETTY'S TIP

If bell peppers are in season, use one red and one green pepper to jazz up the color of this chunky chowder.

Beef-Barley-Vegetable Stew

PREP **10 min** COOK **1 hr 55 min** SERVINGS **4**

- 1 tablespoon vegetable oil
- 1 pound beef stew meat, cut into 1-inch pieces
- 1 cup dry red wine or water
- 1 teaspoon chopped fresh or 1/4 teaspoon dried rosemary leaves, crumbled
- 1/4 teaspoon pepper
- 1 clove garlic, finely chopped
- 1 can (10 1/2 ounces) condensed beef broth
- 1 can (14 1/2 ounces) whole tomatoes, undrained
- 1/2 cup uncooked barley
- 1 cup broccoli flowerets
- 2 medium carrots, sliced (1 cup)
- 1 medium onion, cut into wedges
- 4 ounces medium mushrooms, cut in half (1 1/4 cups)

1. Heat oil in 4-quart Dutch oven over medium heat. Cook beef in oil, stirring occasionally, until brown. Stir wine, rosemary, pepper, garlic, broth and tomatoes into beef, breaking up tomatoes. Heat to boiling; reduce heat to low. Cover and simmer 1 hour.
2. Stir in barley. Cover and simmer about 30 minutes or until beef is almost tender. Stir in remaining ingredients. Cover and simmer about 20 minutes or until vegetables are tender.

1 SERVING Calories 420 (Calories from Fat 155) | Fat 17g (Saturated 6g) | Cholesterol 70mg | Sodium 620mg | Carbohydrate 34g (Dietary Fiber 7g) | Protein 30g % DAILY VALUE Vitamin A 100% | Vitamin C 34% | Calcium 8% | Iron 28% EXCHANGES 2 Starch, 3 Medium-Fat Meat, 1 Fat CARBOHYDRATE CHOICES 2

BETTY'S TIP

The hearty, healthful ingredients in this savory stew make it a great choice for chilly winter evenings. Enjoy a bowl with a thick wedge of wheat bread and a glass of red wine.

Quick Beef and Vegetable Stew

PREP **5 min** COOK **10 min** SERVINGS **6**

1 pound lean beef boneless sirloin

1 bag (1 pound) frozen stew vegetables, thawed and drained

1 can (15 ounces) chunky garlic-and-herb tomato sauce

1 can (14 ounces) beef broth

2 cans (5 1/2 ounces each) spicy eight-vegetable juice

1. Remove fat from beef. Cut beef into 1/2-inch cubes. Spray 10-inch nonstick skillet with cooking spray; heat over medium-high heat. Cook beef in skillet, stirring occasionally, until brown.
2. Stir in remaining ingredients. Heat to boiling; reduce heat to low. Simmer uncovered 5 minutes, stirring occasionally.

1 SERVING Calories 265 (Calories from Fat 55) | Fat 6g (Saturated 2g) | Cholesterol 65mg | Sodium 860mg | Carbohydrate 25g (Dietary Fiber 3g) | Protein 27g % DAILY VALUE Vitamin A 14% | Vitamin C 24% | Calcium 4% | Iron 18% EXCHANGES 1 Starch, 2 Vegetable, 3 Very Lean Meat, 1/2 Fat CARBOHYDRATE CHOICES 1 1/2

BETTY'S TIP

This satisfying stew has many ingredients that can be substituted for others. Instead of frozen stew vegetables, use your favorite frozen veggie mix, or switch the chunky garlic-and-herb tomato sauce for regular tomato sauce. If you're trying to lower the fat in your diet, use low-fat beef broth instead of regular.

Classic Beef Stew

PREP 15 min **COOK** 3 hr 30 min **SERVINGS** 8

- 1 pound beef stew meat, cut into 1/2-inch pieces
- 1 medium onion, cut into eighths
- 1 package (8 ounces) baby-cut carrots (about 30)
- 1 can (14 1/2 ounces) diced tomatoes, undrained
- 1 can (10 1/2 ounces) condensed beef broth
- 1 can (8 ounces) tomato sauce
- 1/3 cup all-purpose flour
- 1 tablespoon Worcestershire sauce
- 1 teaspoon salt
- 1 teaspoon sugar
- 1 teaspoon dried marjoram leaves
- 1/4 teaspoon pepper
- 1 1/2 pounds new potatoes, cut into fourths (about 12 potatoes)
- 2 cups sliced mushrooms (about 5 ounces) or 1 package (3.4 ounces) fresh shiitake mushrooms, sliced

1. Heat oven to 325°.
2. Mix all ingredients except potatoes and mushrooms in ovenproof 4-quart Dutch oven. Cover and bake 2 hours, stirring once.
3. Stir in potatoes and mushrooms. Cover and bake 1 hour to 1 hour 30 minutes or until beef and vegetables are tender.

1 SERVING Calories 245 (Calories from Fat 65) | Fat 7g (Saturated 3g) | Cholesterol 35mg | Sodium 810mg | Carbohydrate 28g (Dietary Fiber 4g) | Protein 17g % DAILY VALUE Vitamin A 100% | Vitamin C 20% | Calcium 4% | Iron 18% EXCHANGES 1 Starch, 2 Vegetable, 1 1/2 Medium-Fat Meat CARBOHYDRATE CHOICES 2

BETTY'S TIP

Try to cut the meat and veggies into similar sizes so that all the ingredients in this stick-to-your-ribs stew get done at the same time.

Greek Beef and Onion Stew

PREP **15 min** COOK **2 hr 15 min** SERVINGS **6**

3 tablespoons olive or vegetable oil

1 medium onion, chopped (1/2 cup)

2 cloves garlic, finely chopped

2 pounds beef boneless chuck, tip or round, cut into 1-inch cubes

1/2 cup dry red wine or water

2 tablespoons red wine vinegar

1/2 teaspoon salt

1/4 teaspoon coarsely ground pepper

1 dried bay leaf

1 stick cinnamon

1 can (8 ounces) tomato sauce

1 1/2 pounds small white onions, peeled (about 12)

Crumbled feta cheese

1. Heat oil in 4-quart Dutch oven over medium heat. Cook chopped onion and garlic in oil, stirring occasionally, until onion is tender. Remove onion and garlic; set aside. Cook beef in remaining oil in Dutch oven about 25 minutes, stirring occasionally, until all liquid has evaporated and beef is brown; drain.
2. Return onion and garlic to Dutch oven. Stir in remaining ingredients except white onions and cheese. Heat to boiling; reduce heat to low. Cover and simmer 1 hour.
3. Stir in white onions. Cover and simmer about 45 minutes or until beef and white onions are tender. Remove bay leaf and cinnamon. Sprinkle with cheese.

1 SERVING Calories 435 (Calories from Fat 215) | Fat 24g (Saturated 8g) | Cholesterol 95mg | Sodium 520mg | Carbohydrate 15g (Dietary Fiber 3g) | Protein 33g % DAILY VALUE Vitamin A 10% | Vitamin C 10% | Calcium 4% | Iron 22% EXCHANGES 1 Starch, 4 Medium-Fat Meat, 1 Fat CARBOHYDRATE CHOICES 1

BETTY'S TIP

Pita bread triangles are great for dunking into this flavorful stew, and a bowl of Kalamata olives served on the side keeps the Greek theme going.

New England Baked Bean Stew

PREP 10 min COOK 20 min SERVINGS 4

- 1/2 pound boneless, skinless chicken breasts, cut into 1/2-inch pieces
- 1/2 pound fully cooked Polish sausage, cut into 1/2-inch slices
- 1 can (15 to 16 ounces) great northern beans, rinsed and drained
- 1 can (15 to 16 ounces) dark red kidney beans, rinsed and drained
- 1 can (14 1/2 ounces) diced tomatoes with olive oil, garlic and spices, undrained
- 1 tablespoon packed brown sugar
- 4 medium green onions, sliced (1/4 cup)

1. Spray 12-inch nonstick skillet with cooking spray; heat over medium-high heat. Cook chicken in skillet 3 to 5 minutes, stirring occasionally, until brown.
2. Stir in remaining ingredients except onions. Cook uncovered over medium-low heat 8 to 10 minutes, stirring occasionally, until chicken is no longer pink in center.
3. Stir in onions. Cook 3 to 5 minutes, stirring occasionally, until onions are crisp-tender.

1 SERVING Calories 525 (Calories from Fat 170) | Fat 19g (Saturated 6g) | Cholesterol 65mg | Sodium 1150mg | Carbohydrate 64g (Dietary Fiber 15g) | Protein 40g % DAILY VALUE Vitamin A 6% | Vitamin C 12% | Calcium 18% | Iron 48% EXCHANGES 4 Starch, 1 Vegetable, 4 Very Lean Meat, 1 Fat CARBOHYDRATE CHOICES 4

BETTY'S TIP

Pick up a 6-ounce package of cooked chicken breast slices in the meat department of your grocery store, and you can skip the first step altogether.

Chicken Stew with Potatoes

PREP **15 min** COOK **25 min** SERVINGS **4**

2 cups broccoli flowerets

1 cup water

3/4 pound small red potatoes (about 6 potatoes), cut into fourths

3/4 pound boneless, skinless chicken breasts, cut into 1-inch cubes

1 jar (12 ounces) chicken gravy

1. Mix all ingredients in 3-quart saucepan. Heat to boiling, stirring occasionally; reduce heat to low.
2. Cover and simmer 15 to 20 minutes, stirring occasionally, until potatoes are tender and chicken is no longer pink in center.

1 SERVING Calories 330 (Calories from Fat 70) | Fat 8g (Saturated 2g) | Cholesterol 55mg | Sodium 580mg | Carbohydrate 40g (Dietary Fiber 5g) | Protein 25g % DAILY VALUE Vitamin A 24% | Vitamin C 44% | Calcium 6% | Iron 18% EXCHANGES 2 Starch, 2 Vegetable, 2 Lean Meat CARBOHYDRATE CHOICES 2 1/2

BETTY'S TIP

If broccoli isn't one of your family's favorite veggies, use 2 cups of cut green beans instead.

Zesty Autumn Pork Stew

PREP **15 min** COOK **15 min** SERVINGS **4**

1 pound lean pork tenderloin, cut into 1-inch cubes

2 medium sweet potatoes, peeled and cubed (2 cups)

1 medium green bell pepper, chopped (1 cup)

2 cloves garlic, finely chopped

1 cup coarsely chopped cabbage

1 teaspoon Cajun seasoning

1 can (14 1/2 ounces) chicken broth

1. Spray 4-quart Dutch oven with cooking spray; heat over medium-high heat. Cook pork in Dutch oven, stirring occasionally, until brown.
2. Stir in remaining ingredients. Heat to boiling; reduce heat. Cover and simmer about 15 minutes, stirring once, until sweet potatoes are tender.

1 SERVING Calories 240 (Calories from Fat 45) | Fat 5g (Saturated 2g) | Cholesterol 70mg | Sodium 730mg | Carbohydrate 22g (Dietary Fiber 3g) | Protein 29g % DAILY VALUE Vitamin A 100% | Vitamin C 44% | Calcium 4% | Iron 12% EXCHANGES 1 Starch, 2 Vegetable, 3 Very Lean Meat CARBOHYDRATE CHOICES 1 1/2

BETTY'S TIP

Pork tenderloin is easiest to cut when it's still partially frozen. And save some time by using coleslaw mix as a substitute for chopped cabbage.

Southwestern Pork and Potato Stew

PREP **15 min** COOK **35 min** SERVINGS **4**

- 1 pound lean pork boneless shoulder
- 1 tablespoon all-purpose flour
- 1 medium onion, chopped (1/2 cup)
- 3 cloves garlic, finely chopped
- 2 1/4 cups fat-free reduced-sodium chicken broth
- 1 teaspoon dried thyme leaves
- 1/2 teaspoon ground cumin
- 2 tablespoons chopped fresh or canned jalapeño chilies
- 3 cups (from 1-pound bag) frozen broccoli, corn and red peppers (or other combination)

1. Trim fat from pork. Cut pork into 1-inch cubes. Toss pork with flour. Spray 4-quart Dutch oven with cooking spray; heat over medium-high heat. Cook pork, onion and garlic in Dutch oven, stirring occasionally, until pork is brown.
2. Stir broth, thyme, cumin and chilies into pork. Cook 15 minutes.
3. Stir in vegetable mixture. Heat to boiling; reduce heat to low. Cover and simmer about 10 minutes or until pork is no longer pink in center.

1 SERVING Calories 320 (Calories from Fat 135) | Fat 15g (Saturated 5g) | Cholesterol 70mg | Sodium 380mg | Carbohydrate 18g (Dietary Fiber 3g) | Protein 30g % DAILY VALUE Vitamin A 62% | Vitamin C 78% | Calcium 4% | Iron 10% EXCHANGES 1 Starch, 1 Vegetable, 3 Lean Meat, 1 Fat CARBOHYDRATE CHOICES 1

BETTY'S TIP

In a pinch, 1 tablespoon of ready-to-use minced garlic can be used instead of the garlic cloves. Look for jars of it in the produce department of your supermarket.

Spicy Fish Stew

PREP 5 min **COOK** 20 min **SERVINGS** 4

1. Heat 1/4 cup of the clam juice to boiling in 10-inch nonstick skillet. Cook garlic in clam juice 1 minute.
2. Stir in stir-fry vegetables. Cook about 8 minutes, stirring frequently, until liquid has evaporated.
3. Stir in fish, chilies, fish sauce, brown sugar and remaining clam juice. Heat to boiling; reduce heat to medium. Cook uncovered 10 minutes. Serve with rice.

1 SERVING Calories 305 (Calories from Fat 10) | Fat 1g (Saturated 0g) | Cholesterol 30mg | Sodium 610mg | Carbohydrate 56g (Dietary Fiber 2g) | Protein 18g % DAILY VALUE Vitamin A 18% | Vitamin C 32% | Calcium 6% | Iron 18% EXCHANGES 3 Starch, 2 Vegetable, 1/2 Very Lean Meat CARBOHYDRATE CHOICES 4

1/2 cup clam juice

4 cloves garlic, finely chopped

3 cups packaged fresh (refrigerated) stir-fry vegetables

1/2 pound cod fillets, cubed

1 1/2 tablespoons chopped fresh or canned jalapeño chilies

2 tablespoons fish sauce or reduced-sodium soy sauce

1 tablespoon packed brown sugar

4 cups hot cooked rice

BETTY'S TIP

Mix up the flavor of this sweet and spicy stew by experimenting with different kinds of fish. Halibut, orange roughy or haddock will all taste great.

New England Clam Chowder

PREP 10 min COOK 23 min SERVINGS 4

- 1/4 cup cut-up uncooked bacon or lean salt pork
- 1 medium onion, chopped (1/2 cup)
- 2 cans (6 1/2 ounces each) minced clams
- 1 medium potato, finely chopped (1 cup)
- 1/2 teaspoon salt
- Dash of pepper
- 2 cups milk

1. Cook bacon and onion in 2-quart saucepan over medium heat, stirring frequently, until bacon is crisp and onion is tender. Drain clams, reserving liquid. Add enough water, if necessary, to clam liquid to measure 1 cup. Stir clams, clam liquid, potato, salt and pepper into bacon and onion. Heat to boiling; reduce heat to low.
2. Cover and simmer about 15 minutes or until potato is tender. Stir in milk. Heat, stirring occasionally, just until hot (do not boil).

1 SERVING Calories 235 (Calories from Fat 45) | Fat 5g (Saturated 2g) | Cholesterol 70mg | Sodium 490g | Carbohydrate 19g (Dietary Fiber 1g) | Protein 29g % DAILY VALUE Vitamin A 14% | Vitamin C 20% | Calcium 24% | Iron 100% EXCHANGES 1 Starch, 1/2 Milk, 3 Very Lean Meat CARBOHYDRATE CHOICES 1

BETTY'S TIP

If you have access to fresh clams, go ahead and use them instead of canned clams. Chop up 1 pint of shucked fresh clams and stir them, with their liquid, in with the potato, salt and pepper.

Oyster Stew

PREP **10 min** COOK **10 min** SERVINGS **4**

- 1/4 cup butter or margarine
- 1 pint shucked oysters, undrained
- 2 cups milk
- 1/2 cup half-and-half
- 1/2 teaspoon salt
- Dash of pepper

1. Melt butter in 1 1/2-quart saucepan over low heat. Cook oysters in butter, stirring occasionally, just until edges of oysters curl.
2. Heat milk and half-and-half in 2-quart saucepan over medium-low heat until hot. Stir in salt, pepper and oyster mixture; heat until hot.

1 SERVING Calories 285 (Calories from Fat 180) | Fat 20g (Saturated 12g) | Cholesterol 115mg | Sodium 700mg | Carbohydrate 12g (Dietary Fiber 0g) | Protein 14g % DAILY VALUE Vitamin A 20% | Vitamin C 4% | Calcium 24% | Iron 46% EXCHANGES 1 Milk, 1 Medium-Fat Meat, 3 Fat CARBOHYDRATE CHOICES 1

BETTY'S TIP

If fresh oysters are available, by all means use them! When shopping for fresh oysters, look for oysters that are plump, of similar size and smell fresh. The liquid they are packaged in should be clear, not cloudy. Oysters taste best when used within two days.

Shrimp Gumbo

PREP **20 min** COOK **1 hr** SERVINGS **6**

- 1/4 cup butter or margarine
- 2 medium onions, sliced
- 1 medium green bell pepper, cut into thin strips
- 2 cloves garlic, finely chopped
- 2 tablespoons all-purpose flour
- 3 cups beef broth
- 1/2 teaspoon red pepper sauce
- 1/4 teaspoon salt
- 1/4 teaspoon pepper
- 1 dried bay leaf
- 1 package (10 ounces) frozen cut okra, thawed and drained
- 1 can (14 1/2 ounces) whole tomatoes, undrained
- 1 can (6 ounces) tomato paste
- 1 pound uncooked peeled deveined medium shrimp, thawed if frozen and tails peeled
- 3 cups hot cooked rice
- 1/4 cup chopped fresh parsley

1. Melt butter in 4-quart Dutch oven over medium heat. Cook onions, bell pepper and garlic in butter 5 minutes, stirring occasionally. Stir in flour. Cook over medium heat, stirring constantly, until bubbly; remove from heat.
2. Stir in remaining ingredients except shrimp, rice and parsley, breaking up tomatoes. Heat to boiling; reduce heat to low. Simmer uncovered 45 minutes, stirring occasionally.
3. Stir shrimp into gumbo. Cover and simmer about 5 minutes or until shrimp are pink and firm. Remove bay leaf. Serve soup in bowls over rice. Sprinkle with parsley.

1 SERVING Calories 295 (Calories from Fat 80) | Fat 9g (Saturated 5g) | Cholesterol 125mg | Sodium 1,120mg | Carbohydrate 40g (Dietary Fiber 5g) | Protein 19g % DAILY VALUE Vitamin A 34% | Vitamin C 44% | Calcium 12% | Iron 24% EXCHANGES 2 Starch, 2 Vegetable, 1 Lean Meat, 1 Fat CARBOHYDRATE CHOICES 2 1/2

BETTY'S TIP

A shortcut to breaking up the tomatoes in step 2 is to snip them with kitchen scissors.

Vegetarian Chili

PREP **15 min** COOK **20 min** SERVINGS **4**

2 medium potatoes, unpeeled and cut into 1/2-inch cubes (about 10 ounces)

1 medium onion, chopped (1/2 cup)

1 small yellow bell pepper, finely chopped (about 1/2 cup)

1 can (15 to 16 ounces) garbanzo beans, rinsed and drained

1 can (15 to 16 ounces) kidney beans, rinsed and drained

1 can (28 ounces) whole tomatoes, undrained

1 can (8 ounces) tomato sauce

1 tablespoon chili powder

1 teaspoon ground cumin

1 medium zucchini, cut into 1/2-inch slices

1. Place all ingredients except zucchini in 4-quart Dutch oven, breaking up tomatoes. Heat to boiling, stirring occasionally; reduce heat to low. Cover and simmer 10 minutes.
2. Stir in zucchini. Cover and simmer 5 to 7 minutes, stirring occasionally, until potatoes and zucchini and tender.

1 SERVING Calories 400 (Calories from Fat 35) | Fat 4g (Saturated 1g) | Cholesterol 0mg | Sodium 1090mg | Carbohydrate 87g (Dietary Fiber 20g) | Protein 24g % DAILY VALUE Vitamin A 42% | Vitamin C 72% | Calcium 18% | Iron 50% EXCHANGES 5 Starch, 2 Vegetable CARBOHYDRATE CHOICES 6

BETTY'S TIP

Zucchini comes in all sorts of sizes. For this recipe, look for a medium zucchini between 4 and 8 inches long.

Classic Chili

PREP 15 min **COOK** 1 hr 25 min **SERVINGS** 4

- 1 pound lean ground beef
- 1 medium onion, chopped (1/2 cup)
- 1 clove garlic, finely chopped
- 1 can (14 1/2 ounces) diced tomatoes, undrained
- 1 can (8 ounces) tomato sauce
- 1 tablespoon chili powder
- 3/4 teaspoon ground cumin
- 1/4 teaspoon salt
- 1/4 teaspoon pepper
- 1 can (15 or 16 ounces) kidney or pinto beans, rinsed and drained, if desired

1. Cook beef, onion and garlic in 3-quart saucepan over medium heat 8 to 10 minutes, stirring occasionally, until beef is brown; drain.
2. Stir in remaining ingredients except beans. Heat to boiling; reduce heat to low. Cover and simmer 1 hour, stirring occasionally.
3. Stir in beans. Heat to boiling; reduce heat to low. Simmer uncovered about 10 minutes, stirring occasionally, until desired thickness.

1 SERVING Calories 295 (Calories from Fat 155) | Fat 17g (Saturated 6g) | Cholesterol 65mg | Sodium 740mg | Carbohydrate 12g (Dietary Fiber 3g) | Protein 23g % DAILY VALUE Vitamin A 30% | Vitamin C 22% | Calcium 6% | Iron 18% EXCHANGES 2 Vegetable, 3 Medium-Fat Meat CARBOHYDRATE CHOICES 1

Cincinnati-Style Chili For each serving, spoon about 3/4 cup beef mixture over 1 cup hot cooked spaghetti. Sprinkle each serving with 1/4 cup shredded Cheddar cheese and 2 tablespoons chopped onion. Top with sour cream if desired.

BETTY'S TIP

Want to increase the heat? Increase the chili powder, add 1/2 teaspoon red pepper sauce or add a jalapeño chili, seeded and finely chopped, to the mix.

Buffalo-Chicken Chili

PREP **15 min** COOK **30 min** SERVINGS **4**

- 1 tablespoon vegetable oil
- 1 large onion, chopped (1 cup)
- 1 medium red or yellow bell pepper, chopped (1 cup)
- 2 cups cubed cooked chicken
- 1 cup chicken broth
- 1 tablespoon chili powder
- 5 to 6 drops red pepper sauce
- 2 cans (15 to 16 ounces each) pinto beans, drained
- 1 can (28 ounces) crushed tomatoes, undrained
- 1 can (15 ounces) tomato sauce with tomato bits
- 1/4 cup sliced celery
- 1/4 cup crumbled blue cheese

1. Heat oil in 3-quart saucepan over medium-high heat. Cook onion and bell pepper in oil about 5 minutes, stirring occasionally, until crisp-tender.
2. Stir in remaining ingredients except celery and blue cheese. Heat to boiling; reduce heat to medium-low. Simmer uncovered 10 to 15 minutes, stirring occasionally. Serve topped with celery and blue cheese.

1 SERVING Calories 540 (Calories from Fat 155) | Fat 17g (Saturated 5g) | Cholesterol 65mg | Sodium 1760mg | Carbohydrate 78g (Dietary Fiber 24g) | Protein 43g % DAILY VALUE Vitamin A 50% | Vitamin C 90% | Calcium 24% | Iron 50% EXCHANGES 4 Starch, 3 Vegetable, 3 Lean Meat, 1 Fat CARBOHYDRATE CHOICES 3 1/2

BETTY'S TIP

Buffalo-chicken wings are spicy, deep-fried chicken wings that are served with celery sticks and blue-cheese dressing. We've taken those great flavors and created a terrific chili topped with crumbled blue cheese and celery.

Spicy Chicken Chili

PREP **5 min** COOK **15 min** SERVINGS **4**

1 pound boneless, skinless chicken breast halves

1 can (14 1/2 ounces) salsa-style chunky tomatoes, undrained

1/2 cup shredded reduced-fat Cheddar cheese (2 ounces)

1. Remove fat from chicken. Cut chicken into 3/4-inch pieces. Spray 12-inch nonstick skillet with cooking spray; heat over medium-high heat. Cook chicken in skillet 3 to 5 minutes, stirring frequently, until light brown.
2. Stir in tomatoes and beans; reduce heat to medium-low. Cook uncovered 8 to 10 minutes, stirring frequently, until chicken is no longer pink in center. Sprinkle each serving with 2 tablespoons cheese.

1 SERVING Calories 250 (Calories from Fat 45) | Fat 5g (Saturated 2g) | Cholesterol 70mg | Sodium 1070mg | Carbohydrate 21g (Dietary Fiber 5g, Sugars 5g) | Protein 35g % DAILY VALUE Vitamin A 16% | Vitamin C 20% | Calcium 12% | Iron 18% EXCHANGES 1 Starch, 4 Very Lean Meat, 1 Vegetable CARBOHYDRATE CHOICES 1 1/2

BETTY'S TIP

For added heat and flavor, use Southwestern salsa-style diced tomatoes with green chilies or Southwestern-style diced tomatoes with chili spices.

White Chili

PREP 15 min COOK 25 min SERVINGS 6

1. Heat oil in 4-quart Dutch oven over medium heat. Cook onions and garlic in oil, stirring occasionally, until onions are tender.
2. Stir in remaining ingredients except chicken. Heat to boiling; reduce heat to low. Simmer uncovered 20 minutes. Stir in chicken; simmer until hot.

1 SERVING Calories 235 (Calories from Fat 55) | Fat 6g (Saturated 1g) | Cholesterol 40mg | Sodium 920mg | Carbohydrate 28g (Dietary Fiber 7g) | Protein 24g % DAILY VALUE Vitamin A 2% | Vitamin C 6% | Calcium 28% | Iron 16% EXCHANGES 2 Starch, 2 1/2 Very Lean Meat CARBOHYDRATE CHOICES 2

1 tablespoon vegetable oil

2 medium onions, chopped (1 cup)

2 cloves garlic, finely chopped

3 cups chicken broth

2 tablespoons chopped fresh cilantro or 1/2 teaspoon ground coriander

2 tablespoons lime juice

1 teaspoon ground cumin

1/2 teaspoon dried oregano leaves

1/4 teaspoon red pepper sauce

1/4 teaspoon salt

1 can (11 ounces) white shoepeg or whole kernel corn, drained

1 can (15 to 16 ounces) great northern beans, drained

1 can (15 to 16 ounces) butter beans, drained

2 cups chopped cooked chicken breast

BETTY'S TIP

Provide bowls of shredded cheese, crushed tortilla chips, chopped green onions, diced tomatoes, chopped fresh cilantro, sliced avocado and sour cream so everyone can "accessorize" their chili as they see fit.

Sizzling Skillets and Stir-Fries

Skillet Beef Stew 70
Beef Stroganoff 71
Beef-Taco-Rice Skillet 72
Easy Taco Dinner 73
Penne with Beef and Sun-Dried Tomatoes 75
Stir-Fried Beef and Broccoli 76
Easy Weeknight Beef-Veggie Mix 77
Caesar Chicken with Orzo 79
Chicken Paprika 80
Chicken Penne à la Marengo 82
Asparagus-Dijon-Chicken Fettuccine 83
Citris Ginger Chicken 85
Fettuccine with Chicken in Orange-Cherry Sauce 86
Chicken and Pasta Stir-Fry 89
Chicken-Vegetable Stroganoff 90
Teriyaki Chicken Stir-Fry 91
Easy Chicken Alfredo 93
Easy Mexican Chicken and Beans 94
Szechuan Chicken and Pasta 97
Vegetable Chicken Stir-Fry 99
Country-French Turkey and Red Potatoes 100
Glazed Turkey and Pea Pods 101
Smoked Turkey Lo Mein 102
Cheesy Turkey, Rice and Broccoli 103
Oriental Turkey and Rice 104
Turkey-Pasta Primavera 105
Peppery Cajun Pork Pasta 106
Sausage with Fettuccine 107
Creamy Bow-Ties with Ham and Vegetables 109
Pork Chop Dinner with Rice and Veggies 110
Pork and Julienne Potatoes 112
Pork with Squash and Onions 113
Polynesian Pork Stir-Fry 115
Pork Tenderloin with Prosciutto 116
Halibut Asparagus Stir-Fry 119
Easy Seafood Risotto 120
Shrimp Scampi Fettuccine 123
Shrimp and Scallops in Wine Sauce 124
Honey-Garlic Shrimp and Linguine 125
Ginger-Peanut-Shrimp Stir-Fry 126
Italian Shrimp Linguine 127
Tuna Primavera 128
Southwest Cheese 'n Pasta 129
Mostaccioli with Vodka Sauce 131
Blue Cheese Tenders 132
Swiss Potato and Cheese Skillet 134
Vegetable Paella 135
Potatoes, Green Beans and Tomatoes with Tofu 137

Skillet Beef Stew

PREP 10 min COOK 30 min SERVINGS 4

- 1 pound lean ground beef
- 1 jar (18 ounces) seasoned gravy for beef
- 1/4 cup ketchup
- 8 unpeeled small red potatoes, cut into fourths
- 2 cups frozen whole or cut green beans (from 1-pound bag), thawed and drained

1. Spray 12-inch nonstick skillet with cooking spray; heat over medium-high heat. Cook beef in skillet 3 to 5 minutes, stirring frequently, until light brown.
2. Stir gravy, ketchup and potatoes into beef. Heat to boiling; reduce heat to medium-low. Cover and cook 10 minutes.
3. Stir in beans. Cover and cook 10 to 15 minutes, stirring occasionally, until vegetables are tender.

1 SERVING Calories 410 (Calories from Fat 160) | Fat 18g (Saturated 8g) | Cholesterol 65mg | Sodium 980mg | Carbohydrate 34g (Dietary Fiber 4g) | Protein 29g % DAILY VALUE Vitamin A 12% | Vitamin C 12% | Calcium 4% | Iron 24% EXCHANGES 2 Starch, 1 Vegetable, 3 Medium-Fat Meat CARBOHYDRATE CHOICES 2

Skillet Turkey Stew Substitute ground turkey for the ground beef and turkey gravy for the beef gravy.

BETTY'S TIP

Leaving the skins on the potatoes not only pumps up the flavor and nutrients of this family-friendly skillet dish, it also cuts down on the prep work.

Beef Stroganoff

PREP 15 min COOK 30 min SERVINGS 6

1 1/2 pounds beef boneless top loin steak, about 1 inch thick

2 tablespoons butter or margarine

1 1/2 cups beef broth

2 tablespoons ketchup

1 teaspoon salt

1 clove garlic, finely chopped

1 medium onion, chopped (1/2 cup)

1 package (8 ounces) sliced mushrooms (3 cups)

3 tablespoons all-purpose flour

1 container (8 ounces) sour cream or plain yogurt

3 cups cooked egg noodles

1. Trim fat from beef. Cut beef with grain into 2-inch strips; cut strips across grain into 1/8-inch slices. Cut longer slices in half. Melt butter in 10-inch skillet over medium-high heat. Cook beef in butter 8 to 10 minutes, stirring occasionally, until brown.
2. Reserve 1/3 cup broth. Stir remaining broth, the ketchup, salt and garlic into beef. Heat to boiling; reduce heat to low. Cover and simmer about 10 minutes or until beef is tender. Stir in onion and mushrooms. Cover and simmer about 5 minutes or until onion is tender.
3. Shake the reserved 1/3 cup broth and the flour in tightly covered jar or container. Gradually stir into beef mixture. Heat to boiling. Boil about 1 minute, stirring constantly, until thickened. Reduce heat to low.
4. Stir in sour cream. Heat until hot. (Do not boil or mixture will curdle.) Serve beef over noodles.

1 SERVING Calories 435 (Calories from Fat 190) | Fat 21g (Saturated 10g) | Cholesterol 125mg | Sodium 820mg | Carbohydrate 29g (Dietary Fiber 2g) | Protein 32g % DAILY VALUE Vitamin A 12% | Vitamin C 2% | Calcium 6% | Iron 22% EXCHANGES 2 Starch, 4 Lean Meat, 1 Fat CARBOHYDRATE CHOICES 2

BETTY'S TIP

Try stretching the flavor boundaries of this classic dish by using chanterelle, morel or shiitake mushrooms instead of regular white mushrooms.

Beef-Taco-Rice Skillet

PREP 5 min COOK 14 min STAND 10 min SERVINGS 5

- 1 pound lean ground beef
- 1 envelope (1 1/4 ounces) taco seasoning mix
- 1 1/2 cups water
- 1 cup thick-and-chunky salsa
- 1 cup frozen whole kernel corn (from 1-pound bag)
- 1 1/2 cups uncooked instant rice
- 3/4 cup shredded taco-seasoned cheese (4 ounces)
- 1 cup shredded lettuce
- 1 medium tomato, chopped (3/4 cup)
- Sour cream, if desired

1. Cook beef in 10-inch skillet over medium heat 8 to 10 minutes, stirring occasionally, until brown; drain.
2. Stir seasoning mix, water, salsa and corn into beef. Heat to boiling; stir in rice. Boil 1 minute; remove from heat. Cover and let stand 8 minutes.
3. Fluff rice mixture with fork; sprinkle with cheese. Cover and let stand 1 to 2 minutes or until cheese is melted. Sprinkle lettuce around edge of skillet; sprinkle tomato in circle next to lettuce. Serve with sour cream.

1 SERVING Calories 440 (Calories from Fat 170) | Fat 19g (Saturated 9g) | Cholesterol 70mg | Sodium 670mg | Carbohydrate 44g (Dietary Fiber 3g) | Protein 26g % DAILY VALUE Vitamin A 30% | Vitamin C 12% | Calcium 14% | Iron 20% EXCHANGES 3 Starch, 2 High-Fat Meat CARBOHYDRATE CHOICES 3

BETTY'S TIP

On the slim chance you have leftovers, turn them into taco filling or use them in wrap sandwiches for lunch the next day.

Easy Taco Dinner

PREP 15 min COOK 22 min SERVINGS 6

1 pound lean ground beef

1 large onion, chopped (about 1 cup)

1 envelope (1 1/4 ounces) taco seasoning mix

1 cup water

1 package (12 ounces) tortilla chips

1/2 head iceberg lettuce, shredded

2 medium tomatoes, chopped (1 1/2 cups)

1 can (2 1/4 ounces) sliced ripe olives, drained

1 cup shredded Cheddar or Monterey Jack cheese (4 ounces)

2/3 cup sour cream

1. Cook beef and onion in 10-inch skillet over medium heat 8 to 10 minutes, stirring occasionally, until beef is brown; drain.
2. Stir in seasoning mix and water. Heat to boiling; reduce heat to low. Simmer uncovered, stirring occasionally, 10 minutes. Spoon beef mixture onto chips. Top with remaining ingredients.

1 SERVING Calories 615 (Calories from Fat 340) | Fat 38g (Saturated 13g) | Cholesterol 80mg | Sodium 850mg | Carbohydrate 47g (Dietary Fiber 6g) | Protein 25g % DAILY VALUE Vitamin A 30% | Vitamin C 10% | Calcium 18% | Iron 24% EXCHANGES 3 Starch, 2 Medium-Fat Meat, 5 Fat CARBOHYDRATE CHOICES 3

BETTY'S TIP

Kids will find this dinner much easier to eat than regular tacos because there are no crumbly taco shells to contend with, and the cook gets the benefit of not having to heat the taco shells—everyone wins! Set out bowls of toppings so everyone can top their taco dinner as they like.

Penne with Beef and Sun-Dried Tomatoes

PREP 10 min COOK 20 min SERVINGS 4

- 1 1/2 cups uncooked penne pasta (6 ounces)
- 1 pound beef boneless sirloin steak, cut into thin strips
- 1/2 teaspoon peppered seasoned salt
- 1/2 cup sun-dried tomatoes packed in olive oil and herbs, drained and cut into thin strips
- 2 tablespoons oil from sun-dried tomatoes
- 4 medium green onions, sliced (1/4 cup)
- 1 jar (6 to 6 1/2 ounces) marinated artichoke hearts, drained
- 2 tablespoons chopped fresh basil leaves

1. Cook and drain pasta as directed on package.
2. While pasta is cooking, spray 12-inch nonstick skillet with cooking spray; heat over medium-high heat. Add beef to skillet; sprinkle with peppered seasoned salt. Cook 2 to 3 minutes, stirring occasionally, just until brown.
3. Stir tomatoes, 1 tablespoon of the oil and the onions into beef. Cook 1 to 2 minutes, stirring frequently, until hot. Stir in artichoke hearts, pasta and the remaining 1 tablespoon oil. Cook 1 to 2 minutes, stirring constantly, until hot. Sprinkle with basil.

1 SERVING Calories 395 (Calories from Fat 125) | Fat 14g (Saturated 3g) | Cholesterol 60mg | Sodium 390mg | Carbohydrate 42g (Dietary Fiber 5g) | Protein 31g % DAILY VALUE Vitamin A 10% | Vitamin C 16% | Calcium 4% | Iron 26% EXCHANGES 2 1/2 Starch, 1 Vegetable, 3 Lean Meat CARBOHYDRATE CHOICES 3

BETTY'S TIP

Don't throw out the leftover sun-dried tomato oil. It adds pizzazz when added to salad dressings or drizzled over French bread.

Stir-Fried Beef and Broccoli

PREP 15 min COOK 10 min SERVINGS 4

- 1/2 cup cold water
- 2 tablespoons cornstarch
- 2 tablespoons soy sauce
- 1 pound beef boneless sirloin steak
- 2 tablespoons vegetable oil
- 1/4 teaspoon ground ginger
- 1/4 teaspoon garlic powder
- 1 bag (1 pound) frozen chopped broccoli, thawed and drained
- 1 cup orange juice
- 4 cups hot cooked rice

1. Mix water, cornstarch and soy sauce; set aside. Trim fat from beef. Cut beef with grain into 2-inch strips; cut strips across grain into 1/8-inch slices.
2. Heat 12-inch skillet or wok over medium-high heat. Add oil; rotate skillet to coat bottom. Add beef, ginger and garlic powder; stir-fry about 3 minutes or until beef is brown. Add broccoli; stir-fry 2 minutes.
3. Stir in orange juice; heat to boiling. Stir in cornstarch mixture; cook and stir about 1 minute or until thickened. Serve beef mixture with rice.

1 SERVING Calories 460 (Calories from Fat 100) | Fat 11g (Saturated 2g) | Cholesterol 55mg | Sodium 530mg | Carbohydrate 62g (Dietary Fiber 4g) | Protein 28g % DAILY VALUE Vitamin A 36% | Vitamin C 50% | Calcium 8% | Iron 28% EXCHANGES 3 1/2 Starch, 1 Vegetable, 2 Lean Meat, 1 Fat CARBOHYDRATE CHOICES 4

BETTY'S TIP

A fresh spinach salad with sliced red onion and mushrooms nicely complements this citrus-kissed stir-fry. For added zip, top the salad with crumbled Gorgonzola or blue cheese.

Easy Weeknight Beef-Veggie Mix

PREP **20 min** COOK **10 min** SERVINGS **5**

1. Melt butter in 10-inch skillet over low heat. Stir in cornstarch. Stir tomatoes, bell pepper, onion and garlic into butter mixture. Cook about 5 minutes, stirring frequently, until hot.
2. Stir beef, raisins and salt into vegetable mixture. Cook about 5 minutes, stirring frequently, until beef and raisins are hot.

1 SERVING Calories 160 (Calories from Fat 45) | Fat 5g (Saturated 1g) | Cholesterol 45mg | Sodium 300mg | Carbohydrate 11g (Dietary Fiber 1g) | Protein 18g % DAILY VALUE Vitamin A 12% | Vitamin C 20% | Calcium 0% | Iron 10% EXCHANGES 2 Vegetable, 2 Lean Meat CARBOHYDRATE CHOICES 1

1 tablespoon butter or margarine

1 teaspoon cornstarch

2 medium tomatoes, chopped (1 1/2 cups)

1 small green bell pepper, chopped (1/2 cup)

1 small onion, chopped (1/4 cup)

1 clove garlic, finely chopped

2 cups bite-size pieces cooked beef

3 tablespoons raisins

1/2 teaspoon salt

BETTY'S TIP

Get ahead of the game by chopping the tomatoes, bell pepper, onion and garlic the night before. Store in a tightly sealed container in the refrigerator.

Caesar Chicken with Orzo

PREP **5 min** COOK **27 min** SERVINGS **4**

1 tablespoon vegetable oil

4 boneless, skinless chicken breast halves (about 1 1/4 pounds)

1 can (14 ounces) chicken broth

1 cup water

1 cup uncooked orzo or rosamarina pasta (6 ounces)

1 bag (1 pound) frozen baby whole carrots, green beans and yellow beans (or other combination)

3 tablespoons Caesar dressing

1/8 teaspoon coarsely ground pepper

1. Heat oil in 10-inch skillet over medium-high heat. Cook chicken in oil about 10 minutes, turning once, until brown. Remove chicken from skillet; keep warm.
2. Add broth and water to skillet; heat to boiling. Stir in pasta; heat to boiling. Cook uncovered 8 to 10 minutes, stirring occasionally, until pasta is tender. Stir in frozen vegetables and dressing. Add chicken. Sprinkle with pepper.
3. Heat to boiling; reduce heat to low. Simmer uncovered about 5 minutes or until vegetables are crisp-tender and juice of chicken is no longer pink when centers of thickest pieces are cut.

1 SERVING Calories 405 (Calories from Fat 125) | Fat 14g (Saturated 3g) | Cholesterol 75mg | Sodium 670mg | Carbohydrate 49g (Dietary Fiber 6g) | Protein 39g % DAILY VALUE Vitamin A 100% | Vitamin C 22% | Calcium 10% | Iron 26% EXCHANGES 2 Starch, 1 Vegetable, 4 Lean Meat CARBOHYDRATE CHOICES 3

BETTY'S TIP

Warmed purchased focaccia bread and fresh pear slices or clusters of red grapes make tasty sides to this dish.

Chicken Paprika

PREP 15 min COOK 12 min SERVINGS 4

- 2 medium onions, cut lengthwise in half, then cut crosswise into very thin slices
- 2 medium stalks celery, sliced (1 cup)
- 4 cloves garlic, finely chopped
- 2 tablespoons paprika
- 1/4 teaspoon pepper
- 1 1/2 cups cut-up cooked chicken
- 1/2 cup ready-to-serve chicken broth
- 1 cup reduced-fat sour cream
- Hot cooked wide egg noodles, if desired
- Chopped fresh parsley, if desired

1. Spray 10-inch nonstick skillet with cooking spray; heat over medium heat. Cook onions, celery and garlic in skillet about 5 minutes, stirring frequently, until onions are tender. Stir in paprika and pepper. Cook 1 minute, stirring constantly.
2. Stir in chicken and broth. Heat to boiling; reduce heat to medium. Stir sour cream into liquid in skillet. Heat over medium heat just until heated through. Serve over noodles. Sprinkle with parsley.

1 SERVING Calories 220 (Calories from Fat 100) | Fat 11g (Saturated 6g) | Cholesterol 65mg | Sodium 220mg | Carbohydrate 11g (Dietary Fiber 2g) | Protein 19g % DAILY VALUE Vitamin A 52% | Vitamin C 6% | Calcium 10% | Iron 10% EXCHANGES 1/2 Starch, 1 Vegetable, 2 Medium-Fat Meat CARBOHYDRATE CHOICES 1

BETTY'S TIP

This updated version of Chicken Paprikash allows you to enjoy all the traditional spicy flavor of the dish with less fat and sodium and fewer calories than old-time recipes. For a touch of authenticity, use fiery Hungarian paprika, but use only 1 tablespoon to start and then add more to taste.

Chicken Penne à la Marengo

PREP 15 min COOK 25 min SERVINGS 4

- 1 pound boneless, skinless chicken breasts, cut into 1-inch pieces
- 1 can (14 ounces) chicken broth
- 2 cups uncooked penne pasta (6 ounces)
- 1 medium green bell pepper, cut into 1-inch pieces (1 cup)
- 1 can (14 1/2 ounces) Italian-style stewed tomatoes, undrained
- 1/4 cup dry white wine or chicken broth
- 1 tablespoon tomato paste
- 1 can (2 1/4 ounces) sliced ripe olives, drained

1. Spray 12-inch nonstick skillet with cooking spray; heat over medium-high heat. Cook chicken 2 to 3 minutes, stirring frequently, until brown.
2. Stir broth into chicken; heat to boiling. Stir in pasta and bell pepper. Heat to boiling; reduce heat to medium. Cover and cook 10 minutes, stirring occasionally.
3. Stir in tomatoes, wine and tomato paste. Cook uncovered 5 to 10 minutes, stirring occasionally, until chicken is no longer pink in center and pasta is tender. Stir in olives.

1 SERVING Calories 365 (Calories from Fat 65) | Fat 7g (Saturated 2g) | Cholesterol 70mg | Sodium 1080mg | Carbohydrate 45g (Dietary Fiber 4g) | Protein 34g % DAILY VALUE Vitamin A 10% | Vitamin C 34% | Calcium 66% | Iron 22% EXCHANGES 2 1/2 Starch, 2 Vegetable, 3 Very Lean Meat CARBOHYDRATE CHOICES 3

BETTY'S TIP

Napoleon's chef is believed to have created this famous dish after the Battle of Marengo in 1800. In this version, the pasta is cooked right in the sauce for an easy one-dish meal.

Asparagus-Dijon-Chicken Fettuccine

PREP 10 min COOK 17 min STAND 5 min SERVINGS 5

1 tablespoon butter or margarine

1 pound boneless, skinless chicken breasts, cut into 1-inch pieces

1 can (4 ounces) mushroom pieces and stems, drained

1 medium onion, chopped (1/2 cup)

1 package (6.8 ounces) fettuccine Alfredo skillet-dinner mix for chicken

1 cup milk

2 1/2 cups water

2 tablespoons Dijon mustard

1 package (10 ounces) frozen asparagus cuts, thawed and drained

1. Melt butter in 10-inch skillet over high heat. Cook chicken, mushrooms and onion in butter 3 to 5 minutes, stirring occasionally, until chicken is white.
2. Stir Sauce Mix from skillet-dinner mix, the milk, water and mustard into chicken mixture. Heat to boiling, stirring occasionally. Stir in uncooked Pasta; reduce heat to low. Cover and simmer about 10 minutes, stirring occasionally, until pasta is tender.
3. Stir in asparagus. Cover and simmer 2 minutes, stirring occasionally; remove from heat. Uncover and let stand about 5 minutes or until sauce thickens. Stir before serving.

1 SERVING Calories 290 (Calories from Fat 90) | Fat 10g (Saturated 3g) | Cholesterol 60mg | Sodium 1030mg | Carbohydrate 34g (Dietary Fiber 3g) | Protein 29g % DAILY VALUE Vitamin A 10% | Vitamin C 10% | Calcium 10% | Iron 12% EXCHANGES 2 Starch, 1 Vegetable, 3 Very Lean Meat CARBOHYDRATE CHOICES 2

Dijon-Chicken Fettuccine with Green Peas Use a 10-ounce package of frozen green peas, thawed and drained, instead of the asparagus cuts.

BETTY'S TIP

A tossed salad with mandarin orange segments and vinaigrette dressing would taste great with this delicious entrée.

Citrus Ginger Chicken

PREP 10 min **COOK** 20 min **SERVINGS** 4

1/2 cup orange juice

1/4 cup lime juice

2 tablespoons honey

1 teaspoon finely chopped gingerroot

1 teaspoon chopped fresh or 1/4 teaspoon dried thyme leaves

1/4 teaspoon salt

1/4 teaspoon black and red pepper blend

4 boneless, skinless chicken breast halves (about 1 1/4 pounds)

1 tablespoon butter or margarine

1 medium seedless orange, peeled and cut into slices

Additional fresh thyme leaves, if desired

1. Mix orange juice, lime juice, honey, gingerroot and 1 teaspoon thyme in medium bowl.
2. Spray 10-inch nonstick skillet with cooking spray; heat over medium-high heat. Sprinkle salt and pepper blend over chicken. Cook chicken in skillet 3 to 4 minutes, turning once, until brown. Stir in orange juice mixture. Heat to boiling; reduce heat to medium-low. Cover and cook 8 to 10 minutes or until chicken is no longer pink when centers of thickest pieces are cut. Remove chicken from skillet.
3. Heat sauce in skillet to boiling. Add butter. Cook, stirring constantly, until butter is melted and sauce is slightly thickened. Serve sauce over chicken and orange slices. Sprinkle with additional thyme.

1 SERVING Calories 235 (Calories from Fat 65) | Fat 7g (Saturated 3g) | Cholesterol 80mg | Sodium 240mg | Carbohydrate 17g (Dietary Fiber 1g) | Protein 27g % DAILY VALUE Vitamin A 4% | Vitamin C 26% | Calcium 2% | Iron 6% EXCHANGES 1 Fruit, 4 Very Lean Meat, 1 Fat CARBOHYDRATE CHOICES 1

BETTY'S TIP

Serve this citrus-flavored chicken dish with rice or couscous and cooked beets tossed with butter.

Fettucine and Chicken in Orange-Cherry Sauce

PREP 10 min COOK 15 min SERVINGS 4

- 6 ounces uncooked fettuccine
- 1/2 pound cut-up boneless chicken breast for stir-fry
- 1/4 teaspoon salt
- 1 1/2 cups or 1 package (9 ounces) frozen whole green beans
- 1 cup orange juice
- 1 tablespoon cornstarch
- 1 tablespoon orange marmalade
- 1/4 cup dried cherries
- 1/4 cup chopped walnuts, toasted* if desired

1. Cook and drain fettuccine as directed on package.
2. While fettuccine is cooking, spray 12-inch nonstick skillet with cooking spray; heat over medium heat. Cook chicken and salt in skillet 2 to 3 minutes, stirring occasionally, until chicken is brown. Stir in frozen green beans. Cover and cook over medium heat 3 to 4 minutes, stirring occasionally, until beans are crisp-tender.
3. Mix orange juice and cornstarch until smooth. Stir orange juice mixture, marmalade and cherries into chicken mixture. Heat to boiling, stirring constantly; reduce heat to medium. Cover and cook 2 to 3 minutes, stirring occasionally, until beans are tender and chicken is no longer pink in center. Add fettuccine to chicken mixture; toss. Sprinkle each serving with walnuts.

*How to toast nuts: Bake nuts uncovered in ungreased shallow pan in a 350° oven about 10 minutes, stirring occasionally, until golden brown. Or cook in ungreased heavy skillet over medium-low heat 5 to 7 minutes, stirring frequently until browning begins, then stirring constantly until golden brown.

1 SERVING: Calories 325 (Calories from Fat 70) | Fat 8g (Saturated 1g) | Cholesterol 70mg | Sodium 190mg | Carbohydrate 49g (Dietary Fiber 6g) | Protein 20g % DAILY VALUE: Vitamin A 4% | Vitamin C 26% | Calcium 6% | Iron 18% EXCHANGES 3 Starch, 1 Lean Meat, 1 Vegetable, 1/2 Fat CARBOHYDRATE CHOICES 3

BETTY'S TIP

Boneless chicken breast for stir-fry is available in most larger grocery stores, but if you can't find it, cut boneless, skinless chicken breast halves into thin strips.

Chicken-and-Pasta Stir-Fry

PREP **10 min** COOK **14 min** SERVINGS **4**

2 cups uncooked farfalle (bow-tie) pasta (4 ounces)

1 pound asparagus, cut into 2-inch pieces (3 cups)

2 medium onions, sliced

1 1/2 cups chicken broth

1 pound boneless, skinless chicken breast halves, cut into 1-inch pieces

3 tablespoons chopped fresh or 1 tablespoon dried basil leaves

3 tablespoons chopped sun-dried tomatoes (not oil-packed)

1/4 teaspoon pepper

Freshly grated Parmesan cheese, if desired

1. Cook and drain pasta as directed on package.
2. Spray 12-inch skillet with cooking spray; heat over medium heat. Cook asparagus, onions and 1 cup of the broth in skillet 5 to 7 minutes, stirring occasionally, until liquid has evaporated. Remove mixture from skillet.
3. Spray skillet with cooking spray; heat over medium-high heat. Add chicken; stir-fry about 5 minutes or until no longer pink in center.
4. Return asparagus mixture to skillet. Stir in remaining 1/2 cup broth, the basil, tomatoes, pepper and pasta. Cook about 2 minutes, stirring frequently, until mixture is hot. Sprinkle with cheese.

1 SERVING Calories 290 (Calories from Fat 45 | Fat 5g (Saturated 1g) | Cholesterol 70mg | Sodium 510mg | Carbohydrate 31g (Dietary Fiber 3g) | Protein 33g % DAILY VALUE Vitamin A 6% | Vitamin C 14% | Calcium 4% | Iron 16% EXCHANGES 2 Starch, 4 Very Lean Meat CARBOHYDRATE CHOICES 2

BETTY'S TIP

If you'd like to serve six, this is an easy recipe to stretch. Add more veggies, like broccoli flowerets or sliced carrots, and more pasta, too. For interest, use a different shape or color of pasta.

Chicken-Vegetable Stroganoff

PREP 15 min COOK 15 min SERVINGS 4

- 1 1/2 cups (from 1-pound bag) frozen broccoli, cauliflower and carrots (or other combination)
- 1 1/2 cups sliced mushrooms (4 ounces)
- 1 large onion, sliced
- 2 cups chicken broth
- 1 tablespoon chopped fresh or 1 teaspoon dried marjoram leaves
- 1/4 teaspoon pepper
- 3 to 3 3/4 cups uncooked egg noodles (6 to 7 ounces)
- 2 cups cut-up cooked chicken or turkey
- 1 container (8 ounces) sour cream
- 1/3 cup water
- 2 tablespoons all-purpose flour

1. Heat broccoli mixture, mushrooms, onion, broth, marjoram, pepper and noodles to boiling in 10-inch skillet; reduce heat to low.
2. Cover and simmer about 8 minutes, stirring occasionally, until noodles and vegetables are tender.
3. Stir in chicken. Mix sour cream, water and flour; stir into chicken mixture. Heat to boiling. Boil and stir 1 minute.

1 SERVING Calories 445 (Calories from Fat 170) | Fat 19g (Saturated 9g) | Cholesterol 135mg | Sodium 620mg | Carbohydrate 40g (Dietary Fiber 3g) | Protein 31g % DAILY VALUE Vitamin A 22% | Vitamin C 12% | Calcium 10% | Iron 20% EXCHANGES 2 Starch, 2 Vegetable, 3 Medium-Fat Meat CARBOHYDRATE CHOICES 2 1/2

BETTY'S TIP

For a health twist, use low-sodium chicken broth and reduced-fat sour cream in this stroganoff.

Teriyaki Chicken Stir-Fry

PREP **5 min** COOK **10 min** SERVINGS **4**

- 1 pound boneless, skinless chicken breast strips for stir-fry
- 1/2 cup teriyaki baste and glaze
- 3 tablespoons lemon juice
- 1 bag (1 pound) frozen broccoli, carrots, water chestnuts and red peppers (or other combination)
- Hot cooked rice, couscous, or noodles, if desired

1. Spray 12-inch nonstick skillet with cooking spray; heat over medium-high heat. Cook chicken 3 to 4 minutes, stirring frequently, until chicken is no longer pink in center.
2. Stir remaining ingredients except rice into chicken. Heat to boiling, stirring constantly; reduce heat to low. Cover and simmer about 6 minutes or until vegetables are crisp-tender. Serve with rice.

1 SERVING Calories 215 (Calories from Fat 45) | Fat 5g (Saturated 1g) | Cholesterol 70mg | Sodium 1850mg | Carbohydrate 15g (Dietary Fiber 3g) | Protein 30g % DAILY VALUE Vitamin A 26% | Vitamin C 32% | Calcium 6% | Iron 14% EXCHANGES 3 Very Lean Meat, 3 Vegetable, 1 Fat CARBOHYDRATE CHOICES 1

BETTY'S TIP

Take care not to confuse teriyaki baste and glaze with teriyaki sauce or marinade. The first is a thick and brown-colored sauce, while the second has a watery consistency. Both can be found in the Asian foods section of your supermarket.

Easy Chicken Alfredo

PREP 10 min COOK 11 min SERVINGS 4

- 2 tablespoons olive or vegetable oil
- 1 1/4 pounds boneless, skinless chicken breasts, cut into thin strips
- 2 medium zucchini, sliced (4 cups)
- 1 large red bell pepper, cut into thin strips (1 cup)
- 1 container (10 ounces) refrigerated Alfredo sauce
- Grated fresh Parmesan cheese

1. Heat oil in 12-inch skillet over medium-high heat. Cook chicken in oil 5 to 6 minutes, stirring occasionally, until chicken is no longer pink in center.
2. Add zucchini and bell pepper; cook about 5 minutes, stirring frequently, until vegetables are crisp-tender.
3. Stir in Alfredo sauce. Sprinkle with cheese.

1 SERVING Calories 575 (Calories from Fat 370) | Fat 41g (Saturated 21g) | Cholesterol 165mg | Sodium 570mg | Carbohydrate 15g (Dietary Fiber 3g) | Protein 39g % DAILY VALUE Vitamin A 52% | Vitamin C 80% | Calcium 36% | Iron 12% EXCHANGES 1 Starch, 5 Lean Meat, 5 Fat CARBOHYDRATE CHOICES 1

BETTY'S TIP

Pierogies are potato-filled dumplings. If you can't find them, you can easily use frozen cooked gnocchi to make Chicken with Potato Gnocchi.

Easy Mexican Chicken and Beans

PREP **8 min** COOK **20 min** SERVINGS **4**

- 1 pound cut-up boneless chicken breast for stir-fry
- 1 envelope (1 1/4 ounces) taco seasoning mix
- 1 can (15 to 16 ounces) black or pinto beans, rinsed and drained
- 1 can (11 ounces) whole-kernel corn with red and green peppers, undrained
- 1/4 cup water
- Flour tortillas, if desired

1. Spray 10-inch nonstick skillet with cooking spray. Cook chicken in skillet over medium-high heat 8 to 10 minutes, stirring occasionally, until no longer pink in center.
2. Stir in seasoning mix, beans, corn and water. Cook over medium-high heat 8 to 10 minutes, stirring frequently, until sauce is slightly thickened. Serve with tortillas.

1 SERVING Calories 335 (Calories from Fat 45) | Fat 5g (Saturated 1g) | Cholesterol 70mg | Sodium 780mg | Carbohydrate 48g (Dietary Fiber 12g) | Protein 37g
% DAILY VALUE Vitamin A 10% | Vitamin C 10% | Calcium 8% | Iron 24%
EXCHANGES 2 Starch, 3 Vegetable, 3 1/2 Very Lean Meat CARBOHYDRATE CHOICES 2 1/2

BETTY'S TIP

Make a weekday Mexican fiesta by serving this tasty dish topped with sour cream, salsa and green chilies. Olé! Chips and guacamole are always popular, too.

Szechuan Chicken and Pasta

PREP 5 min COOK 25 min SERVINGS 4

1 pound boneless, skinless chicken breast halves, cut into 3/4- to 1-inch pieces

1 medium onion, cut into thin wedges

2 cups water

1 1/2 cups uncooked fusilli pasta (3 ounces)

1 package (1 pound 5 ounces) frozen Szechuan stir-fry mix with vegetables, Szechuan sauce and peanuts

1. Spray 12-inch nonstick skillet with cooking spray; heat over medium-high heat. Add chicken and onion; stir-fry 3 to 5 minutes or until chicken is light brown.
2. Stir in water; heat to boiling. Stir in pasta. Cook 8 to 10 minutes, stirring occasionally, until pasta is almost tender (do not drain).
3. Stir in packet of Sauce Mix from stir-fry mix until well blended. Stir in Vegetables from stir-fry mix. Reduce heat to medium. Cover and cook 8 to 9 minutes, stirring occasionally, until vegetables are crisp-tender. Sprinkle with Peanuts from stir-fry mix.

1 SERVING Calories 380 (Calories from Fat 90) | Fat 10g (Saturated 2g) | Cholesterol 50mg | Sodium 620mg | Carbohydrate 49g (Dietary Fiber 7g) | Protein 30g % DAILY VALUE Vitamin A 18% | Vitamin C 38% | Calcium 8% | Iron 22% EXCHANGES 3 Starch, 1 Vegetable, 2 Lean Meat CARBOHYDRATE CHOICES 3

BETTY'S TIP

For an additional time-saver, look for thinly presliced chicken breast strips in the meat aisle (the package may be labeled "chicken for stir-fry"). You'll need about 1 pound of strips for this recipe.

Vegetable Chicken Stir-Fry

PREP **5 min** COOK **7 min** SERVINGS **4**

- 2 tablespoons vegetable oil
- 1 pound boneless, skinless chicken breast halves or thighs, cut into 1-inch pieces
- 3 cups cut-up assorted vegetables (shredded carrots, bell peppers, broccoli flowerets)
- 1 clove garlic, finely chopped
- 1/2 cup stir-fry sauce

1. Heat 1 tablespoon of the oil in 12-inch skillet or wok over high heat. Add chicken; stir-fry about 3 minutes or until no longer pink in center. Remove from skillet.
2. Heat remaining 1 tablespoon oil in skillet. Add vegetables and garlic; stir-fry about 2 minutes or until vegetables are crisp-tender.
3. Add chicken and stir-fry sauce. Cook and stir about 2 minutes or until hot.

1 SERVING Calories 235 (Calories from Fat 100) | Fat 11g (Saturated 2g) | Cholesterol 70mg | Sodium 1900mg | Carbohydrate 9g (Dietary Fiber 3g) | Protein 28g % DAILY VALUE Vitamin A 66% | Vitamin C 78% | Calcium 4% | Iron 10% EXCHANGES 2 Vegetable, 3 1/2 Lean Meat CARBOHYDRATE CHOICES 1/2

BETTY'S TIP

Add toasty crunch with toasted wonton wrappers! You'll find wonton wrappers in the produce or freezer section of most grocery stores. Cut wonton wrappers into thin strips, and bake on ungreased cookie sheet at 350° for 5 to 7 minutes or until light golden brown. Top each serving with whole or broken toasted wonton strips.

Country-French Turkey and Red Potatoes

PREP **10 min** COOK **18 min** SERVINGS **4**

- 1/4 cup all-purpose flour
- 1/8 teaspoon pepper
- 1 pound uncooked turkey breast slices, about 1/4 inch thick
- 1 pound mushrooms, cut in half
- 8 large shallots, cut into fourths
- 8 small red potatoes (about 3/4 pound), cut into 6 wedges
- 1/3 cup dry white wine or chicken broth
- 1/2 teaspoon dried rosemary leaves

1. Mix flour and pepper in shallow dish or resealable plastic food-storage bag. Toss turkey with flour mixture. Spray 12-inch nonstick skillet with cooking spray; heat over medium heat. Cook turkey in skillet about 5 minutes, turning once, until brown. Remove turkey from skillet; keep warm.
2. Add mushrooms and shallots to skillet. Cook about 3 minutes, stirring frequently, until shallots are tender. Stir in remaining ingredients. Heat to boiling, stirring constantly. Boil and stir 2 minutes. Add turkey; reduce heat to low. Cover and simmer about 6 minutes, stirring occasionally, until turkey is no longer pink in center.

1 SERVING Calories 290 (Calories from Fat 20) | Fat 2g (Saturated 1g) | Cholesterol 75mg | Sodium 150mg | Carbohydrate 32g (Dietary Fiber 5g) | Protein 34g % DAILY VALUE Vitamin A 8% | Vitamin C 18% | Calcium 6% | Iron 26% EXCHANGES 2 Starch, 4 Very Lean Meat CARBOHYDRATE CHOICES 2

BETTY'S TIP

Shallots look like mini onions and taste like a mild mix of garlic and onion. You can usually find them near the onions in the produce section of the supermarket.

Glazed Turkey and Pea Pods

PREP **15 min** COOK **10 min** SERVINGS **4**

1. Cut turkey breast slices into bite-size pieces. Toss turkey and 1 teaspoon cornstarch. Mix broth, 1 tablespoon cornstarch, the hoisin sauce, gingerroot and pepper; set aside.
2. Heat 12-inch skillet or wok over medium-high heat. Add 1 tablespoon of the oil to skillet; rotate skillet to bottom. Add turkey; stir-fry about 4 minutes or until turkey is white. Remove turkey from skillet.
3. Add remaining 1 tablespoon oil to skillet; rotate skillet to bottom. Add pea pods, bell pepper and onions; stir-fry 4 to 5 minutes or until vegetables are crisp-tender. Stir in hoisin sauce mixture. Cook and stir about 1 minute or until thickened. Stir in turkey; heat through. Stir in noodles and cashews. Serve immediately.

1 SERVING Calories 495 (Calories from Fat 215) | Fat 24g (Saturated 4g) | Cholesterol 75mg | Sodium 640mg | Carbohydrate 35g (Dietary Fiber 5g) | Protein 35g % DAILY VALUE Vitamin A 55% | Vitamin C 80% | Calcium 6% | Iron 24% EXCHANGES 2 Starch, 1 Vegetable, 4 Lean Meat, 2 Fat CARBOHYDRATE CHOICES 2

1 pound uncooked turkey breast slices, about 1/4 inch thick

1 teaspoon cornstarch

3/4 cup chicken broth

1 tablespoon cornstarch

3 tablespoons hoisin sauce

2 teaspoons chopped gingerroot or 1 teaspoon ground ginger

1/8 teaspoon pepper

2 tablespoons vegetable oil

2 cups snow (Chinese) pea pods, strings removed

1 large red or green bell pepper, cut into 3/4-inch pieces

2 cups frozen small whole onions (from 1-pound bag), thawed and drained

2 cups chow mein noodles

1/2 cup coarsely chopped cashews or peanuts

Photo on page 68.

BETTY'S TIP

You can use a 6-ounce package of frozen snow (Chinese) pea pods, thawed and drained, instead of the fresh pea pods, if you have them on hand.

Smoked Turkey Lo Mein

PREP 30 min COOK 3 min SERVINGS 4

- 6 dried black (shiitake) mushrooms
- 1/2 pound fully cooked smoked 97%-fat-free turkey breast, cut into 1/2-inch cubes (1 1/2 cups)
- 1 cup frozen green peas (from 1-pound bag)
- 1 package (about 7.31 ounces) fresh (refrigerated) stir-fry noodles with soy sauce–flavored sauce
- 3/4 cup water
- 1 tablespoon oyster sauce
- 2 green onions, chopped (2 tablespoons)

1. Soak mushrooms in hot water about 20 minutes or until soft; drain. Rinse with warm water; drain. Squeeze out excess moisture. Remove and discard stems; cut caps into thin strips.
2. Spray 12-inch nonstick skillet or nonstick wok with cooking spray; heat over medium-high heat. Add turkey; stir-fry about 1 minute or until brown. Stir in mushrooms, peas, contents of Sauce Packet from noodles, water and oyster sauce. Add noodles; separate and stir-fry about 2 minutes or until heated through. Sprinkle with onions.

1 SERVING Calories 190 (Calories from Fat 45) | Fat 5g (Saturated 2g) | Cholesterol 30mg | Sodium 1080mg | Carbohydrate 21g (Dietary Fiber 3g) | Protein 15g % DAILY VALUE Vitamin A 8% | Vitamin C 4% | Calcium 6% | Iron 10% EXCHANGES 1 Starch, 1 Vegetable, 1 1/2 Lean Meat CARBOHYDRATE CHOICES 1 1/2

BETTY'S TIP

Instead of throwing away the mushroom stems, save them for future use in sautés, soups and sauces. They can be kept for up to three days when covered and stored in the fridge, or they can be frozen for up to six months.

Cheesy Turkey, Rice and Broccoli

PREP 10 min COOK 17 min STAND 5 min SERVINGS 4

1 pound turkey breast tenderloins, cut into 1-inch pieces

1 package (10 ounces) frozen broccoli with low-fat cheese-flavored sauce

1 2/3 cups uncooked instant brown rice

1 cup sliced mushrooms (3 ounces)

1/2 cup sliced water chestnuts

1 1/2 cups fat-free chicken broth

1 teaspoon chopped fresh or 1/2 teaspoon dried thyme leaves

1/2 teaspoon salt

5 medium green onions, sliced (1/3 cup)

1. Spray 12-inch skillet with cooking spray; heat over medium heat. Cook turkey in skillet about 5 minutes, stirring occasionally, until no longer pink in center.
2. While turkey is cooking, microwave broccoli in pouch on High 1 minute to easily remove from package.
3. Add broccoli mixture to turkey. Stir in remaining ingredients. Heat to boiling; reduce heat to low. Cover and simmer about 10 minutes, stirring occasionally, until most of liquid is absorbed. Let stand 5 minutes before serving.

1 SERVING Calories 305 (Calories from Fat 25) | Fat 3g (Saturated 1g) | Cholesterol 60mg | Sodium 600mg | Carbohydrate 43g (Dietary Fiber 5g) | Protein 31g % DAILY VALUE Vitamin A 12% | Vitamin C 14% | Calcium 12% | Iron 4% EXCHANGES 2 Starch, 2 Vegetable, 3 Very Lean Meat CARBOHYDRATE CHOICES 3

BETTY'S TIP

Regardless of whether it's fresh or frozen, one-half cup of chopped broccoli provides 90 percent of your RDA for vitamin A and 100 percent of vitamin C. With this tasty recipe, it's easy to go green.

Oriental Turkey and Rice

PREP 5 min COOK 30 min SERVINGS 4

- 1 pound ground turkey breast
- 1 package (7.3 ounces) rice Oriental skillet-dinner mix for hamburger
- 4 cups water
- 1 can (16 ounces) chow mein vegetables, drained
- 1 can (8 ounces) sliced water chestnuts, drained
- 2 cups chow mein noodles

1. Cook turkey in 10-inch skillet over medium heat, stirring frequently, until no longer pink; drain.
2. Stir uncooked Rice and Sauce Mix from skillet-dinner mix, the water, vegetables and water chestnuts into turkey. Heat to boiling, stirring occasionally; reduce heat to low.
3. Cover and simmer about 25 minutes or until rice is tender. Uncover and cook until desired consistency. Serve over noodles.

1 SERVING Calories 490 (Calories from Fat 100) | Fat 11g (Saturated 2g) | Cholesterol 50mg | Sodium 1150mg | Carbohydrate 68g (Dietary Fiber 4g) | Protein 30g % DAILY VALUE Vitamin A 8% | Vitamin C 10% | Calcium 4% | Iron 28% EXCHANGES 4 Starch, 1 Vegetable, 2 Lean Meat CARBOHYDRATE CHOICES 4 1/2

BETTY'S TIP

If you'd like to serve this dish with a side, grab a bag of Oriental salad greens and top the salad with drained canned mandarin orange segments and toasted slivered almonds.

Turkey-Pasta Primavera

PREP 10 min COOK 8 min SERVINGS 4

1. Cook and drain fettuccine as directed on package.
2. While fettuccine is cooking, heat dressing in 10-inch skillet over medium-high heat. Cook vegetables in dressing, stirring occasionally, until crisp-tender.
3. Stir turkey, salt and tomatoes into vegetables. Cook about 3 minutes or just until turkey is hot. Spoon turkey mixture over fettuccine. Sprinkle with cheese and parsley.

1 SERVING Calories 435 (Calories from Fat 115) | Fat 13g (Saturated 3g) | Cholesterol 120mg | Sodium 880mg | Carbohydrate 52g (Dietary Fiber 6g) | Protein 34g % DAILY VALUE Vitamin A 80% | Vitamin C 46% | Calcium 16% | Iron 26% EXCHANGES 3 Starch, 1 Vegetable, 3 Lean Meat CARBOHYDRATE CHOICES 3 1/2

1 package (9 ounces) refrigerated fettuccine or linguine

2 tablespoons Italian dressing

1 bag (1 pound) frozen broccoli, cauliflower and carrots (or other combination), thawed and drained

2 cups cut-up cooked turkey or chicken

1 teaspoon salt

2 large tomatoes, seeded and chopped (2 cups)

1/4 cup freshly grated Parmesan cheese

2 tablespoons chopped fresh parsley

BETTY'S TIP

Need to thaw veggies in a hurry? Place them in a colander and run cool water over them until thawed but still cold.

Peppery Cajun Pork Pasta

PREP 20 min COOK 15 min SERVINGS 6

- 8 ounces uncooked fettuccine
- 1 pound pork tenderloin
- 4 teaspoons Cajun seasoning
- 1 tablespoon vegetable oil
- 1 large red onion, chopped (1 1/2 cups)
- 2 large zucchini, chopped (2 1/2 cups)
- 1/4 teaspoon salt
- 3 medium roma (plum) tomatoes, chopped (1 cup)
- 1 can (15 to 16 ounces) black-eyed peas, rinsed and drained
- 1/4 cup lemon juice
- 1 teaspoon dried oregano leaves
- 1/4 teaspoon freshly ground pepper
- Red pepper sauce, if desired

1. Cook and drain fettuccine as directed on package.
2. While fettuccine is cooking, cut pork into 1/4-inch slices; sprinkle with Cajun seasoning. Heat oil in 12-inch nonstick skillet over medium-high heat. Cook pork in oil 4 to 6 minutes, turning occasionally, until pork is no longer pink in center. Remove from skillet; keep warm.
3. Spray same skillet with cooking spray; heat over medium-high heat. Cook onion in skillet about 4 minutes, stirring frequently, until onion begins to brown. Stir in zucchini and salt. Cook about 4 minutes, stirring frequently, until vegetables are tender. Stir in remaining ingredients. Cook about 1 minute, stirring frequently, until hot.
4. Toss vegetable mixture and fettuccine. Serve pork over fettuccine mixture, or toss pork with fettuccine mixture.

1 SERVING Calories 290 (Calories from Fat 65) | Fat 7g (Saturated 2g) | Cholesterol 80mg | Sodium 300mg | Carbohydrate 46g (Dietary Fiber 8g) | Protein 29g % DAILY VALUE Vitamin A 20% | Vitamin C 16% | Calcium 6% | Iron 26% EXCHANGES 2 1/2 Starch, 2 Vegetable, 2 Very Lean Meat CARBOHYDRATE CHOICES 3

BETTY'S TIP

Black-eyed peas, a common staple in the South, are actually a legume. They are available dried, canned or frozen. If you like, substitute a 10-ounce package of frozen black-eyed peas for the canned; just thaw before cooking.

Sausage with Fettuccine

PREP 10 min COOK 8 min SERVINGS 4

1 package (9 ounces) refrigerated spinach or regular fettuccine

2 cans (15 ounces each) chunky garlic-and-herb tomato sauce

1 bag (1 pound) frozen stir-fry bell peppers and onions, thawed and drained

1 ring (1 pound) fully cooked fat-free Polish or kielbasa sausage, cut into 1/2-inch pieces

Finely shredded Parmesan cheese, if desired

1. Cook and drain fettuccine as directed on package; keep warm.
2. Heat tomato sauce, bell pepper mixture and sausage to boiling in same saucepan. Serve sauce over fettuccine, or toss fettuccine with sauce mixture. Serve with cheese.

1 SERVING Calories 380 (Calories from Fat 25) | Fat 3g (Saturated 3g) | Cholesterol 110mg | Sodium 2310mg | Carbohydrate 67g (Dietary Fiber 7g) | Protein 29g % DAILY VALUE Vitamin A 36% | Vitamin C 70% | Calcium 8% | Iron 30% EXCHANGES 4 Starch, 1 Vegetable, 2 Very Lean Meat CARBOHYDRATE CHOICES 4 1/2

Fettuccine Alfredo with Sausage Use Alfredo pasta sauce instead of the chunky garlic-and-herb tomato sauce. Check Alfredo pasta sauce label for heating instructions; some should not be boiled.

BETTY'S TIP

A slice of crusty garlicky bread complements this Italian dish. To make your own, brush cut sides of French bread with olive oil and sprinkle with garlic powder or garlic salt, then sprinkle with grated Parmesan cheese. Broil on a cookie sheet until edges of bread are golden brown and bread is hot.

Creamy Bow-Ties with Ham and Vegetables

PREP 10 min COOK 15 min SERVINGS 4

- 2 cups uncooked farfalle (bow-tie) pasta or wide egg noodles (4 ounces)
- 1/2 cup soft cream cheese with chives and onion
- 3/4 cup half-and-half
- 1 cup baby-cut carrots, cut lengthwise in half if large
- 8 ounces asparagus, cut into 1 1/2-inch pieces
- 1 1/2 cups cooked ham strips (1 × 1/4-inch)
- 1/4 teaspoon dried marjoram leaves

1. Cook and drain pasta as directed on package.
2. While pasta is cooking, mix cream cheese and half-and-half in 12-inch nonstick skillet. Cook over medium heat 2 to 3 minutes, stirring constantly, until melted and smooth.
3. Stir in carrots. Cook 4 minutes, stirring occasionally. Stir in asparagus. Cover and cook 4 to 5 minutes, stirring occasionally, until vegetables are crisp-tender.
4. Stir in ham, pasta and marjoram. Cook, stirring occasionally, just until hot.

1 SERVING Calories 425 (Calories from Fat 180) | Fat 20g (Saturated 11g) | Cholesterol 75mg | Sodium 860mg | Carbohydrate 40g (Dietary Fiber 3g) | Protein 21g % DAILY VALUE Vitamin A 100% | Vitamin C 8% | Calcium 10% | Iron 16% EXCHANGES 2 Starch, 2 Lean Meat, 2 Vegetable, 2 1/2 Fat CARBOHYDRATE CHOICES 2 1/2

BETTY'S TIP

Fresh asparagus is easy to prepare. Just rinse the stalks with cool water to remove any grit in the tips, and snap off the ends where they naturally break. Then cut into pieces of the desired size. Or to save time, use frozen asparagus cuts.

Pork Chop Dinner with Rice and Veggies

PREP **5 min** COOK **25 min** SERVINGS **6**

- 6 pork boneless loin chops, 1/2 inch thick (about 1 1/4 pounds)
- 2 cans (10 3/4 ounces each) condensed reduced-fat cream of mushroom soup
- 1 bag (1 pound) frozen baby peas, carrots, pea pods and corn (or other combination), thawed and drained
- 1 can (14 ounces) chicken broth
- 2 cups uncooked instant brown rice

1. Spray 12-inch nonstick skillet with cooking spray; heat over medium heat. Cook pork in skillet about 5 minutes, turning once, until brown. Remove pork from skillet; keep warm.
2. Heat soup, vegetables and broth to boiling in same skillet, stirring occasionally. Stir in rice; reduce heat to low. Cover and simmer 5 minutes.
3. Top with pork. Cover and simmer 10 to 15 minutes longer or until pork is no longer pink in center and rice is tender.

1 SERVING Calories 485 (Calories from Fat 115) | Fat 13g (Saturated 4g) | Cholesterol 70mg | Sodium 1160mg | Carbohydrate 65g (Dietary Fiber 6g) | Protein 33g % DAILY VALUE Vitamin A 80% | Vitamin C 8% | Calcium 6% | Iron 14% EXCHANGES 4 Starch, 1 Vegetable, 2 1/2 Lean Meat CARBOHYDRATE CHOICES 4

BETTY'S TIP

Because brown rice contains oil in its bran, it should be used within six months of purchasing.

Pork and Julienne Potatoes

PREP 15 min COOK 32 min SERVINGS 4

- 2 tablespoons butter or margarine
- 4 pork boneless loin chops, about 3/4 inch thick (about 1 1/4 pounds)
- 1 medium onion, cut in half and sliced
- 2 teaspoons dried sage leaves
- 1 package (4.6 ounces) julienne potato mix
- 2 1/3 cups boiling water
- 1/3 cup milk

1. Melt butter in 12-inch skillet over medium-high heat. Cook pork, onion and sage in butter 9 minutes, turning pork once.
2. Mix Potatoes and Sauce Mix from potato mix, the boiling water and milk in medium bowl. Reduce skillet heat to medium. Pour potato mixture over pork. Cover and cook 19 to 23 minutes, stirring occasionally, until pork is no longer pink in center. If potatoes are too saucy, cook uncovered 4 to 5 minutes longer, stirring occasionally, until desired consistency.

1 SERVING Calories 335 (Calories from Fat 145) | Fat 16g (Saturated 7g) | Cholesterol 80mg | Sodium 650mg | Carbohydrate 22g (Dietary Fiber 2g) | Protein 26g % DAILY VALUE Vitamin A 6% | Vitamin C 2% | Calcium 6% | Iron 4% EXCHANGES 1 1/2 Starch, 3 Lean Meat, 1 Fat CARBOHYDRATE CHOICES 1 1/2

Chicken and Julienne Potatoes Boneless, skinless chicken breasts can be used instead of the pork.

BETTY'S TIP

A side salad of sliced tomatoes and cucumber sprinkled with a squeeze of fresh lemon juice, salt and pepper adds color and crunch to this meat-and-potatoes meal.

Pork with Squash and Onions

PREP 15 min COOK 22 min SERVINGS 4

- 4 lean pork loin or rib chops, about 1/2 inch thick (about 1 pound)
- 1 teaspoon dried sage leaves
- 1/2 teaspoon salt
- 1/4 teaspoon pepper
- 2 cloves garlic, finely chopped
- 1 medium onion, cut into 1/4-inch slices
- 1/2 cup chicken broth
- 1 acorn squash (about 1 1/2 pounds)
- 1 medium unpeeled cooking apple, cored and cut into eighths
- 1/4 teaspoon salt
- 1/4 teaspoon pepper

1. Trim fat from pork. Mix sage, 1/2 teaspoon salt, 1/4 teaspoon pepper and garlic; rub on both sides of pork.
2. Cook pork in 10-inch nonstick skillet over medium heat about 3 minutes on each side until brown. Place onion on pork. Pour broth around pork. Heat to boiling; reduce heat to low.
3. Cut squash crosswise into 1-inch slices; remove seeds and fibers. Cut each slice into fourths. Place squash and apple on pork; sprinkle with 1/4 teaspoon salt and 1/4 teaspoon pepper. Cover and simmer about 15 minutes or until pork is no longer pink when cut near bone and squash is tender.

1 SERVING Calories 255 (Calories from Fat 80) | Fat 9g (Saturated 3g) | Cholesterol 65mg | Sodium 620mg | Carbohydrate 25g (Dietary Fiber 6g) | Protein 25g % DAILY VALUE Vitamin A 8% | Vitamin C 12% | Calcium 6% | Iron 10% EXCHANGES 1 Starch, 2 Vegetable, 2 Lean Meat CARBOHYDRATE CHOICES 1 1/2

BETTY'S TIP

If you like, you can leave out the fresh acorn squash and serve the squash on the side instead. Just microwave frozen cooked squash as directed on the package, and serve it alongside the pork, onion and apple.

Polynesian Pork Stir-Fry

PREP 15 min COOK 10 min SERVINGS 4

1/4 cup shredded coconut

1 pound pork tenderloin, cut into 1/8-inch slices

1 small onion, cut into thin wedges

1 teaspoon finely chopped gingerroot

1/4 teaspoon salt

1 medium sweet potato, peeled and cut into 1 1/2- × 1/4-inch strips (1 1/2 cups)

1 1/2 cups frozen snap pea pods (from 1-pound bag)

1/4 cup stir-fry sauce

1 can (8 ounces) pineapple tidbits or chunks in juice, drained and juice reserved

1 tablespoon honey

1. Cook coconut in 10-inch nonstick skillet over medium heat 2 to 3 minutes, stirring constantly, just until golden brown. Remove from skillet.
2. Spray same skillet with cooking spray. Cook pork, onion, gingerroot and salt in skillet over medium-high heat, stirring occasionally, until pork is brown. Stir in sweet potato and frozen pea pods. Cover and cook over medium heat 4 to 6 minutes, stirring occasionally, until potato is tender.
3. Stir in stir-fry sauce, pineapple juice and honey until pork mixture is coated. Stir in pineapple; cook until heated through. Sprinkle each serving with coconut.

1 SERVING Calories 330 (Calories from Fat 65) | Fat 7g (Saturated 3g) | Cholesterol 70mg | Sodium 770mg | Carbohydrate 40g (Dietary Fiber 4g) | Protein 30g % DAILY VALUE Vitamin A 100% | Vitamin C 38% | Calcium 6% | Iron 18% EXCHANGES 1 Starch, 1 Fruit, 4 Very Lean Meat, 1 Fat CARBOHYDRATE CHOICES 2 1/2

BETTY'S TIP

To make your preparation easier, purchase chopped gingerroot in the produce section of your supermarket.

Pork Tenderloin with Prosciutto

PREP 10 min COOK 35 min SERVINGS 6

- 1 1/2 pounds pork tenderloin
- 2 tablespoons olive oil
- 1/4 cup chopped imported prosciutto or fully cooked ham (about 2 ounces)
- 2 tablespoons chopped fresh sage leaves
- 2 tablespoons chopped fresh parsley
- 2 tablespoons chopped sun-dried tomatoes in oil
- 1 small onion, chopped (1/4 cup)
- 1/2 cup dry white wine or chicken broth
- 1/2 cup whipping (heavy) cream or half-and-half
- 1/2 teaspoon pepper
- 1/4 teaspoon salt

1. Cut pork diagonally across grain into 1/2-inch slices. Heat oil in 12-inch skillet over medium-high heat. Cook prosciutto, sage, parsley, tomatoes and onion in oil about 5 minutes, stirring frequently, until onion is tender.
2. Add pork to skillet. Cook about 10 minutes, turning pork occasionally, until pork is light brown. Stir in remaining ingredients. Heat to boiling; reduce heat. Simmer uncovered about 20 minutes, stirring occasionally, until pork is no longer pink in center and sauce is thickened.

1 SERVING Calories 255 (Calories from Fat 145) | Fat 16g (Saturated 6g) | Cholesterol 90mg | Sodium 290mg | Carbohydrate 3g (Dietary Fiber 1g) | Protein 26g % DAILY VALUE Vitamin A 6% | Vitamin C 4% | Calcium 2% | Iron 8% EXCHANGES 4 Lean Meat, 1 Fat CARBOHYDRATE CHOICES 0

BETTY'S TIP

Italian prosciutto, slowly cured and aged, is usually sweet tasting and is an ideal accompaniment to appetizers and other meat dishes. In this recipe, it marries well with the subtle yet zealous flavor of sun-dried tomatoes. Italian cooks enjoy simple, natural flavors such as these, and you can too!

Halibut Asparagus Stir-Fry

PREP 15 min COOK 10 min SERVINGS 4

1 pound halibut, swordfish or tuna fillets, cut into 1-inch pieces

1 medium onion, thinly sliced

3 cloves garlic, finely chopped

1 teaspoon finely chopped gingerroot

1 package (10 ounces) frozen asparagus cuts, thawed and drained

1 package (8 ounces) sliced mushrooms (3 cups)

1 medium tomato, cut into thin wedges

2 tablespoons reduced-sodium soy sauce

1 tablespoon lemon juice

1. Spray 10-inch nonstick skillet with cooking spray; heat over medium-high heat. Add fish, onion, garlic, gingerroot and asparagus; stir-fry 2 to 3 minutes or until fish almost flakes with fork.
2. Carefully stir in remaining ingredients. Cook until heated through and fish flakes easily with fork. Serve with additional soy sauce if desired.

1 SERVING Calories 140 (Calories from Fat 20) | Fat 2g (Saturated 0g) | Cholesterol 50mg | Sodium 350mg | Carbohydrate 11g (Dietary Fiber 3g) | Protein 22g % DAILY VALUE Vitamin A 8% | Vitamin C 22% | Calcium 4% | Iron 10% EXCHANGES 2 Vegetable, 2 1/2 Very Lean Meat CARBOHYDRATE CHOICES 1

BETTY'S TIP

Does fresh asparagus sound good? No need to peel the stalks—just break off the tough ends as far down as the stalks snap easily and wash them well. Cut stalks into 1-inch pieces and cook in same manner as the frozen asparagus.

Easy Seafood Risotto

PREP 5 min COOK 20 min SERVINGS 4

- 1 tablespoon olive or vegetable oil
- 1 medium onion, chopped (1/2 cup)
- 1 can (14 1/2 ounces) chicken broth
- 1 cup uncooked medium or long-grain white rice
- 1 cup baby-cut carrots, cut lengthwise in half
- 1/2 cup water
- 1/2 teaspoon garlic pepper
- 2 cups prewashed fresh baby spinach leaves
- 1 package (8 ounces) refrigerated imitation crabmeat chunks
- 1/4 cup shredded Parmesan cheese

1. Heat oil in 12-inch nonstick skillet over medium-high heat. Cook onion in oil 2 to 3 minutes, stirring occasionally, until crisp-tender. Stir in broth; heat to boiling. Stir in rice; reduce heat. Cover and simmer 10 minutes without stirring.
2. Stir in carrots, water and garlic pepper. Cover and simmer 8 to 10 minutes without stirring until rice is tender.
3. Stir in spinach until wilted. Stir in crabmeat and cheese.

1 SERVING Calories 330 (Calories from Fat 65) | Fat 7g (Saturated 2g) | Cholesterol 20mg | Sodium 1080mg | Carbohydrate 50g (Dietary Fiber 2g) | Protein 18g % DAILY VALUE Vitamin A 60% | Vitamin C 6% | Calcium 12% | Iron 14% EXCHANGES 3 Starch, 1 Vegetable, 1 Medium-Fat Meat CARBOHYDRATE CHOICES 3

BETTY'S TIP

Risotto, a tender and brothy Italian rice dish, requires careful attention and constant stirring. Relax! This shortcut recipe saves you about 20 minutes—and cooks fine all by itself without constant stirring. The result? Just as tasty and delicious as traditional risotto.

Shrimp Scampi Fettuccine

PREP 10 min **COOK** 12 min **SERVINGS** 2 or 3

- 3/4 pound uncooked peeled deveined medium shrimp, thawed if frozen and tails peeled
- 4 ounces uncooked fettuccine
- 1 tablespoon olive or vegetable oil
- 1 medium green onion, sliced (1 tablespoon)
- 1 clove garlic, finely chopped
- 2 teaspoons chopped fresh or 1/2 teaspoon dried basil leaves
- 2 teaspoons chopped fresh parsley or 3/4 teaspoon dried parsley flakes
- 1 tablespoon lemon juice
- 1/8 teaspoon salt
- Grated Parmesan cheese, if desired

1. Rinse shrimp with cold water; pat dry with paper towels. Set aside.
2. Cook and drain fettuccine as directed on package. Keep warm.
3. While fettuccine is cooking, heat oil in 10-inch skillet over medium heat. Cook shrimp, onion, garlic, basil, parsley, lemon juice and salt in oil 2 to 3 minutes, stirring frequently, just until shrimp are pink and firm. (Do not overcook.) Remove skillet from heat.
4. Add fettuccine to skillet; toss fettuccine and shrimp mixture in skillet. Sprinkle with cheese.

1 SERVING Calories 375 (Calories from Fat 90) | Fat 10g (Saturated 2g) | Cholesterol 290mg | Sodium 440mg | Carbohydrate 38g (Dietary Fiber 2g) | Protein 33g % DAILY VALUE Vitamin A 12% | Vitamin C 6% | Calcium 8% | Iron 36% EXCHANGES 2 1/2 Starch, 4 1/2 Very Lean Meat, 1 Fat CARBOHYDRATE CHOICES 2 1/2

BETTY'S TIP

If you choose to use fresh fettuccine instead of dried, keep in mind it will cook much faster. Try to start the shrimp as soon as the fettuccine begins to cook.

Shrimp and Scallops in Wine Sauce

PREP 20 min COOK 10 min SERVINGS 4

- 2 tablespoons olive or vegetable oil
- 1 clove garlic, finely chopped
- 2 medium green onions, sliced (2 tablespoons)
- 2 medium carrots, thinly sliced (1 cup)
- 1 tablespoon chopped fresh parsley or 1 teaspoon parsley flakes
- 1 pound uncooked peeled deveined medium shrimp, thawed if frozen and tails peeled
- 1 pound sea scallops, cut in half
- 1/2 cup dry white wine or chicken broth
- 1 tablespoon lemon juice
- 1/4 to 1/2 teaspoon crushed red pepper

1. Heat oil in 12-inch nonstick skillet over medium heat. Cook garlic, onions, carrots and parsley in oil about 5 minutes, stirring occasionally, until carrots are crisp-tender.
2. Stir in remaining ingredients. Cook 4 to 5 minutes, stirring frequently, until shrimp are pink and firm and scallops are white.

1 SERVING Calories 220 (Calories from Fat 70) | Fat 8g (Saturated 1g) | Cholesterol 185mg | Sodium 350mg | Carbohydrate 6g (Dietary Fiber 1g) | Protein 31g % DAILY VALUE Vitamin A 100% | Vitamin C 6% | Calcium 12% | Iron 26% EXCHANGES 1 Vegetable, 4 Lean Meat, 1 Fat CARBOHYDRATE CHOICES 1/2

BETTY'S TIP

For this recipe, pick up sea scallops, the larger ones that measure up to 2 inches, and cut in half. You can also use bay scallops, which are much smaller (only 1/2 inch), but don't cut them. Sea scallops will have a more tender texture for this dish.

Honey-Garlic Shrimp and Linguine

PREP 10 min COOK 15 min SERVINGS 4

1 package (9 ounces) refrigerated linguine

1 tablespoon water

1 bag (1 pound) frozen baby peas, carrots, pea pods and corn (or other combination)

1/2 cup coarsely chopped red bell pepper

1 pound uncooked peeled deveined medium or large shrimp, thawed if frozen and tails peeled

1/2 cup roasted garlic and herbs marinade (from 14-ounce bottle)

1 tablespoon honey

1. Cook and drain linguine as directed on package; keep warm.
2. Heat water in 12-inch nonstick skillet over medium-high heat. Add frozen vegetables and bell pepper. Cook 2 to 3 minutes, stirring frequently.
3. Stir in shrimp. Cook 5 to 7 minutes, stirring frequently, until vegetables are crisp-tender and shrimp are pink and firm. Stir in marinade and honey. Cook, stirring frequently, until hot. Serve over linguine.

1 SERVING Calories 430 (Calories from Fat 20) | Fat 2g (Saturated 0g) | Cholesterol 160mg | Sodium 1650mg | Carbohydrate 77g (Dietary Fiber 8g) | Protein 33g % DAILY VALUE Vitamin A 38% | Vitamin C 38% | Calcium 8% | Iron 40% EXCHANGES 5 Starch, 2 Very Lean Meat CARBOHYDRATE CHOICES 5

BETTY'S TIP

Whole-grain rolls and sliced watermelon make great side dishes to this light shrimp dish.

Ginger-Peanut-Shrimp Stir-Fry

PREP 15 min STAND 15 min COOK 12 min SERVINGS 4

- 3 tablespoons soy sauce
- 3 teaspoons grated gingerroot
- 1/4 teaspoon red pepper sauce
- 1 clove garlic, finely chopped
- 3/4 pound uncooked peeled deveined medium shrimp, thawed if frozen and tails peeled
- 2 tablespoons vegetable oil
- 2 cups cooked spaghetti or vermicelli
- 6 medium green onions, cut into 1-inch pieces
- 9 ounces snow (Chinese) pea pods, strings removed
- 1 tablespoon vegetable oil
- 3 tablespoons creamy peanut butter
- 1/4 cup chopped peanuts

1. Mix soy sauce, gingerroot, pepper sauce and garlic in large resealable plastic food-storage bag. Add shrimp; seal bag. Let stand 15 minutes.
2. Heat 2 tablespoons oil in 10-inch skillet or wok over medium-high heat. Add spaghetti, onions and pea pods; stir-fry until onions are crisp-tender. Remove mixture from skillet.
3. Heat 1 tablespoon oil in skillet. Add shrimp; stir-fry until shrimp are pink and firm. Stir in spaghetti mixture. Stir in peanut butter until mixture is coated; cook until hot. Sprinkle with peanuts.

1 SERVING Calories 400 (Calories from Fat 200) | Fat 22g (Saturated 4g) | Cholesterol 120mg | Sodium 930mg | Carbohydrate 31g (Dietary Fiber 5g) | Protein 25g % DAILY VALUE Vitamin A 10% | Vitamin C 28% | Calcium 8% | Iron 28% EXCHANGES 2 Starch, 2 1/2 Lean Meat, 2 Fat CARBOHYDRATE CHOICES 2

BETTY'S TIP

This sassy stir-fry tastes great with mugs of icy-cold Chinese beer or freshly squeezed lemonade.

Italian Shrimp Linguine

PREP 15 min COOK 15 min SERVINGS 5

- 8 ounces uncooked linguine
- 3/4 cup reduced-calorie Italian dressing
- 1 1/2 teaspoons grated lemon peel
- 3 cloves garlic, finely chopped
- 3/4 pound uncooked peeled deveined medium shrimp, thawed if frozen and tails peeled
- 3 cups broccoli flowerets
- 1 medium yellow summer squash, cut lengthwise in half, then cut crosswise into slices (1 1/2 cups)
- 2 tablespoons water
- 8 cherry tomatoes, cut in half
- 12 extra-large pitted ripe olives, cut in half
- 1/4 cup chopped fresh basil leaves
- Grated Parmesan cheese, if desired

1. Cook and drain linguine as directed on package; keep warm. Mix dressing, lemon peel and garlic; set aside.
2. Spray 12-inch nonstick skillet with cooking spray; heat over medium-high heat. Cook shrimp about 2 minutes, stirring frequently, until shrimp are pink and firm. Remove shrimp from skillet.
3. Spray skillet with cooking spray; heat over medium-high heat. Cook broccoli and squash in skillet about 1 minute, stirring frequently. Add water. Cover and cook about 3 minutes, stirring occasionally, until vegetables are crisp-tender (add water if necessary to prevent sticking).
4. Stir dressing mixture into skillet; cook 30 seconds. Stir in tomatoes, olives, basil, shrimp and linguine; heat until hot. Sprinkle with cheese.

1 SERVING Calories 310 (Calories from Fat 70) | Fat 8g (Saturated 1g) | Cholesterol 100mg | Sodium 660mg | Carbohydrate 45g (Dietary Fiber 4g) | Protein 19g % DAILY VALUE Vitamin A 24% | Vitamin C 44% | Calcium 8% | Iron 24% EXCHANGES 2 Starch, 3 Vegetable, 1 Medium-Fat Meat CARBOHYDRATE CHOICES 3

Italian Chicken Linguine Use 3/4 pound boneless, skinless chicken breasts, cut into 1-inch pieces. Cook the chicken 3 to 4 minutes, stirring frequently, or until no longer pink in center.

BETTY'S TIP

A sharp paring knife comes in handy when deveining shrimp. First, use the knife to make a shallow cut down the back of the shrimp. Then use the tip of the knife to pull out the dark vein. Rinse the shrimp under cold water.

Tuna Primavera

PREP 15 min COOK 20 min SERVINGS 5

- 1 package (8.25 ounces) creamy pasta skillet-dinner mix for tuna
- 2 tablespoons butter or margarine
- 1 can (6 ounces) tuna in water, drained
- 1/2 cup milk
- 3 1/2 cups hot water
- 2 medium carrots, cut into 1/8-inch slices (1 cup)
- 1 cup frozen broccoli cuts (from 1-pound bag)
- 1 jar (4 1/2 ounces) sliced mushrooms, drained

1. Mix uncooked Pasta and Sauce Mix from skillet-dinner mix, the butter, tuna, milk, water and carrots in 12-inch skillet. Heat to boiling, stirring occasionally; reduce heat. Cover and simmer 10 minutes, stirring occasionally.
2. Stir broccoli and mushrooms into tuna mixture. Cover and simmer about 10 minutes or until vegetables are tender.

1 SERVING Calories 325 (Calories from Fat 115) | Fat 13g (Saturated 3g) | Cholesterol 40mg | Sodium 1020mg | Carbohydrate 36g (Dietary Fiber 3g) | Protein 16g % DAILY VALUE Vitamin A 100% | Vitamin C 14% | Calcium 10% | Iron 12% EXCHANGES 2 Starch, 1 Vegetable, 1 Lean Meat, 2 Fat CARBOHYDRATE CHOICES 2 1/2

BETTY'S TIP

If you're in a hurry, omit the fresh carrots and frozen broccoli cuts, and use 2 cups of a frozen broccoli blend instead.

Southwest Cheese 'n Pasta

PREP **5 min** COOK **17 min** SERVINGS **6**

1 1/2 cups milk

1 cup green salsa (salsa verde)

1 can (15 ounces) cream-style corn

1 can (11 ounces) whole kernel corn with red and green peppers, drained

3 cups uncooked cavatappi pasta or elbow macaroni (8 ounces)

8 ounces process American cheese loaf, cut into cubes

1. Mix all ingredients except cheese in 12-inch nonstick skillet. Heat to boiling, stirring occasionally; reduce heat. Cover and cook 10 to 14 minutes, stirring frequently, until pasta is tender.
2. Add cheese to pasta mixture; stir until cheese is melted.

1 SERVING Calories 420 (Calories from Fat 135) | Fat 15g (Saturated 8g) | Cholesterol 40mg | Sodium 960mg | Carbohydrate 54g (Dietary Fiber 5g) | Protein 18g % DAILY VALUE Vitamin A 18% | Vitamin C 16% | Calcium 30% | Iron 14% EXCHANGES 3 1/2 Starch, 1 High-Fat Meat, 1 Fat CARBOHYDRATE CHOICES 3 1/2

Southwest Ham 'n Cheese Pasta Stir 2 cups of cubed fully cooked ham into the pasta in skillet; heat through.

BETTY'S TIP

Round out this meal with coleslaw and crusty rolls and finish with slices of cool, refreshing watermelon.

Mostaccioli with Vodka Sauce

PREP **20 min** COOK **40 min** SERVINGS **6**

3 tablespoons butter or margarine

1 tablespoon olive oil

2 cloves garlic, finely chopped

1 small onion, chopped (1/4 cup)

1/4 cup chopped imported prosciutto or fully cooked ham (about 2 ounces)

2 boneless, skinless chicken breasts (about 1/2 pound), cut into 1-inch pieces

1/2 cup vodka or chicken broth

1/2 cup whipping (heavy) cream

1/2 cup sliced pitted imported Kalamata or large pitted ripe olives

1 tablespoon chopped fresh parsley

1/2 teaspoon pepper

1 package (16 ounces) mostaccioli or penne rigate pasta

1/4 cup freshly grated or shredded imported Parmesan cheese

1. Heat butter and oil in 10-inch skillet over medium-high heat. Cook garlic and onion in butter mixture about 5 minutes, stirring occasionally, until onion is tender.
2. Stir in prosciutto and chicken. Cook about 5 minutes, stirring occasionally, until chicken is brown. Stir in vodka. Cook uncovered until liquid has evaporated.
3. Stir in whipping cream, olives, parsley and pepper. Heat to boiling; reduce heat. Simmer uncovered about 30 minutes, stirring frequently, until thickened.
4. While sauce is simmering, cook and drain pasta as directed on package. Add pasta to sauce; toss gently until pasta is evenly coated. Sprinkle with cheese.

1 SERVING Calories 530 (Calories from Fat 180) | Fat 20g (Saturated 9g) | Cholesterol 70mg | Sodium 330mg | Carbohydrate 62g (Dietary Fiber 3g) | Protein 23g % DAILY VALUE Vitamin A 10% | Vitamin C 2% | Calcium 10% | Iron 20% EXCHANGES 4 Starch, 2 Lean Meat, 2 Fat CARBOHYDRATE CHOICES 4

BETTY'S TIP

This is a modern pasta recipe popular in northern Italy. Cooks intrigued by different ways of cooking shortcut pastas found vodka to be an innovative addition to their repertoire. Brandy or grappa is sometimes substituted for the vodka.

Blue Cheese Tenders

PREP **5 min** COOK **12 min** SERVINGS **4**

- 1 tablespoon vegetable oil
- 1 pound chicken breast tenders
- 1 tablespoon lemon juice
- 1 clove garlic, finely chopped
- 1/3 cup blue cheese dressing
- Hot cooked farfalle (bow-tie) pasta, if desired
- Crumbled blue cheese, if desired

1. Heat oil in 10-inch skillet over medium-high heat. Cook chicken, lemon juice and garlic in oil 8 to 10 minutes, stirring occasionally, until chicken is no longer pink in center.
2. Stir in dressing. Cook 2 to 4 minutes, stirring frequently, until hot. Serve over farfalle. Sprinkle with blue cheese.

1 SERVING Calories 230 (Calories from Fat 110) | Fat 12g (Saturated 2g) | Cholesterol 70mg | Sodium 350mg | Carbohydrate 5g (Dietary Fiber 0g) | Protein 26g % DAILY VALUE Vitamin A 0% | Vitamin C 0% | Calcium 2% | Iron 4% EXCHANGES 1 Vegetable, 3 1/2 Lean Meat, 1/2 Fat CARBOHYDRATE CHOICES 0

BETTY'S TIP

The combination of toasted walnuts and blue cheese is a marriage made in heaven. To toast walnuts, place them in an uncovered shallow pan and toast in a 350° oven about 10 minutes, stirring occasionally, until golden brown.

Swiss Potato and Cheese Skillet

PREP 10 min COOK 26 min SERVINGS 4

- 1 tablespoon butter or margarine
- 1 cup chopped onions
- 1 package (28 ounces) frozen chunky-style seasoned hash-brown potatoes
- 1/4 cup water
- 2 cups shredded Swiss or Gruyère cheese (8 ounces)
- Dash nutmeg, if desired

1. Melt butter in 12-inch nonstick skillet over medium heat. Cook onions in butter 2 to 3 minutes, stirring frequently, until tender. Stir potatoes and water into skillet. Cover and cook 15 to 20 minutes, stirring occasionally, until potatoes are tender.
2. Sprinkle potatoes with cheese; reduce heat to low. Cover and cook 2 to 3 minutes or until cheese is melted. Sprinkle with nutmeg.

1 SERVING Calories 500 (Calories from Fat 170) | Fat 19g (Saturated 11g) | Cholesterol 50mg | Sodium 960mg | Carbohydrate 61g (Dietary Fiber 6g) | Protein 21g % DAILY VALUE Vitamin A 14% | Vitamin C 18% | Calcium 58% | Iron 6% EXCHANGES 4 Starch, 2 High-Fat Meat, 2 Fat CARBOHYDRATE CHOICES 4

BETTY'S TIP

A fresh spinach salad with chopped hard-cooked eggs makes a tasty accompaniment to this skillet meal.

Vegetable Paella

PREP 10 min COOK 15 min STAND 5 min SERVINGS 4

- 2 tablespoons olive or vegetable oil
- 2 cloves garlic, finely chopped
- 1 large red onion, cut into thin wedges
- 1 cup uncooked quick-cooking brown rice
- 1 cup vegetable or chicken broth
- 1/2 teaspoon saffron threads, crushed
- 1 bag (1 pound) frozen petite peas, baby whole carrots, snow peas and baby cob corn (or other combination)
- 1 can (14 1/2 ounces) stewed tomatoes, undrained

1. Heat oil in 12-inch nonstick skillet over medium-high heat. Cook garlic and onion in oil, stirring frequently, until onion is tender.
2. Stir in remaining ingredients. Heat to boiling; reduce heat to medium-low. Cover and cook 5 minutes, stirring occasionally; remove from heat. Let stand covered 5 minutes.

1 SERVING Calories 335 (Calories from Fat 80) | Fat 9g (Saturated 1g) | Cholesterol 0mg | Sodium 590mg | Carbohydrate 62g (Dietary Fiber 8g) | Protein 9g % DAILY VALUE Vitamin A 100% | Vitamin C 24% | Calcium 8% | Iron 14% EXCHANGES 3 1/2 Starch, 1 Vegetable, 1/2 Fat CARBOHYDRATE CHOICES 4

Vegetable Chicken Paella Remove half of the paella from the skillet; keep warm. Stir 1/2 cup of cubed cooked chicken or turkey into the remaining paella in skillet; heat through.

BETTY'S TIP

Saffron gives paella its characteristic bright yellow color and distinct flavor, but it can be a bit pricey. If you like, the same amount of turmeric can be substituted for the saffron.

Potatoes, Green Beans and Tomatoes with Tofu

PREP 10 min COOK 20 min SERVINGS 5

- 2 tablespoons olive or vegetable oil
- 1/2 cup coarsely chopped red onion
- 5 small red potatoes, sliced (2 1/2 cups)
- 2 cups frozen cut green beans
- 1/2 teaspoon Italian seasoning
- 1/2 teaspoon garlic salt
- 1 package (14 ounces) firm tofu, cut into 1/2-inch cubes
- 2 roma (plum) tomatoes, thinly sliced
- 1 hard-cooked egg, chopped

1. Heat oil in 12-inch skillet over medium-high heat. Cook onion in oil 2 minutes, stirring frequently. Stir in potatoes; reduce heat to medium-low. Cover and cook about 10 minutes, stirring occasionally, until potatoes are tender.
2. Stir in green beans, Italian seasoning and garlic salt. Cover and cook about 6 minutes, stirring occasionally, until beans are tender and potatoes are light golden brown.
3. Stir in tofu and tomatoes. Cook about 2 minutes, stirring occasionally and gently, just until hot. Sprinkle each serving with egg.

1 SERVING Calories 205 (Calories from Fat 100) | Fat 11g (Saturated 2g) | Cholesterol 85mg | Sodium 140mg | Carbohydrate 20g (Dietary Fiber 3g) | Protein 10g % DAILY VALUE Vitamin A 12% | Vitamin C 10% | Calcium 12% | Iron 12% EXCHANGES 1 Starch, 1 Vegetable, 1 Very Lean Meat, 1 1/2 Fat CARBOHYDRATE CHOICES 1

BETTY'S TIP

No takers for tofu? This dish, filled with tender red potatoes and green beans, might change their minds. For vegans, just leave off the egg.

Comforting Casseroles

Wild Rice and Beef Casserole 140
Texas Tater Casserole 141
Quick Lasagna 143
Curried Beef Casserole 144
Spinach-Lasagna Casserole 145
Garlic Shepherd's Pie 146
Beef and Potatoes au Gratin 148
Beef and Bulgur Casserole 149
Cheesy Pizza Casserole 150
Deep-Dish Spaghetti Pie 151
Western Beef Casserole au Gratin 152
Baked Ravioli and Meatballs 153
California Chicken Bake 155
Chicken and Cashew Bake 156
Chicken with Cider Glaze 157
Hot Chicken Salad with Sage Biscuits 158
Wild Rice and Chicken Casserole 159
Ranch Potatoes and Chicken Casserole 160
Country Chicken and Pasta Bake 161
Chicken-Vegetable Strata 162
Chicken and Rice Bake 163
Layered Chicken–Black Bean Enchiladas 164
Chicken Drumstick Cacciatore Casserole 165
Baked Chicken Gumbo 167
Three-Herb Chicken 168
Chicken Legs with Vegetables 169
Maple-Glazed Turkey and Rice Casserole 170
Turkey Divan 171
Turkey, Carrot and Noodle Bake 172
Turkey and Corn Bread Stuffing Casserole 173
Easy Turkey Lasagna 175
Turkey with Italian Roasted Vegetables 176
Turkey and Tortilla Casserole 177
Ham and Brie Bake 178
Sausage and Pizza Bake 179
Mashed Potato and Sausage Casserole 180
Lamb and Lentil Casserole 181
Lamb with Sweet Peppers and Garlic Sauce 182
Baked Salmon with Cilantro 185
Gremolata-Topped Sea Bass 186
Parmesan-Shrimp Pasta Bake 187
Baked Tuna and Noodles with Mushroom Sauce 188
Tuna Twist Casserole 189
Cheddar Strata with Onions 190
Mozzarella and Pesto Strata 191
Vegetable Strata 192
Easy Cheese Strata 193
Stacked Enchilada Bake 195
Easy Cheesy Manicotti 197

Wild Rice and Beef Casserole

PREP 5 min COOK 10 min BAKE 40 min SERVINGS 4

- 1 pound lean ground beef
- 1 package (6.2 ounces) fast-cooking long-grain and wild rice mix
- 1 can (10 3/4 ounces) condensed tomato soup
- 1/4 cup milk
- 1/4 teaspoon pepper
- 1 cup shredded Cheddar cheese (4 ounces)

1. Heat oven to 350°. Spray 2-quart casserole with cooking spray. Cook beef in 10-inch skillet over medium heat 8 to 10 minutes, stirring occasionally, until brown; drain.
2. While beef is cooking, make rice mix as directed on package—except omit butter. Stir rice mixture, soup, milk and pepper into beef. Spoon into casserole.
3. Cover and bake 30 minutes. Sprinkle with cheese. Bake uncovered 5 to 10 minutes longer or until cheese is melted and mixture is hot.

1 SERVING Calories 460 (Calories from Fat 240) | Fat 27g (Saturated 13g) | Cholesterol 95mg | Sodium 850mg | Carbohydrate 24g | (Dietary Fiber 1g) | Protein 31g % DAILY VALUE Vitamin A 14% | Vitamin C 8% | Calcium 18% | Iron 16% EXCHANGES 1 1/2 Starch, 4 Medium-Fat Meat, 1 Fat CARBOHYDRATE CHOICES 1 1/2

Wild Rice and Turkey Casserole Substitute 1 pound ground turkey breast for the ground beef.

BETTY'S TIP

Did you know you can purchase precooked ground beef crumbles? Just stir them into the remaining ingredients and knock 10 minutes off your prep time. Look for plain and flavored varieties in the meat or freezer section of your grocery store.

Texas Tater Casserole

PREP 10 min COOK 10 min BAKE 50 min SERVINGS 6

1. Heat oven to 375°. Cook beef, onion, celery and garlic in 10-inch skillet over medium heat 8 to 10 minutes, stirring occasionally, until beef is brown; drain.
2. Stir soup, corn, picante sauce, chili powder and pepper into beef mixture. Spoon into ungreased 2 1/2-quart casserole. Top with potato nuggets.
3. Bake uncovered 40 minutes. Sprinkle with cheese. Bake 5 to 10 minutes longer or until bubbly and cheese is melted.

1 SERVING Calories 540 (Calories from Fat 280) | Fat 31g (Saturated 14g) | Cholesterol 70mg | Sodium 1680mg | Carbohydrate 45g (Dietary Fiber 5g) | Protein 25g % DAILY VALUE Vitamin A 50% | Vitamin C 14% | Calcium 16% | Iron 18% EXCHANGES 2 Starch, 3 Vegetable, 2 Medium-Fat Meat, 4 Fat CARBOHYDRATE CHOICES 3

1 pound lean ground beef

1 large onion, chopped (1 cup)

1 medium stalk celery, chopped (1/2 cup)

2 cloves garlic, finely chopped

2 cans (10 3/4 ounces each) condensed Cheddar cheese soup

1 can (11 ounces) whole kernel corn with red and green peppers, drained

1/2 cup picante sauce

2 teaspoons chili powder

1/4 teaspoon pepper

1 package (16 ounces) frozen potato nuggets

1/2 cup shredded taco-seasoned cheese (2 ounces)

BETTY'S TIP

There's no need to peel garlic cloves when you're putting them through a garlic press. Just pop the clove—skin and all—into the press, then squeeze. The garlic flesh will be forced through the mesh, while the skin stays in the press.

Quick Lasagna

PREP 15 min COOK 7 min BAKE 40 min STAND 10 min SERVINGS 4

- 1/2 pound lean ground beef
- 1 clove garlic, finely chopped
- 1 teaspoon Italian seasoning
- 1 cup spaghetti sauce
- 6 frozen precooked lasagna noodles (each about 8 × 2 1/2 inches)
- 1 container (12 ounces) reduced-fat cottage cheese (1 1/2 cups)
- 1 cup shredded mozzarella cheese (4 ounces)
- 2 tablespoons grated Parmesan cheese

1. Heat oven to 400°. Cook beef and garlic in 10-inch skillet over medium-high heat 5 to 7 minutes, stirring occasionally, until beef is brown; drain. Stir Italian seasoning and spaghetti sauce into beef. Spread 1/4 cup meat sauce in ungreased square pan, 8 × 8 × 2 inches.
2. Arrange 2 noodles on sauce, so they do not overlap or touch sides of pan. Spread about 1/2 cup of the remaining sauce over noodles. Spread about 1/2 cup cottage cheese over sauce. Sprinkle with about 1/3 cup mozzarella cheese.
3. Repeat step 2 two times, using remaining noodles, sauce, cottage cheese and mozzarella cheese. Sprinkle with Parmesan cheese.
4. Spray piece of aluminum foil large enough to cover square pan with cooking spray. Tightly cover pan with foil, sprayed side down. Bake 30 minutes. Carefully remove foil. Bake about 10 minutes longer or until lasagna is hot and bubbly. Let stand 10 minutes before cutting.

1 SERVING Calories 460 (Calories from Fat 160) | Fat 18g (Saturated 8g) | Cholesterol 55mg | Sodium 890mg | Carbohydrate 39g (Dietary Fiber 2g) | Protein 36g % DAILY VALUE Vitamin A 14% | Vitamin C 8% | Calcium 32% | Iron 14% EXCHANGES 2 1/2 Starch, 4 1/2 Lean Meat CARBOHYDRATE CHOICES 2 1/2

BETTY'S TIP

If you're out of cottage cheese but have some ricotta cheese in the fridge, you can use that instead.

Curried Beef Casserole

PREP 10 min COOK 15 min BAKE 45 min SERVINGS 4

- 2 1/2 cups uncooked wagon wheel pasta (about 6 ounces)
- 1 pound lean ground beef
- 1 medium onion, chopped (1/2 cup)
- 2 tablespoons butter or margarine
- 2 tablespoons all-purpose flour
- 1 tablespoon curry powder
- 1/2 teaspoon salt
- 1/4 teaspoon crushed red pepper
- 2 cups milk
- 1 container (8 ounces) sour cream
- 1/2 cup dry-roasted peanuts
- 1 package (10 ounces) frozen mixed vegetables, thawed and drained

1. Heat oven to 350°. Spray 2-quart casserole with cooking spray. Cook and drain pasta as directed on package.
2. While pasta is cooking, cook ground beef and onion in 10-inch skillet over medium heat 8 to 10 minutes, stirring frequently, until beef is brown and onion is tender; drain. Remove beef mixture from skillet.
3. Melt butter in same skillet over medium heat. Stir flour, curry powder, salt and red pepper into butter. Cook, stirring constantly, until smooth and bubbly; remove from heat. Stir in milk. Heat to boiling, stirring constantly. Boil and stir 1 minute; remove from heat. Stir in sour cream and peanuts.
4. Mix pasta, beef mixture, vegetables and sour cream mixture in casserole. Cover and bake about 45 minutes or until hot.

1 SERVING Calories 750 (Calories from Fat 405) | Fat 45g (Saturated 17g) | Cholesterol 110mg | Sodium 680mg | Carbohydrate 53g (Dietary Fiber 6g) | Protein 39g % DAILY VALUE Vitamin A 72% | Vitamin C 10% | Calcium 28% | Iron 36% EXCHANGES 2 1/2 Starch, 1 Vegetable, 1 Milk, 3 High-Fat Meat, 3 Fat CARBOHYDRATE CHOICES 3 1/2

BETTY'S TIP

Curry powder tends to be a love-it or leave-it type of seasoning. If you're not sure if your family will like this Indian blend of spices, herbs and seeds, you may not want to use a whole tablespoon the first time you make this beefy casserole.

Spinach-Lasagna Casserole

PREP 25 min **BAKE** 50 min **SERVINGS** 7

1 package (10 ounces) frozen chopped spinach

1 cup shredded mozzarella cheese (4 ounces)

1/2 cup small curd creamed cottage cheese

1/4 cup grated Parmesan cheese

1 pound lean ground beef

1 clove garlic, finely chopped

1 package (6.4 ounces) lasagna skillet-dinner mix for hamburger

3 cups hot water

1. Heat oven to 375°. Rinse spinach with cold water to separate; drain thoroughly. Mix mozzarella, cottage and Parmesan cheeses; set aside.
2. Cook beef and garlic in 10-inch skillet over medium heat 8 to 10 minutes, stirring occasionally, until beef is brown; drain.
3. Mix beef mixture, spinach, uncooked Pasta and Sauce Mix from skillet-dinner mix and water in ungreased 2-quart casserole or rectangular baking dish, 11 × 7 × 1 1/2 inches. Spoon cheese mixture evenly over top.
4. Bake uncovered 40 to 50 minutes or until top is golden brown and sauce is bubbly.

1 SERVING Calories 305 (Calories from Fat 125) | Fat 14g (Saturated 6g) | Cholesterol 50mg | Sodium 920mg | Carbohydrate 24g (Dietary Fiber 2g) | Protein 23g % DAILY VALUE Vitamin A 50% | Vitamin C 2% | Calcium 22% | Iron 10% EXCHANGES 1 Starch, 2 Vegetable, 2 Medium-Fat Meat, 1 Fat CARBOHYDRATE CHOICES 1 1/2

BETTY'S TIP

To get out as much moisture as you possibly can from the spinach, squeeze the spinach in a paper towel or two after you drain it.

Garlic Shepherd's Pie

PREP 10 min COOK 15 min BAKE 30 min SERVINGS 6

- 1 pound lean ground beef
- 1 medium onion, chopped (1/2 cup)
- 2 cups (from 1-pound bag) frozen baby beans and carrots (or other combination)
- 1 cup sliced mushrooms (3 ounces)
- 1 can (14 1/2 ounces) diced tomatoes, undrained
- 1 jar (12 ounces) beef gravy
- 2 tablespoons chili sauce
- 1/2 teaspoon dried basil leaves
- 1/8 teaspoon pepper
- 1/2 package (7.2-ounce size) roasted garlic mashed potato mix (1 pouch)
- Water, milk, margarine or butter called for on potato mix package
- 2 teaspoons shredded Parmesan cheese

1. Heat oven to 350°. Cook beef and onion in 12-inch nonstick skillet over medium heat 8 to 10 minutes, stirring occasionally, until beef is brown; drain well. Stir in frozen vegetables, mushrooms, tomatoes, gravy, chili sauce, basil and pepper. Heat to boiling; reduce heat. Cover and simmer about 10 minutes or until vegetables are tender.
2. Make potatoes as directed on package for 4 servings, using 1 pouch potatoes and seasoning, water, milk and margarine; let stand 3 to 5 minutes.
3. Spoon beef mixture into ungreased square baking dish, 8 × 8 × 2 inches, or 2-quart casserole. Spoon potatoes onto beef mixture around edge of dish. Sprinkle with cheese. Bake uncovered 25 to 30 minutes or until potatoes are firm and beef mixture is bubbly.

1 SERVING Calories 350 (Calories from Fat 155) | Fat 17g (Saturated 8g) | Cholesterol 60mg | Sodium 620mg | Carbohydrate 27g (Dietary Fiber 4g) | Protein 21g % DAILY VALUE Vitamin A 98% | Vitamin C 22% | Calcium 10% | Iron 14% EXCHANGES 1 1/2 Starch, 1 Vegetable, 2 Medium-Fat Meat, 1 1/2 Fat CARBOHYDRATE CHOICES 2

BETTY'S TIP

Shepherd's Pie was originally created as a handy way to use up leftovers. If you'd prefer, you can use ground pork or ground turkey in place of the ground beef.

Beef and Potatoes au Gratin

PREP 15 min **COOK** 15 min **BAKE** 30 min **STAND** 5 min **SERVINGS** 4

- 4 cups water
- 3 medium potatoes, cut into 1/4-inch slices (about 3 cups)
- 1 pound lean ground beef
- 1 medium stalk celery, thinly sliced (1/2 cup)
- 3 tablespoons butter or margarine
- 3 tablespoons all-purpose flour
- 1 tablespoon chopped fresh or 1 teaspoon dried chervil leaves
- 1 teaspoon yellow mustard
- 1/4 teaspoon salt
- 1/4 teaspoon pepper
- 2 cups milk
- 1 1/4 cups shredded sharp process American cheese (5 ounces)
- 3 tablespoons chopped fresh parsley
- 1/4 cup dry bread crumbs
- 1 tablespoon chopped fresh parsley
- 2 teaspoons butter or margarine, melted

1. Heat oven to 375°. Heat water and potatoes to boiling in 2 1/2-quart saucepan; reduce heat to medium. Cook uncovered 8 to 10 minutes or just until potatoes are tender; drain. Set aside.
2. While potatoes are cooking, cook ground beef and celery in 10-inch skillet over medium heat 8 to 10 minutes, stirring frequently, until beef is brown; drain. Remove beef mixture from skillet; set aside.
3. Melt 3 tablespoons butter in same skillet over medium heat. Stir flour, chervil, mustard, salt and pepper into butter. Cook, stirring constantly, until bubbly; remove from heat. Stir in milk. Heat to boiling, stirring constantly. Boil and stir 1 minute. Stir in cheese until melted. Stir in 3 tablespoons parsley.
4. Layer half of the potatoes in ungreased 2-quart casserole. Layer with beef mixture and remaining potatoes. Pour cheese sauce over potatoes. Bake uncovered 20 to 25 minutes or until bubbly.
5. Mix bread crumbs, 1 tablespoon parsley and 2 teaspoons melted butter; sprinkle over potatoes. Bake about 5 minutes longer or until crumbs are brown and crisp. Let stand 5 minutes before serving.

1 SERVING Calories 675 (Calories from Fat 370) | Fat 41g (Saturated 17g) | Cholesterol 110mg | Sodium 1000mg | Carbohydrate 35g (Dietary Fiber 2g) | Protein 34g % DAILY VALUE Vitamin A 32% | Vitamin C 10% | Calcium 36% | Iron 18% EXCHANGES 1 1/2 Starch, 1 Milk, 3 Medium-Fat Meat, 5 Fat CARBOHYDRATE CHOICES 2

BETTY'S TIP

If you love kitchen gadgets, you may want to try a mandoline. This hand-operated machine has blades that adjust for thin to thick slicing of firm vegetables and fruits.

Beef and Bulgur Casserole

PREP 15 min COOK 15 min BAKE 35 min SERVINGS 4

1. Heat oven to 375°. Cook ground beef, bell pepper and onion in 10-inch skillet over medium heat 8 to 10 minutes, stirring frequently, until beef is brown; drain.
2. Stir tomatoes, water, raisins, oregano, Worcestershire sauce, salt and pepper sauce into beef mixture, breaking up tomatoes. Heat to boiling. Stir in bulgur; reduce heat to low. Cover and simmer 5 minutes. Stir in squash and walnuts. Spoon mixture into ungreased 2-quart casserole.
3. Cover and bake 20 minutes; stir. Cover and bake about 15 minutes longer or until bulgur is tender and mixture is heated through.

1 SERVING Calories 500 (Calories from Fat 225) | Fat 25g (Saturated 7g) | Cholesterol 65mg | Sodium 560mg | Carbohydrate 50g (Dietary Fiber 14g) | Protein 29g % DAILY VALUE Vitamin A 12% | Vitamin C 36% | Calcium 10% | Iron 24% EXCHANGES 3 Starch, 1 Vegetable, 2 1/2 Medium-Fat Meat, 1 Fat CARBOHYDRATE CHOICES 3

1 pound lean ground beef or ground pork

1 small green bell pepper, chopped (about 1/2 cup)

1 medium onion, chopped (about 1/2 cup)

1 can (14 1/2 ounces) whole tomatoes, undrained

1/2 cup water

1/3 cup raisins

2 tablespoons chopped fresh or 2 teaspoons dried oregano leaves

1 tablespoon Worcestershire sauce

1/2 teaspoon salt

1/2 teaspoon red pepper sauce

1 cup uncooked bulgur

2 small yellow summer squash, cut lengthwise in half and sliced

1/3 cup coarsely chopped walnuts

BETTY'S TIP

Bulgur is whole wheat that has been cooked, dried and then broken into coarse fragments. You may have tasted it before in a tabbouleh salad. You'll find it shelved along with the other grains at your grocery store.

Cheesy Pizza Casserole

PREP 15 min BAKE 35 min SERVINGS 6

- 3 cups uncooked rigatoni pasta (9 ounces)
- 1/2 pound lean ground beef
- 1/4 cup sliced ripe olives
- 1 can (4 ounces) mushroom pieces and stems, drained
- 1 jar (26 to 28 ounces) vegetable primavera pasta sauce
- 1 cup shredded mozzarella cheese (4 ounces)

1. Heat oven to 350°. Cook and drain pasta as directed on package.
2. While pasta is cooking, cook beef in 10-inch skillet over medium-high heat 5 to 7 minutes, stirring occasionally, until beef is brown; drain. Mix pasta, beef and remaining ingredients except cheese in ungreased 2 1/2-quart casserole.
3. Cover and bake about 30 minutes or until hot and bubbly. Sprinkle with cheese. Bake uncovered about 5 minutes longer or until cheese is melted.

1 SERVING Calories 455 (Calories from Fat 135) | Fat 15g (Saturated 5g) | Cholesterol 30mg | Sodium 920mg | Carbohydrate 60g (Dietary Fiber 4g) | Protein 20g % DAILY VALUE Vitamin A 20% | Vitamin C 16% | Calcium 18% | Iron 20% EXCHANGES 4 Starch, 1 Medium-Fat Meat CARBOHYDRATE CHOICES 4

Cheesy Italian Sausage Casserole Use bulk Italian sausage instead of ground beef.

BETTY'S TIP

Try serving this yummy pizza and pasta casserole with toasted garlic bread and a tossed salad. A fruit-flavored sorbet or ice does the trick for dessert.

Deep-Dish Spaghetti Pie

PREP 15 min COOK 15 min BAKE 30 min STAND 5 min SERVINGS 6

- 6 ounces uncooked spaghetti
- 2 eggs, slightly beaten
- 1/4 cup grated Parmesan cheese
- 1 pound lean ground beef
- 1/4 cup chopped onion
- 1 jar (14 ounces) spaghetti sauce
- 1 can (11 ounces) vacuum-packed whole kernel corn, drained
- 1 small green bell pepper, cut into rings
- 1 cup shredded mozzarella cheese (4 ounces)

1. Heat oven to 350°. Spray pie plate, 10 × 1 1/2 inches, or square pan, 9 × 9 × 2 inches, with cooking spray.
2. Cook spaghetti as directed on package; drain. Rinse with hot water; drain. Mix spaghetti, eggs and Parmesan cheese. Press spaghetti mixture evenly over bottom and up sides of pie plate to form crust; set aside.
3. Cook ground beef and onion in 12-inch skillet over medium heat 8 to 10 minutes, stirring occasionally, until beef is brown; drain. Stir spaghetti sauce and corn into beef mixture. Spoon evenly over spaghetti crust. Top with bell pepper; sprinkle with cheese.
4. Bake 25 to 30 minutes. Let stand 5 minutes before serving.

1 SERVING Calories 440 (Calories from Fat 170) | Fat 19g (Saturated 8g) | Cholesterol 130mg | Sodium 700mg | Carbohydrate 39g (Dietary Fiber 3g) | Protein 27g % DAILY VALUE Vitamin A 10% | Vitamin C 15% | Calcium 24% | Iron 20% EXCHANGES 2 1/2 Starch, 3 Medium-Fat Meat CARBOHYDRATE CHOICES 2 1/2

BETTY'S TIP

This kid-friendly casserole will serve up smiles when you add breadsticks and some carrot sticks on the side. If your kids don't like green bell peppers, feel free to leave them out.

Western Beef Casserole au Gratin

PREP 15 min COOK 10 min BAKE 35 min STAND 5 min SERVINGS 6

- 1 1/2 cups water
- 3/4 cup milk
- 2 cups mashed potato flakes
- 1/2 pound lean ground beef
- 1/3 cup chopped onion
- 1 can (8 ounces) tomato sauce
- 1/4 teaspoon garlic powder
- 1/8 teaspoon pepper
- 1 can (15 1/4 ounces) whole kernel corn, drained
- 2 cups shredded Cheddar cheese (8 ounces)
- 1 can (4.5 ounces) chopped green chiles, drained
- 1 medium tomato, chopped (3/4 cup)

1. Heat oven to 350°. Spray rectangular baking dish, 11 × 7 × 1 1/2, with cooking spray. Make mashed potatoes as directed on package using 1 1/2 cups water, 3/4 cup milk and 2 cups mashed potato flakes. Keep warm.
2. Cook ground beef and onion in 12-inch skillet over medium heat 8 to 10 minutes, stirring occasionally, until beef is brown; drain. Stir tomato sauce, garlic powder and pepper into beef mixture. Spoon into baking dish. Spoon corn evenly over beef mixture. Spread potatoes evenly over corn; sprinkle with cheese. Top with green chiles.
3. Bake 30 to 35 minutes or until bubbly around edges and cheese is melted. Let stand 5 minutes. Top with chopped tomato.

1 SERVING Calories 400 (Calories from Fat 180) | Fat 20g (Saturated 11g) | Cholesterol 65mg | Sodium 720mg | Carbohydrate 34g (Dietary Fiber 4g) | Protein 20g % DAILY VALUE Vitamin A 20% | Vitamin C 24% | Calcium 34% | Iron 10% EXCHANGES 2 Starch, 2 High-Fat Meat, 1 Fat CARBOHYDRATE CHOICES 2

BETTY'S TIP

Green chiles and corn give this casserole a southwestern flair. Pick up some corn bread muffins on the way home from work, and your meal is made.

Baked Ravioli and Meatballs

PREP 15 min COOK 10 min BAKE 35 min SERVINGS 6

1 package (25 ounces) frozen cheese-filled ravioli

1 package (20 ounces) frozen cooked meatballs, thawed

1 jar (28 ounces) low-sodium spaghetti sauce

1 1/2 cups shredded mozzarella cheese (6 ounces)

1. Heat oven to 375°. Spray rectangular baking dish, 13 × 9 × 2 inches, with cooking spray.
2. Cook and drain ravioli as directed on package. Spoon ravioli into baking dish; top with meatballs and sauce. Sprinkle with cheese.
3. Bake 30 to 35 minutes or until cheese is melted and casserole is hot.

1 SERVING Calories 840 (Calories from Fat 400) | Fat 44g (Saturated 20g) | Cholesterol 165mg | Sodium 1060mg | Carbohydrate 68g (Dietary Fiber 8g) | Protein 43g % DAILY VALUE Vitamin A 34% | Vitamin C 4% | Calcium 60% | Iron 30% EXCHANGES 4 1/2 Starch, 4 High-Fat Meat, 2 Fat CARBOHYDRATE CHOICES 4 1/2

BETTY'S TIP

This is a great recipe for involving the kids. Depending on their age, they could spoon the ravioli and meatballs into the baking dish or sprinkle the cheese on top.

California Chicken Bake

PREP 15 min **BAKE** 1 hr 10 min **SERVINGS** 4

- 2 cups shredded taco-seasoned cheese (8 ounces)
- 3/4 cup uncooked regular long-grain rice
- 1/4 cup chopped fresh cilantro
- 1 cup salsa
- 1 cup water
- 4 boneless, skinless chicken breast halves (about 1 1/4 pounds)

1. Heat oven to 350°. Spray rectangular baking dish, 11 × 7 × 1 1/2 inches, with cooking spray.
2. Reserve 1/2 cup cheese. Mix remaining cheese, the rice, cilantro, salsa and water in large bowl. Spread evenly in baking dish. Arrange chicken on rice mixture.
3. Bake 55 to 65 minutes or until juice of chicken is no longer pink when centers of thickest pieces are cut and rice is tender. Sprinkle with reserved 1/2 cup cheese. Bake uncovered 5 minutes longer or until cheese is melted.

1 SERVING Calories 500 (Calories from Fat 200) | Fat 22g (Saturated 14g) | Cholesterol 130mg | Sodium 970mg | Carbohydrate 34g (Dietary Fiber 0g) | Protein 42g % DAILY VALUE Vitamin A 20% | Vitamin C 0% | Calcium 40% | Iron 14% EXCHANGES 2 Starch, 5 Lean Meat, 1 1/2 Fat CARBOHYDRATE CHOICES 2

BETTY'S TIP

Here's a quick trick to test the rice for doneness. Remove a small amount from the casserole and let it cool slightly. Then taste it. It's done when the rice is tender in the center.

Chicken and Cashew Bake

PREP **15 min** COOK **5 min** BAKE **40 min** SERVINGS **4**

2 medium stalks celery, thinly sliced (1 cup)

1/4 cup chopped onion

1 tablespoon water

3 cups cubed cooked chicken breast

1 1/2 cups frozen green peas (from 1-pound bag)

1/4 cup chopped salted cashews

1/4 cup water or chicken broth

1 can (10 3/4 ounces) condensed 98% fat–free cream of chicken soup with 30% less sodium

1 jar (2 ounces) sliced pimientos, drained

1/4 cup chow mein noodles

1/4 cup salted cashew halves

1. Heat oven to 350°. Spray 1 1/2-quart casserole and 3-quart saucepan with cooking spray. Heat saucepan over medium-high heat; add celery, onion and 1 tablespoon water. Cover and cook 3 to 4 minutes, stirring occasionally, until vegetables are crisp-tender.
2. Stir in remaining ingredients except chow mein noodles and cashew halves. Pour into casserole.
3. Bake 30 to 35 minutes. Sprinkle chow mein noodles and cashew halves evenly over casserole. Bake 5 minutes longer or until hot.

1 SERVING Calories 430 (Calories from Fat 150) | Fat 17g (Saturated 4g) | Cholesterol 90mg | Sodium 640mg | Carbohydrate 28g (Dietary Fiber 4g) | Protein 40g % DAILY VALUE Vitamin A 20% | Vitamin C 34% | Calcium 6% | Iron 20% EXCHANGES 1 1/2 Starch, 1 Vegetable, 5 Lean Meat CARBOHYDRATE CHOICES 2

BETTY'S TIP

If you'd like to decrease the fat and calories of this chow mein–like casserole, simply reduce the amount of cashews and chow mein noodles.

Chicken with Cider Glaze

PREP 5 min **BAKE** 1 min **SERVINGS** 4

- 2 to 2 1/2 pounds broiler-fryer chicken pieces, skin removed
- 1/2 teaspoon salt
- 1/4 teaspoon black peppercorns, crushed
- 1/2 cup apple cider
- 1/2 cup roasted-apple marinade or applesauce
- Chopped fresh parsley, if desired

1. Heat oven to 375°. Place chicken in ungreased rectangular pan, 13 × 9 × 2 inches. Sprinkle with salt and pepper. Pour cider and marinade over chicken.
2. Cover and bake 30 minutes; turn chicken. Bake uncovered 20 to 30 minutes longer or until juice of chicken is no longer pink when centers of thickest pieces are cut. Sprinkle with parsley.

1 SERVING Calories 205 (Calories from Fat 65) | Fat 7g (Saturated 2g) | Cholesterol 80mg | Sodium 370mg | Carbohydrate 9g (Dietary Fiber 0g) | Protein 26g % DAILY VALUE Vitamin A 0% | Vitamin C 0% | Calcium 2% | Iron 6% EXCHANGES 1/2 Fruit, 4 Very Lean Meat, 1 Fat CARBOHYDRATE CHOICES 1/2

BETTY'S TIP

Roasted-apple marinade is a bottled fat-free dressing and marinade made from fresh apples that have been roasted and mixed with champagne vinegar, sugar and spices. It is deep brown in color with a toasty, savory apple flavor. Look for it along with the salad dressings or marinades in your grocery store.

Hot Chicken Salad with Sage Biscuits

PREP **20 min** BAKE **20 min** SERVINGS **6**

- 1/4 cup mayonnaise or salad dressing
- 2 tablespoons Original Bisquick mix
- 2 cups cut-up cooked chicken
- 1/4 cup shredded Cheddar cheese (1 ounce)
- 2 medium stalks celery, sliced (1 cup)
- 2 medium green onions, sliced (2 tablespoons)
- 2 1/4 cups Original Bisquick mix
- 3/4 cup milk
- 1/2 teaspoon dried sage leaves

Photo on page 138.

1. Heat oven to 425°. Mix mayonnaise and 2 tablespoons Bisquick mix in medium bowl until well blended. Stir in chicken, cheese, celery and onions; set aside.
2. Mix remaining ingredients just until soft dough forms. Place on surface sprinkled with Bisquick mix; roll in Bisquick mix to coat. Shape into a ball; knead 10 times. Roll dough 1/2 inch thick. Cut with 1 1/2-inch round cutter dipped in Bisquick mix. Place close together around edge of ungreased 2-quart casserole.
3. Spoon chicken mixture into mound in center of biscuits. Bake uncovered 18 to 20 minutes or until biscuits are golden brown and chicken mixture is hot.

1 SERVING Calories 370 (Calories from Fat 170) | Fat 19g (Saturated 5g) | Cholesterol 55mg | Sodium 820mg | Carbohydrate 31g (Dietary Fiber 1g) | Protein 19g % DAILY VALUE Vitamin A 4% | Vitamin C 2% | Calcium 16% | Iron 12% EXCHANGES 2 Starch, 2 Medium-Fat Meat, 11/2 Fat CARBOHYDRATE CHOICES 2

BETTY'S TIP

For an extra-special touch, sprinkle this warm salad with toasted sliced almonds and dried cranberries, and garnish with fresh sage leaves.

Wild Rice and Chicken Casserole

PREP 10 min **BAKE** 1 hr 5 min **SERVINGS** 6

- 2 cups cut-up cooked chicken or turkey
- 1/2 cup frozen green peas (from 1-pound bag)
- 2 1/4 cups boiling water
- 1/3 cup milk
- 1 small onion, chopped (1/4 cup)
- 1 can (10 3/4 ounces) condensed cream of mushroom soup
- 1 package (6 ounces) seasoned long-grain and wild rice

1. Heat oven to 350°.
2. Mix all ingredients including seasoning packet from rice mix in ungreased 2-quart casserole.
3. Cover and bake 45 to 50 minutes or until rice is tender. Uncover and bake 10 to 15 minutes longer or until liquid is absorbed.

1 SERVING Calories 210 (Calories from Fat 65) | Fat 7g (Saturated 2g) | Cholesterol 45mg | Sodium 440mg | Carbohydrate 19g (Dietary Fiber 1g) | Protein 17g % DAILY VALUE Vitamin A 6% | Vitamin C 4% | Calcium 6% | Iron 10% EXCHANGES 1 Starch, 2 Lean Meat, 1/2 Fat CARBOHYDRATE CHOICES 1

Wild Rice and Ham Casserole Substitute 2 cups cut-up ham for the chicken.

BETTY'S TIP

Mushroom lovers may like to add a small can of sliced mushrooms, drained, to this wild rice casserole.

Ranch Potatoes and Chicken Casserole

PREP 15 min **BAKE** 43 min **STAND** 5 min **SERVINGS** 4 to 6

- 1 package (5.1 ounces) ranch potato mix
- 4 slices process American cheese
- 2 cups cut-up cooked chicken
- 1 package (10 ounces) frozen chopped broccoli, thawed and drained
- 2 1/4 cups boiling water
- 1 package (3 ounces) cream cheese, cut into cubes and softened

1. Heat oven to 400°. Spray 2-quart casserole with cooking spray.
2. Layer uncooked Potatoes from potato mix, the American cheese, chicken and broccoli in casserole. Mix boiling water, Sauce Mix from potato mix and cream cheese; pour over broccoli.
3. Bake uncovered 35 to 40 minutes or until potatoes are tender. Sprinkle with Topping from potato mix. Bake 3 minutes longer. Let stand 5 minutes before serving.

1 SERVING Calories 415 (Calories from Fat 180) | Fat 20g (Saturated 10g) | Cholesterol 105mg | Sodium 1140mg | Carbohydrate 33g (Dietary Fiber 4g) | Protein 30g % DAILY VALUE Vitamin A 24% | Vitamin C 20% | Calcium 18% | Iron 8% EXCHANGES 2 Starch, 3 Medium-Fat Meat, 1 Fat CARBOHYDRATE CHOICES 2

BETTY'S TIP

For the sake of convenience, you may want to use a 9-ounce package of frozen diced cooked chicken, thawed, in place of the 2 cups cut-up chicken.

Country Chicken and Pasta Bake

PREP 10 min COOK 15 min BAKE 30 min SERVINGS 6

- 2 cups uncooked radiatore (nugget) pasta (6 ounces)
- 3 cups cubed cooked chicken
- 2 jars (12 ounces each) chicken gravy
- 1 bag (1 pound) frozen broccoli, carrots and cauliflower (or other combination)
- 1/4 teaspoon dried thyme leaves
- 1/4 teaspoon salt
- 1/2 cup herb-seasoned stuffing crumbs
- 2 tablespoons butter or margarine, melted

1. Heat oven to 375°. Cook and drain pasta as directed on package.
2. Mix pasta and remaining ingredients except stuffing and butter. Spread in ungreased rectangular baking dish, 11 × 7 × 1 1/2 inches. Sprinkle with stuffing; drizzle with butter.
3. Cover and bake about 30 minutes or until hot.

1 SERVING Calories 390 (Calories from Fat 115) | Fat 16g (Saturated 6g) | Cholesterol 75mg | Sodium 900mg | Carbohydrate 37g (Dietary Fiber 4g) | Protein 37g % DAILY VALUE Vitamin A 60% | Vitamin C 20% | Calcium 6% | Iron 16% EXCHANGES 2 Starch, 1 Vegetable, 3 Lean Meat, 1 Fat CARBOHYDRATE CHOICES 2 1/2

BETTY'S TIP

When cooking pasta to be used in a casserole, cook only the minimum amount of time listed on the package because the pasta will continue to cook and absorb liquid while baking in the casserole.

Chicken-Vegetable Strata

PREP 15 min **CHILL** 2 hr **BAKE** 1 hr 15 min **STAND** 10 min **SERVINGS** 4

- 4 to 5 slices whole wheat or rye bread
- 1 1/2 cups cut-up cooked chicken or turkey
- 1 1/2 cups (from 1-pound bag) frozen broccoli, green beans, onions and red pepper (or other combination)
- 1 cup shredded Cheddar cheese (4 ounces)
- 4 eggs, slightly beaten
- 2 cups milk
- 1 1/2 teaspoons chopped fresh or 1/2 teaspoon dried oregano leaves
- 1 1/2 teaspoons chopped fresh or 1/2 teaspoon dried thyme leaves
- 1 teaspoon onion powder
- 1/4 teaspoon pepper

1. Trim crust edges from bread slices; cut each bread slice diagonally into 4 triangles. Arrange half of the bread in ungreased square pan, 8 × 8 × 2 inches. Top with chicken and vegetables. Sprinkle with cheese. Top with remaining bread.
2. Mix remaining ingredients; pour over bread. Cover and refrigerate at least 2 hours but no longer than 24 hours, occasionally pressing bread down into egg mixture.
3. Heat oven to 325°. Cover pan with aluminum foil; bake 30 minutes. Uncover and bake about 45 minutes longer or until knife inserted in center comes out clean. Let stand 10 minutes before serving.

1 SERVING Calories 435 (Calories from Fat 190) | Fat 21g (Saturated 10g) | Cholesterol 300mg | Sodium 500mg | Carbohydrate 25g (Dietary Fiber 3g) | Protein 37g % DAILY VALUE Vitamin A 38% | Vitamin C 26% | Calcium 36% | Iron 14% EXCHANGES 1 1/2 Starch, 1 Vegetable, 4 Medium-Fat Meat CARBOHYDRATE CHOICES 1 1/2

BETTY'S TIP

This is a great dish to turn to when you want a make-ahead meal that's ready to bake without last-minute fuss. If you like, you can also leave your bread untrimmed.

Chicken and Rice Bake

PREP 15 min BAKE 1 hr 30 min STAND 5 min SERVINGS 6

1 package (6 ounces) long-grain and wild rice

3- to 3 1/2-pound cut-up broiler-fryer chicken, skinned if desired

2 medium stalks celery, sliced (1 cup)

1 jar (4.5 ounces) whole mushrooms, drained

2 cups water

1 can (10 3/4 ounces) condensed cream of chicken or cream of celery soup

Paprika

1. Heat oven to 350°. Spray rectangular baking dish, 13 × 9 × 2 inches, with cooking spray. Pour uncooked rice from rice mix evenly into baking dish. Sprinkle seasoning mix from rice mix evenly over rice. Arrange chicken over rice; arrange celery and mushrooms around chicken.
2. Mix water and soup in 2-quart saucepan; heat to boiling. Pour soup mixture evenly over chicken and vegetables. Sprinkle with paprika. Cover with aluminum foil.
3. Bake 1 hour; remove foil. Bake 20 to 30 minutes longer or until juice of chicken is no longer pink when centers of thickest pieces are cut. Let stand 5 minutes before serving.

1 SERVING Calories 390 (Calories from Fat 150) | Fat 17g (Saturated 5g) | Cholesterol 95mg | Sodium 910mg | Carbohydrate 26g (Dietary Fiber 1g) | Protein 33g % DAILY VALUE Vitamin A 8% | Vitamin C 0% | Calcium 4% | Iron 15% EXCHANGES 1 1/2 Starch, 4 Lean Meat, 1 Fat CARBOHYDRATE CHOICES 1 1/2

BETTY'S TIP

Chances are you've used paprika before, but do you know what it is? It's actually a powder made from grinding sweet red pepper pods. It's a good idea to store it in a cool, dark place for no longer than six months.

Layered Chicken–Black Bean Enchiladas

PREP 25 min **BAKE** 40 min **STAND** 10 min **SERVINGS** 6

- 2 cups chopped cooked chicken
- 2 tablespoons chopped fresh cilantro
- 1 can (15 ounces) black beans, rinsed and drained
- 1 can (4.5 ounces) chopped green chiles
- 1 can (10 ounces) enchilada sauce
- 8 corn tortillas (5 or 6 inches in diameter)
- 1 1/2 cups shredded Colby–Monterey Jack cheese (6 ounces)
- 1 container (8 ounces) sour cream

1. Heat oven to 375°. Spray rectangular baking dish, 11 × 7 × 1 1/2 inches, with cooking spray. Mix chicken, cilantro, black beans and chiles in medium bowl.
2. Spread 2 tablespoons of the enchilada sauce in bottom of baking dish. Place 4 tortillas over sauce, overlapping as necessary. Spoon half of the chicken mixture over tortillas; sprinkle with 1/2 cup cheese. Spoon half of the remaining enchilada sauce and half of the sour cream randomly over cheese. Repeat with remaining tortillas, chicken mixture, 1/2 cup cheese, the enchilada sauce and sour cream.
3. Cover with aluminum foil. Bake 30 to 35 minutes or until hot. Sprinkle remaining 1/2 cup cheese over casserole. Bake uncovered 5 minutes longer or until cheese is melted. Let stand 10 minutes before serving.

1 SERVING Calories 440 (Calories from Fat 210) | Fat 23g (Saturated 12g) | Cholesterol 85mg | Sodium 640mg | Carbohydrate 30g (Dietary Fiber 6g) | Protein 28g % DAILY VALUE Vitamin A 14% | Vitamin C 8% | Calcium 34% | Iron 14% EXCHANGES 2 Starch, 3 Lean Meat, 2 1/2 Fat CARBOHYDRATE CHOICES 2

BETTY'S TIP

Spanish rice and a green salad tossed with jicama sticks and orange segments make tasty accompaniments to this Mexican specialty.

Chicken Drumstick Cacciatore Casserole

PREP 15 min **BAKE** 45 min **SERVINGS** 4

1. Heat oven to 375°. Spray rectangular baking dish, 11 × 7 × 1 1/2 inches, with cooking spray.
2. Gently mix rice, zucchini, broth, tomatoes and mushrooms in baking dish. Arrange chicken over rice mixture. Sprinkle with paprika. Cover with aluminum foil.
3. Bake 30 minutes. Uncover and bake 10 to 15 minutes longer or until juice of chicken is no longer pink when centers of thickest pieces are cut.

1 SERVING Calories 380 (Calories from Fat 55) | Fat 6g (Saturated 2g) | Cholesterol 80mg | Sodium 740mg | Carbohydrate 48g (Dietary Fiber 3g) | Protein 33g % DAILY VALUE Vitamin A 20% | Vitamin C 20% | Calcium 8% | Iron 24% EXCHANGES 3 Starch, 1 Vegetable, 3 Lean Meat CARBOHYDRATE CHOICES 3

1 cup uncooked regular long–grain rice

1 medium zucchini, sliced

1 can (14 ounces) chicken broth

1 can (14.5 ounces) diced tomatoes with Italian–style herbs, undrained

1 jar (4.5 ounces) sliced mushrooms, drained

8 chicken drumsticks, skin removed

1 teaspoon paprika

BETTY'S TIP

Here's a quick trick to removing the skin from the drumsticks: Use a paper towel to grab the skin and pull it from the large end to the small end of the leg. The paper towel makes it easy to get a grip on the slippery skin.

Baked Chicken Gumbo

PREP 35 min BAKE 45 min SERVINGS 4

3 slices bacon, cut into 1-inch pieces

4 skinless chicken thighs (about 1 1/4 pounds)

1 large green bell pepper, chopped (about 1 1/2 cups)

1 large onion, chopped (about 1 cup)

1 medium stalk celery, chopped (about 1/2 cup)

3 cloves garlic, finely chopped

1 package (10 ounces) frozen cut okra, thawed and drained

1 cup chicken broth

3/4 cup uncooked quick-cooking brown rice

1/2 teaspoon pepper

1/4 teaspoon ground red pepper (cayenne)

2 tablespoons chopped fresh parsley

1. Cook bacon in 10-inch skillet over medium heat, stirring occasionally, until crisp. Remove bacon with slotted spoon and drain. Drain all but 1 tablespoon fat from skillet.
2. Heat oven to 350°. Cook chicken thighs in bacon fat over low heat about 15 minutes or until light brown on all sides. Remove chicken from skillet.
3. Cook bell pepper, onion, celery and garlic in drippings in skillet about 3 minutes, stirring frequently, until vegetables are crisp-tender. Stir in okra, broth, rice, pepper and red pepper. Heat to boiling; remove from heat. Pour rice mixture into ungreased rectangular baking dish, 11 × 7 × 1 1/2 inches. Place chicken on top.
4. Cover with aluminum foil. Bake 40 to 45 minutes or until juice of chicken is no longer pink when centers of thickest pieces are cut and rice is tender. Sprinkle with parsley and bacon.

1 SERVING Calories 320 (Calories from Fat 80) | Fat 9g (Saturated 3g) | Cholesterol 45mg | Sodium 390mg | Carbohydrate 38g (Dietary Fiber 6g) | Protein 22g % DAILY VALUE Vitamin A 8% | Vitamin C 38% | Calcium 10% | Iron 14% EXCHANGES 2 Starch, 2 Vegetable, 2 Very Lean Meat, 1 Fat CARBOHYDRATE CHOICES 2 1/2

BETTY'S TIP

Okra is a common ingredient in many southern dishes, especially gumbo. It serves to both thicken this stew-like dish and add flavor. In fact, gumbo is actually a derivation of the African word for "okra."

Three-Herb Chicken

PREP 5 min MARINATE 3 hr BAKE 1 hr 15 min SERVINGS 4

- 1/2 cup olive or vegetable oil
- 1/2 cup lime juice
- 2 tablespoons chopped fresh or 2 teaspoons dried basil leaves
- 2 tablespoons chopped fresh or 2 teaspoons dried oregano leaves
- 2 tablespoons chopped fresh or 2 teaspoons dried thyme leaves
- 1 teaspoon onion powder
- 1/4 teaspoon lemon pepper
- 4 chicken thighs (about 1 pound)
- 4 chicken drumsticks (about 1 pound)

1. Mix all ingredients except chicken thighs and drumsticks in resealable heavy-duty plastic bag or glass bowl. Add chicken; turn to coat with marinade. Seal bag or cover dish; refrigerate 3 to 4 hours, turning occasionally.
2. Heat oven to 375°. Grease rack of broiler pan. Remove chicken from marinade; reserve marinade. Place chicken on rack in broiler pan. Bake uncovered 30 minutes; turn chicken. Brush with marinade. Bake uncovered about 45 minutes longer or until juice of chicken is no longer pink when centers of thickest pieces are cut. Discard any remaining marinade.

1 SERVING Calories 425 (Calories from Fat 280) | Fat 31g (Saturated 7g) | Cholesterol 110mg | Sodium 120mg | Carbohydrate 2g (Dietary Fiber 0g) | Protein 35g % DAILY VALUE Vitamin A 4% | Vitamin C 4% | Calcium 4% | Iron 14% EXCHANGES 5 Lean Meat, 3 Fat CARBOHYDRATE CHOICES 0

BETTY'S TIP

Looking for some sides to serve with this juicy chicken? Hot cooked saffron rice tossed with some butter, along with a side of green beans or peas, tastes great with this flavorful dish.

Chicken Legs with Vegetables

PREP 10 min BAKE 1 hr SERVINGS 4

8 chicken drumsticks or thighs (about 1 1/4 pounds), skin removed

1 pound Yukon gold potatoes, cut into fourths

1 medium red or green bell pepper, cut into strips

1 medium onion, cut into wedges

2 tablespoons chopped fresh or 2 teaspoons dried marjoram leaves

3 tablespoons olive or vegetable oil

1 teaspoon garlic salt

1. Heat oven to 375°. Place chicken, potatoes, bell pepper and onion in ungreased rectangular pan, 13 × 9 × 2 inches. Mix remaining ingredients; sprinkle over chicken and vegetables.
2. Bake uncovered 30 minutes; turn chicken. Bake uncovered 25 to 30 minutes longer or until juice of chicken is no longer pink when centers of thickest pieces are cut.

1 SERVING Calories 380 (Calories from Fat 160) | Fat 18g (Saturated 4g) | Cholesterol 90mg | Sodium 320mg | Carbohydrate 28g (Dietary Fiber 3g) | Protein 30g % DAILY VALUE Vitamin A 16% | Vitamin C 58% | Calcium 4% | Iron 22% EXCHANGES 2 Starch, 3 1/2 Lean Meat, 1 Fat CARBOHYDRATE CHOICES 2

BETTY'S TIP

Yukon gold potatoes are medium-size potatoes with thin yellow skins and golden yellow flesh. They have a mild, slightly sweet flavor and a smooth, moist texture.

Maple-Glazed Turkey and Rice Casserole

PREP 15 min BAKE 1 hr 15 min SERVINGS 4

- 1 package (6 ounces) long-grain and wild rice mix
- 1 1/2 cups water
- 2-pound bone-in skin-on turkey breast half
- 3 tablespoons maple-flavored syrup
- 1/2 teaspoon ground cinnamon
- 1/2 cup chopped walnuts

1. Heat oven to 350°. Mix Rice and Seasoning Packet from rice mix and water in ungreased square baking dish, 8 × 8 × 2 inches.
2. Place turkey breast half, skin side up, on rice mixture. Drizzle with maple syrup. Sprinkle with cinnamon. Insert meat thermometer so tip is in thickest part of turkey.
3. Cover and bake about 55 minutes. Sprinkle with walnuts. Bake uncovered 15 to 20 minutes longer or until rice is tender, thermometer reads 170° and juice of turkey is no longer pink when center is cut.

1 SERVING Calories 475 (Calories from Fat 180) | Fat 20g (Saturated 4g) | Cholesterol 105mg | Sodium 260mg | Carbohydrate 45g (Dietary Fiber 1g) | Protein 29g % DAILY VALUE Vitamin A 2% | Vitamin C 0% | Calcium 4% | Iron 12% EXCHANGES 3 Starch, 3 Lean Meat, 1 1/2 Fat CARBOHYDRATE CHOICES 3

BETTY'S TIP

A green vegetable, such as Brussels sprouts or French green beans, would be a nice complement to this casserole. And why not pick up an apple pie from your favorite bakery for a special dessert?

Turkey Divan

PREP 25 min **BAKE** 20 min **SERVINGS** 6

1 1/2 pounds fresh broccoli spears

2 tablespoons water

1/4 cup butter or margarine

1/4 cup all-purpose flour

1/8 teaspoon ground nutmeg

1 cup chicken broth

1/2 cup grated Parmesan cheese

2 tablespoons dry white wine or apple juice

1/2 cup whipping (heavy) cream

6 large slices cooked turkey breast, 1/8 to 1/4 inch thick (about 1 pound)

2 tablespoons grated Parmesan cheese

1. Heat oven to 425°. Place broccoli and water in rectangular microwavable dish, 11 × 7 × 1 1/2 inches. Cover with plastic wrap, folding back one edge or corner 1/4 inch to vent steam. Microwave on High 6 to 8 minutes or until tender; drain.
2. Meanwhile, melt butter in 2-quart saucepan over low heat. Stir flour and nutmeg into butter. Cook, stirring constantly, until smooth and bubbly; remove from heat. Stir in broth. Heat to boiling, stirring constantly. Boil and stir 1 minute; remove from heat. Stir in 1/2 cup cheese, the wine and whipping cream.
3. Arrange hot broccoli in ungreased rectangular baking dish, 13 × 9 × 2 inches. Top with turkey. Pour cheese sauce over turkey. Sprinkle with 2 tablespoons cheese.
4. Bake uncovered 15 to 20 minutes or until sauce is bubbly and cheese is light brown.

1 SERVING Calories 300 (Calories from Fat 160) | Fat 18g (Saturated 11g) | Cholesterol 100mg | Sodium 470mg | Carbohydrate 9g (Dietary Fiber 2g) | Protein 26g % DAILY VALUE Vitamin A 30% | Vitamin C 54% | Calcium 20% | Iron 10% EXCHANGES 2 Vegetable, 3 Lean Meat, 2 Fat CARBOHYDRATE CHOICES 1/2

BETTY'S TIP

Instead of fresh broccoli, two 10-ounce packages of frozen broccoli spears can be used instead. Cook as directed on the package, then continue with step 2.

Turkey, Carrot and Noodle Bake

PREP 15 min COOK 10 min BAKE 40 min SERVINGS 4

- 2 cups uncooked egg noodles (4 ounces)
- 1 pound ground turkey
- 1 medium onion, chopped (1/2 cup)
- 3 medium carrots, thinly sliced (about 1 1/2 cups)
- 2 medium tomatoes, seeded and cut into bite-size pieces
- 1 jar (12 ounces) chicken or turkey gravy
- 1 container (8 ounces) sour cream
- 1 tablespoon chopped fresh or 1 teaspoon dried sage leaves
- 1 tablespoon chopped fresh or 1 teaspoon dried marjoram leaves
- 1/4 teaspoon pepper
- 1/2 cup buttery cracker crumbs
- 1/3 cup chopped pecans or walnuts
- 2 tablespoons butter or margarine, melted

1. Heat oven to 375°. Cook and drain noodles as directed on package.
2. While noodles are cooking, cook turkey and onion in 10-inch skillet over medium heat, stirring frequently, until turkey is no longer pink; drain. Stir carrots, tomatoes, gravy, sour cream, sage, marjoram and pepper into turkey mixture. Place cooked noodles in ungreased rectangular pan, 11 × 7 × 1 1/2 inches. Gently fold in turkey mixture.
3. Cover with aluminum foil. Bake 30 minutes. Mix cracker crumbs, pecans and butter; sprinkle over turkey mixture. Bake uncovered 5 to 10 minutes longer or until hot.

1 SERVING Calories 660 (Calories from Fat 360) | Fat 40g (Saturated 12g) | Cholesterol 140mg | Sodium 880mg | Carbohydrate 42g (Dietary Fiber 2g) | Protein 34g % DAILY VALUE Vitamin A 100% | Vitamin C 14% | Calcium 12% | Iron 20% EXCHANGES 2 Starch, 2 Vegetable, 3 1/2 Medium-Fat Meat, 4 Fat CARBOHYDRATE CHOICES 3

Beef, Carrot and Noodle Bake Substitute 1 pound lean ground beef in place of the ground turkey.

BETTY'S TIP

To make quick work of seeding a tomato, cut the tomato in half along its equator, and squeeze each half to release the seeds.

Turkey and Corn Bread Stuffing Casserole

PREP **10 min** COOK **5 min** BAKE **40 min** SERVINGS **6**

- 1 can (10 3/4 ounces) condensed cream of chicken or celery soup
- 1 1/4 cups milk
- 1 cup frozen green peas (from 1-pound bag)
- 1/2 cup dried cranberries
- 4 medium green onions, sliced (1/4 cup)
- 2 cups cut-up cooked turkey or chicken
- 1 1/2 cups corn bread stuffing mix
- 1 cup Original Bisquick mix
- 1/4 cup milk
- 2 eggs

1. Heat oven to 400°. Spray 3-quart casserole with cooking spray. Heat soup and milk to boiling in 3-quart saucepan, stirring frequently. Stir peas, cranberries and onions into soup mixture. Heat to boiling, stirring frequently; remove from heat. Stir in turkey and stuffing mix. Spoon into casserole.
2. Stir remaining ingredients until blended. Pour over stuffing mixture.
3. Bake uncovered 35 to 40 minutes or until knife inserted in center comes out clean.

1 SERVING Calories 410 (Calories from Fat 135) | Fat 15g (Saturated 4g) | Cholesterol 140mg | Sodium 1000mg | Carbohydrate 43g (Dietary Fiber 3g) | Protein 29g % DAILY VALUE Vitamin A 12% | Vitamin C 4% | Calcium 16% | Iron 16% EXCHANGES 3 Starch, 3 Lean Meat CARBOHYDRATE CHOICES 3

BETTY'S TIP

No dried cranberries on hand? You can leave them out of the recipe, or use dried cherries or raisins instead.

Easy Turkey Lasagna

PREP **25 min** BAKE **45 min** STAND **15 min** SERVINGS **8**

- 3 cups chunky-style spaghetti sauce
- 2 cups chopped cooked turkey
- 1 small zucchini, shredded (1 cup)
- 6 uncooked lasagna noodles
- 1 cup ricotta cheese
- 1/4 cup grated Parmesan cheese
- 1 teaspoon dried oregano leaves
- 2 cups shredded mozzarella cheese (8 ounces)

1. Heat oven to 350°. Mix spaghetti sauce, turkey and zucchini. Spread 1 1/2 cups turkey mixture in ungreased rectangular baking dish, 11 × 7 × 1 1/2 inches. Top with 3 noodles.
2. Mix ricotta cheese, Parmesan cheese and oregano; spread over noodles in dish. Spread with 1 1/2 cups of the turkey mixture. Top with remaining noodles and turkey mixture. Sprinkle with mozzarella cheese.
3. Bake uncovered about 45 minutes or until hot and bubbly. Let stand 15 minutes before cutting.

1 Serving. Calories 315 (Calories from Fat 125) | Fat 14g (Saturated 6g) | Cholesterol 55mg | Sodium 870mg | Carbohydrate 23g (Dietary Fiber 2g) | Protein 26g % DAILY VALUE Vitamin A 14% | Vitamin C 4% | Calcium 36% | Iron 12% EXCHANGES 1 1/2 Starch, 3 Lean Meat, 1 Fat CARBOHYDRATE CHOICES 1 1/2

BETTY'S TIP

You may be tempted to start cutting into this cheesy lasagna right away instead of letting it stand for 15 minutes, but try to resist. If you don't let it stand, the lasagna will be too saucy and won't hold its shape.

Turkey with Italian Roasted Vegetables

PREP 15 min BAKE 40 min SERVINGS 4

- 1 pound turkey breast tenderloins
- 1/2 cup Italian dressing
- 2 medium russet or Idaho baking potatoes, unpeeled, cut into 1-inch cubes
- 1 medium red or green bell pepper, cut into 8 pieces
- 1 medium onion, cut into wedges
- 1 package (8 ounces) whole mushrooms
- 1/2 teaspoon garlic pepper

1. Heat oven to 400°. Line jelly roll pan, 15 1/2 × 10 1/2 × 1 inch, with aluminum foil. Spray foil with cooking spray.
2. Toss all ingredients in large bowl or resealable plastic food-storage bag. Remove turkey and vegetables; place in pan. Discard remaining dressing.
3. Bake 30 to 40 minutes or until juice of turkey is no longer pink when centers of thickest pieces are cut and vegetables are tender.

1 SERVING Calories 380 (Calories from Fat 140) | Fat 15g (Saturated 2g) | Cholesterol 95mg | Sodium 300mg | Carbohydrate 25g (Dietary Fiber 3g) | Protein 37g % DAILY VALUE Vitamin A 2% | Vitamin C 34% | Calcium 4% | Iron 20% EXCHANGES 1 Starch, 2 Vegetable, 4 Lean Meat, 1/2 Fat CARBOHYDRATE CHOICES 1 1/2

Chicken with Italian Roasted Vegetables Substitute 1 pound boneless, skinless chicken breasts in place of the turkey tenderloins.

BETTY'S TIP

Russet potatoes are also called baking potatoes. They are oval in shape and have skin that is brown and rough. In addition to roasting, russet potatoes are good for baking, mashing and frying because they are low in moisture and high in starch.

Turkey and Tortilla Casserole

PREP 10 min **BAKE** 20 min **SERVINGS** 8

- 2 cups green enchilada sauce or green taco sauce
- 8 flour tortillas (about 12 inches in diameter)
- 2 cups cut-up cooked turkey or chicken
- 2 cups shredded mozzarella cheese (8 ounces)
- Guacamole, if desired
- Chopped tomato, if desired

1. Heat oven to 350°. Heat enchilada sauce in 12-inch skillet over medium heat, stirring occasionally, until warm. Dip each tortilla into warm enchilada sauce to coat both sides.
2. Place 4 of the tortillas in ungreased pie plate, 9 × 1 1/4 inches, with edges overlapping. Top with half of the remaining enchilada sauce, 1 cup of the turkey and 1 cup cheese. Arrange 4 tortillas over cheese. Repeat layers, using remaining enchilada sauce, turkey and cheese.
3. Bake uncovered about 20 minutes or until cheese is melted. Serve with guacamole or chopped tomato.

1 SERVING Calories 465 (Calories from Fat 125) | Fat 14g (Saturated 5g) | Cholesterol 45mg | Sodium 920mg | Carbohydrate 58g (Dietary Fiber 4g) | Protein 27g % DAILY VALUE Vitamin A 12% | Vitamin C 6% | Calcium 34% | Iron 24% EXCHANGES 4 Starch, 2 Medium-Fat Meat CARBOHYDRATE CHOICES 4

BETTY'S TIP

Instead of mozzarella cheese, try using one of the Mexican cheese blends available instead. They are usually combinations of some or all of the following: Monterey Jack, Cheddar, asadero or queso blanco cheeses and taco seasonings.

Ham and Brie Bake

PREP 20 min BAKE 30 min SERVINGS 6

- 1/4 cup milk
- 1 tablespoon butter or margarine, melted
- 1 egg
- 6 slices rye bread, cut into cubes (6 cups)
- 1 1/4 cups coarsely chopped fully cooked ham (8 ounces)
- 1 medium pear, peeled and chopped
- 3 green onions, sliced (3 tablespoons)
- 8 ounces Brie cheese, peeled and cut into cubes

1. Heat oven to 350°. Spray square baking dish, 8 × 8 × 2 inches, with cooking spray.
2. Beat milk, butter and egg in medium bowl. Add bread cubes, ham, pear and onions; toss. Spread bread mixture in baking dish. Top with cheese.
3. Bake uncovered 25 to 30 minutes or until pears are tender and cheese is melted.

1 SERVING Calories 295 (Calories from Fat 155) | Fat 17g (Saturated 8g) | Cholesterol 85mg | Sodium 1100mg | Carbohydrate 13g (Dietary Fiber 1g) | Protein 17g % DAILY VALUE Vitamin A 14% | Vitamin C 2% | Calcium 18% | Iron 8% EXCHANGES 1 Starch, 2 1/2 Medium-Fat Meat, 1/2 Fat CARBOHYDRATE CHOICES 1

Turkey and Brie Bake Substitute chopped smoked turkey for the ham.

BETTY'S TIP

This strata-like casserole is a great, hearty dish to serve for brunch. Keep things simple by serving it with steamed asparagus and a variety of fresh fruit.

Sausage and Pizza Bake

PREP 10 min COOK 10 min BAKE 35 min SERVINGS 6

- 3 cups uncooked rotini pasta (9 ounces)
- 1 pound bulk Italian sausage
- 1 medium onion, chopped (1/2 cup)
- 1 small bell pepper, chopped (1/2 cup)
- 1/4 cup water
- 4 ounces sliced Canadian-style bacon, cut into fourths
- 1 jar or can (14 or 15 ounces) pizza sauce
- 1 can (4 ounces) sliced mushrooms, drained
- 3/4 cup shredded pizza cheese blend (3 ounces)

1. Heat oven to 350°. Spray 3-quart casserole with cooking spray. Cook and drain pasta in 3-quart saucepan as directed on package. Return pasta to saucepan.
2. While pasta is cooking, cook sausage and onion in 10-inch skillet over medium heat 8 to 10 minutes, stirring occasionally, until sausage is no longer pink; drain. Stir sausage mixture, bell pepper, water, bacon, pizza sauce and mushrooms into pasta. Spoon pasta mixture into casserole. Sprinkle with cheese.
3. Cover and bake 30 to 35 minutes or until hot and cheese is melted.

1 SERVING Calories 560 (Calories from Fat 200) | Fat 22g (Saturated 8g) | Cholesterol 60mg | Sodium 1270mg | Carbohydrate 56g (Dietary Fiber 4g) | Protein 26g % DAILY VALUE Vitamin A 12% | Vitamin C 20% | Calcium 14% | Iron 18% EXCHANGES 4 Starch, 2 High-Fat Meat CARBOHYDRATE CHOICES 4

BETTY'S TIP

Be sure to thoroughly drain the cooked pasta—a few hard shakes of the colander after the water drains should do it. Excess cooking water clinging to the pasta will dilute the sauce.

Mashed Potato and Sausage Casserole

PREP 20 min COOK 10 min BAKE 57 min SERVINGS 5

- 1 pound bulk pork sausage
- 1 bag (1 pound) frozen mixed vegetables
- 1 cup onion-seasoned beef broth (from 14-ounce can)
- 3 tablespoons all-purpose flour
- 1/2 package (7.2-ounce size) roasted garlic mashed potato mix (1 pouch)
- Water, milk, margarine or butter called for on potato mix package

1. Heat oven to 425°. Spray square baking dish, 8 × 8 × 2 inches, with cooking spray. Cook sausage in 10-inch skillet over medium heat 8 to 10 minutes, stirring frequently, until no longer pink; drain. Mix sausage and frozen vegetables in baking dish. Mix broth and flour in small bowl. Pour over sausage mixture; gently stir.
2. Cover and bake 35 to 45 minutes, stirring occasionally, until mixture is hot, bubbly and slightly thickened.
3. Make potatoes as directed on package for 4 servings, using 1 pouch Potatoes and Seasoning, water, milk and margarine; let stand 3 to 5 minutes. Spoon onto sausage mixture. Bake uncovered 8 to 12 minutes or until potatoes start to brown.

1 SERVING Calories 400 (Calories from Fat 215) | Fat 24g (Saturated 7g) | Cholesterol 40mg | Sodium 950mg | Carbohydrate 30g (Dietary Fiber 4g) | Protein 16g % DAILY VALUE Vitamin A 62% | Vitamin C 32% | Calcium 14% | Iron 8% EXCHANGES 2 Starch, 1 1/2 High-Fat Meat, 2 Fat CARBOHYDRATE CHOICES 2

BETTY'S TIP

You can substitute 1 pound fully cooked kielbasa or Polish sausage, cut into 1/2-inch slices, for the bulk pork sausage. Omit the cooking in step 1, and just mix the kielbasa with the vegetables.

Lamb and Lentil Casserole

PREP 25 min COOK 10 min BAKE 55 min SERVINGS 4

- 2 slices bacon, cut into 1-inch pieces
- 1 tablespoon vegetable oil
- 1 pound lamb boneless loin or shoulder, cut into 3/4-inch pieces
- 3 medium carrots, thinly sliced (about 1 1/2 cups)
- 1 large onion, cut in half and sliced
- 1 can (14 1/2 ounces) stewed tomatoes
- 1 can (8 ounces) tomato sauce
- 1 cup dried lentils, sorted and rinsed
- 1 cup water
- 1 tablespoon packed brown sugar
- 1 tablespoon chopped fresh or 1 teaspoon dried thyme leaves
- 1 tablespoon chopped fresh or 1 teaspoon dried savory leaves
- 1/4 teaspoon salt
- 1/4 teaspoon pepper

1. Heat oven to 350°. Cook bacon in 4-quart Dutch oven over medium heat, stirring occasionally, until bacon is crisp. Remove bacon with slotted spoon; drain. Drain fat from Dutch oven.
2. Heat oil in same Dutch oven over medium heat until hot. Cook lamb in oil, stirring frequently, until brown; drain fat. Stir bacon and remaining ingredients into lamb. Heat to boiling; remove from heat.
3. Spoon lamb mixture into ungreased 2-quart casserole. Cover and bake 50 to 55 minutes, stirring occasionally, until lamb and lentils are tender.

1 SERVING Calories 490 (Calories from Fat 125) | Fat 14g (Saturated 4g) | Cholesterol 85mg | Sodium 900mg | Carbohydrate 50g (Dietary Fiber 14g) | Protein 41g % DAILY VALUE Vitamin A 100% | Vitamin C 24% | Calcium 8% | Iron 42% EXCHANGES 3 Starch, 1 Vegetable, 4 Lean Meat CARBOHYDRATE CHOICES 3

Pork and Lentil Casserole Substitute pork boneless loin or shoulder for the lamb.

BETTY'S TIP

When buying lamb, let color be your guide: Look for lamb that's pinkish red with a velvety texture and a thin, firm layer of fat surrounding it. Keep in mind the darker the meat, the older the animal and stronger the flavor.

Lamb with Sweet Peppers and Garlic Sauce

PREP 15 min **COOK** 20 min **BAKE** 45 min **SERVINGS** 4

- 2 pounds lamb boneless shoulder
- 2 tablespoons olive oil
- 1/4 cup chopped fresh parsley
- 1/4 cup chopped fresh mint leaves
- 4 anchovy fillets in oil, finely chopped
- 4 cloves garlic, finely chopped
- 2 medium green onions, thinly sliced (2 tablespoons)
- 1 medium yellow bell pepper, cut into 1-inch squares
- 1 medium red bell pepper, cut into 1-inch squares
- 1 teaspoon salt
- 1/2 teaspoon pepper
- 1 cup dry white wine or chicken broth
- 3 tablespoons all-purpose flour

1. Heat oven to 375°. Remove fat from lamb. Cut lamb into 1-inch pieces.
2. Heat oil in ovenproof 4-quart Dutch oven over medium-high heat. Cook parsley, mint, anchovies, garlic and onions in oil about 5 minutes, stirring frequently, until onions are tender.
3. Stir in lamb. Cook about 10 minutes, stirring occasionally, until lamb is brown. Stir in bell peppers. Sprinkle with salt and pepper.
4. Shake wine and flour in tightly covered container until smooth; stir into lamb mixture. Heat to boiling. Cover and bake about 45 minutes or until lamb is tender.

1 SERVING Calories 310 (Calories from Fat 145) | Fat 16g (Saturated 5g) | Cholesterol 105mg | Sodium 950mg | Carbohydrate 9g (Dietary Fiber 2g) | Protein 35g % DAILY VALUE Vitamin A 22% | Vitamin C 78% | Calcium 4% | Iron 22% EXCHANGES 2 Vegetable, 4 1/2 Lean Meat CARBOHYDRATE CHOICES 1/2

BETTY'S TIP

This hearty lamb stew works best when baked in a clay casserole, so the wine flavor and moisture will be completely infused into the meat. If you have a clay casserole or pot, go ahead and use it. An aromatic dry white wine such as Vernaccia or Malvasia will suit this dish well and also makes an excellent accompaniment for the dinner.

Baked Salmon with Cilantro

PREP **5 min** BAKE **20 min** SERVINGS **4**

1/4 cup butter or margarine, slightly softened

1 tablespoon chopped fresh cilantro

1/2 teaspoon grated lemon peel

1 pound salmon, snapper or other medium-firm fish fillets, about 1 inch thick

1/4 teaspoon salt

1/4 teaspoon ground cumin

1 tablespoon lemon juice

1. Heat oven to 425°. Line rectangular pan, 13 × 9 × 2 inches, with aluminum foil; spray foil with cooking spray. Mix butter, cilantro and lemon peel. Cover and refrigerate butter while preparing fish.
2. Cut fish into 4 serving pieces. Place fish, skin side down, in pan. Sprinkle with salt and cumin. Drizzle with lemon juice.
3. Bake uncovered 15 to 20 minutes or until fish flakes easily with fork. Carefully lift fish from skin with pancake turner. Top each serving of fish with some cilantro butter mixture.

1 SERVING Calories 260 (Calories from Fat 160) | Fat 18g (Saturated 9g) | Cholesterol 105mg | Sodium 290mg | Carbohydrate 0g (Dietary Fiber 0g) | Protein 24g % DAILY VALUE Vitamin A 12% | Vitamin C 2% | Calcium 2% | Iron 4% EXCHANGES 3 1/2 Medium-Fat Meat CARBOHYDRATE CHOICES 0

BETTY'S TIP

For easy entertaining, just double this recipe. Serve the salmon on a bed of angel-hair pasta or skin-on mashed potatoes on a pretty serving platter. Garnish the platter with cilantro sprigs and slices of lemon.

Gremolata-Topped Sea Bass

PREP 5 min BAKE 20 min SERVINGS 4

- 1/4 cup Italian-style dry bread crumbs
- 1/4 cup chopped fresh parsley
- Grated peel of 1 lemon (1 1/2 to 3 teaspoons)
- 1 tablespoon butter or margarine, melted
- 1 pound sea bass, mahimahi or other medium-firm fish fillets
- 1/4 teaspoon seasoned salt
- 1 tablespoon lemon juice

1. Heat oven to 425°. Line rectangular pan, 13 × 9 × 2 inches, with aluminum foil; spray foil with cooking spray. Mix bread crumbs, parsley, lemon peel and butter.
2. Cut fish into 4 serving pieces. Place fish in pan. Sprinkle with seasoned salt. Drizzle with lemon juice. Spoon crumb mixture over each piece; press lightly.
3. Bake uncovered 15 to 20 minutes or until fish flakes easily with fork.

1 SERVING Calories 150 (Calories from Fat 35) | Fat 4g (Saturated 2g) | Cholesterol 65mg | odium 170mg | Carbohydrate 6g (Dietary Fiber 0g) | Protein 22g % DAILY VALUE Vitamin A 4% | Vitamin C 4% | Calcium 4% | Iron 4% EXCHANGES 3 Very Lean Meat, 1 Fat CARBOHYDRATE CHOICES 1/2

BETTY'S TIP

To save time, use purchased bread crumbs that contain garlic. If the brand you find doesn't list garlic on the label, add 1/4 teaspoon garlic powder to the bread-crumb mixture.

Parmesan-Shrimp Pasta Bake

PREP **15 min** COOK **5 min** BAKE **40 min** SERVINGS **8**

1 package (16 ounces) farfalle (bow-tie) pasta

6 tablespoons butter or margarine

3 cloves garlic, finely chopped

6 tablespoons all-purpose flour

1/3 cup dry vermouth

2 3/4 cups half-and-half

1/2 cup clam juice

1 tablespoon tomato paste

3/4 teaspoon salt

1/4 teaspoon pepper

1 pound uncooked peeled deveined medium shrimp, thawed if frozen and tails peeled

2 tablespoons chopped fresh or 2 teaspoons dried dill weed

3/4 cup freshly grated Parmesan cheese

1. Heat oven to 350°. Spray shallow 2-quart casserole with cooking spray. Cook and drain pasta as directed on package. Melt butter in 2-quart saucepan over medium heat. Cook garlic in butter 1 minute, stirring constantly. Stir in flour. Cook, stirring constantly with wire whisk, until smooth and bubbly.
2. Stir in vermouth. Stir in half-and-half, clam juice, tomato paste, salt and pepper. Cook over medium heat, stirring constantly, until thickened. Stir in shrimp, dill weed and 1/4 cup of the cheese.
3. Stir pasta into shrimp mixture. Pour into casserole. Sprinkle with remaining 1/2 cup cheese. Bake uncovered 35 to 40 minutes or until light brown and hot.

1 SERVING Calories 480 (Calories from Fat 100) | Fat 22g (Saturated 13g) | Cholesterol 115mg | Sodium 560mg | Carbohydrate 53g (Dietary Fiber 2g) | Protein 20g % DAILY VALUE Vitamin A 18% | Vitamin C 2% | Calcium 22% | Iron 20% EXCHANGES 3 Starch, 1 Vegetable, 1 Medium-Fat Meat, 3 Fat CARBOHYDRATE CHOICES 3 1/2

BETTY'S TIP

Need some last-minute substitutions? You can use white wine, chicken broth or clam juice in place of the vermouth. Cocktail sauce or ketchup can be substituted for the tomato paste.

Baked Tuna and Noodles with Creamy Mushroom Sauce

PREP 10 min **COOK** 15 min **BAKE** 40 min **SERVINGS** 6

- 4 cups uncooked egg noodles (8 ounces)
- 2 cans (6 ounces each) tuna, drained
- 1 cup sliced mushrooms (3 ounces)
- 1 1/2 cups sour cream
- 3/4 cup milk
- 1 tablespoon chopped fresh chives
- 1 teaspoon salt
- 1/4 teaspoon pepper
- 1/4 cup dry bread crumbs
- 1/4 cup grated Romano cheese
- 2 tablespoons butter or margarine, melted

1. Heat oven to 350°. Cook and drain noodles as directed on package.
2. Mix noodles, tuna, mushrooms, sour cream, milk, chives, salt and pepper in ungreased 2-quart casserole or square baking dish, 8 × 8 × 2 inches. Mix bread crumbs, cheese and butter; sprinkle over tuna mixture.
3. Bake uncovered 35 to 40 minutes or until hot in center.

1 SERVING Calories 395 (Calories from Fat 170) | Fat 19g (Saturated 9g) | Cholesterol 95mg | Sodium 860mg | Carbohydrate 32g (Dietary Fiber 2g) | Protein 24g % DAILY VALUE Vitamin A 14% | Vitamin C 0% | Calcium 18% | Iron 16% EXCHANGES 2 Starch, 2 1/2 Lean Meat, 2 Fat CARBOHYDRATE CHOICES 2

BETTY'S TIP

Creamy and comforting, this dish is well partnered with a loaf of dilled herb bread and steamed asparagus spears topped with bread crumbs browned in butter.

Tuna Twist Casserole

PREP 10 min **BAKE** 20 min **SERVINGS** 6

1/2 cup reduced-fat Alfredo pasta sauce

2 eggs

1 clove garlic, finely chopped

4 cups cooked tricolor rotelle pasta

2 cups (from 1-pound bag) frozen broccoli, carrots and cauliflower (or other combination), thawed and drained

1 can (12 ounces) tuna in water, drained

1 cup seasoned croutons

1. Heat oven to 350°.
2. Mix Alfredo sauce, eggs and garlic in ungreased square baking dish, 8 × 8 × 2 inches. Stir in pasta, vegetables and tuna. Press lightly in baking dish.
3. Cover and bake about 20 minutes or until set. Sprinkle with croutons.

1 SERVING Calories 285 (Calories from Fat 35) | Fat 4g (Saturated 2g) | Cholesterol 95mg | Sodium 380mg | Carbohydrate 34g (Dietary Fiber 3g) | Protein 24g % DAILY VALUE Vitamin A 22% | Vitamin C 8% | Calcium 8% | Iron 14% EXCHANGES 2 Starch, 1 Vegetable, 2 Lean Meat CARBOHYDRATE CHOICES 2

BETTY'S TIP

Feel free to use regular Alfredo sauce and tuna in oil, but you save 8 grams of fat per serving by using the reduced-fat version of Alfredo sauce and tuna packed in water.

Cheddar Strata with Onions

PREP 5 min COOK 8 min BAKE 1 hr STAND 10 min SERVINGS 6

- 1 teaspoon vegetable oil
- 2 medium onions, sliced
- 8 slices rye bread
- 2 tablespoons Dijon mustard
- 1 1/2 cups shredded Cheddar cheese (6 ounces)
- 1 large tomato, seeded and coarsely chopped (1 cup)
- 1 1/2 cups milk
- 4 eggs

1. Heat oven to 300°. Spray square baking dish, 8 × 8 × 2 inches, with cooking spray. Heat oil in 10-inch nonstick skillet over medium-high heat. Cook onions in oil 6 to 8 minutes, stirring frequently, until golden brown; remove from heat.
2. Trim crusts from bread. Spread mustard on one side of each bread slice. Arrange 4 slices, mustard sides up, in baking dish. Layer 1 cup of the cheese, the tomato and onions on bread. Place remaining bread, mustard sides down, on onions. Beat milk and eggs until well blended. Pour evenly over bread.
3. Bake uncovered about 1 hour or until center is set and bread is golden brown. Sprinkle with remaining 1/2 cup cheese. Let stand 10 minutes before cutting.

1 SERVING Calories 280 (Calories from Fat 145) | Fat 16g (Saturated 8g) | Cholesterol 175mg | Sodium 490mg | Carbohydrate 21g (Dietary Fiber 3g) | Protein 16g % DAILY VALUE Vitamin A 16% | Vitamin C 6% | Calcium 26% | Iron 8% EXCHANGES 1 Starch, 1 Vegetable, 1 1/2 High-Fat Meat, 1/2 Fat CARBOHYDRATE CHOICES 1 1/2

BETTY'S TIP

This dish can be assembled and refrigerated up to 24 hours before baking. You may need to add 5 to 10 minutes to the bake time.

Mozzarella and Pesto Strata

PREP 15 min **CHILL** 2 hr **BAKE** 1 hr **STAND** 5 min **SERVINGS** 8

16 slices French bread, 3/4 inch thick (1/2-pound loaf)

1/2 cup basil pesto

1/2 cup sliced ripe olives

1 cup roasted red bell peppers (from 12-ounce jar), drained and sliced

2 cups shredded mozzarella cheese (8 ounces)

8 eggs

2 cups milk

1/4 teaspoon salt

1/8 teaspoon pepper

2 tablespoons freshly shredded Parmesan cheese

1. Spray rectangular baking dish, 13 × 9 × 2 inches, with cooking spray. Spread one side of each bread slice with pesto. Arrange bread, pesto sides up, in baking dish, cutting to fit if necessary. Sprinkle with olives, bell peppers and mozzarella cheese.
2. Beat eggs, milk, salt and pepper until well blended. Pour evenly over cheese in dish. Sprinkle with Parmesan cheese. Cover and refrigerate at least 2 hours but no longer than 24 hours.
3. Heat oven to 325°. Bake uncovered 55 to 60 minutes or until knife inserted in center comes out clean and top is golden brown. Let stand 5 minutes before cutting.

1 SERVING Calories 405 (Calories from Fat 200) | Fat 22g (Saturated 8g) | Cholesterol 235mg | Sodium 830mg | Carbohydrate 32g (Dietary Fiber 2g) | Protein 22g % DAILY VALUE Vitamin A 22% | Vitamin C 24% | Calcium 42% | Iron 16% EXCHANGES 2 Starch, 2 High-Fat Meat, 1 Fat CARBOHYDRATE CHOICES 2

BETTY'S TIP

Don't throw away that day-old bread! Slightly dried-out bread slices are great for soaking up all the wonderful flavors in this dish.

Vegetable Strata

PREP 15 min **CHILL** 2 hr **BAKE** 1 hr 15 min **STAND** 10 min **SERVINGS** 8

- 8 slices whole wheat bread
- 1 bag (1 pound) frozen broccoli, green beans, pearl onions and red peppers (or other combination), thawed and drained
- 2 cups shredded sharp Cheddar cheese (8 ounces)
- 8 eggs, slightly beaten
- 4 cups milk
- 1/2 teaspoon salt
- 1/2 teaspoon ground mustard
- 1/4 teaspoon pepper
- 1/8 teaspoon ground red pepper (cayenne)

1. Cut each bread slice diagonally into 4 triangles. Arrange half of the bread in ungreased rectangular pan, 13 × 9 × 2 inches. Top with vegetables. Sprinkle with cheese. Top with remaining bread.
2. Beat remaining ingredients until blended; pour over bread. Cover and refrigerate at least 2 hours but no longer than 24 hours.
3. Heat oven to 325°. Cover and bake 30 minutes. Uncover and bake about 45 minutes longer or until knife inserted in center comes out clean. Let stand 10 minutes before cutting.

1 SERVING Calories 325 (Calories from Fat 160) | Fat 18g (Saturated 9g) | Cholesterol 250mg | Sodium 600mg | Carbohydrate 23g (Dietary Fiber 3g) | Protein 21g % DAILY VALUE Vitamin A 26% | Vitamin C 24% | Calcium 36% | Iron 10% EXCHANGES 1 Starch, 1 Milk, 1 High-Fat Meat, 1 Fat CARBOHYDRATE CHOICES 1 1/2

BETTY'S TIP

Instead of whole wheat bread, you can also use white or rye bread in this easy-to-whip-up veggie strata.

Easy Cheese Strata

PREP 15 min **CHILL** 2 hr **BAKE** 1 hr 15 min **STAND** 10 min **SERVINGS** 6

1. Mix butter, mustard and garlic. Spread over each slice bread. Cut each slice into thirds. Line bottom and sides of ungreased square baking dish, 8 × 8 × 2 inches, with enough of the bread slices, buttered sides down.
2. Mix cheese, parsley, onion, salt, Worcestershire sauce, pepper and red pepper. Spread evenly over bread slices in dish. Top with remaining bread slices, buttered sides up. Beat eggs; stir in milk. Pour over bread. Cover and refrigerate at least 2 hours but no longer than 24 hours.
3. Heat oven to 325°. Bake uncovered about 1 hour 15 minutes or until knife inserted in center comes out clean. Let stand 10 minutes before cutting.

1 SERVING Calories 425 (Calories from Fat 260) | Fat 29g (Saturated 12g) | Cholesterol 190mg | Sodium 620mg | Carbohydrate 21g (Dietary Fiber 1g) | Protein 20g % DAILY VALUE Vitamin A 28% | Vitamin C 2% | Calcium 38% | Iron 8% EXCHANGES 1 Starch, 1/2 Milk, 2 High-Fat Meat, 2 Fat CARBOHYDRATE CHOICES 1 1/2

1/3 cup butter or margarine, softened

1/2 teaspoon ground mustard

1 clove garlic, finely chopped

10 slices white bread, crusts removed

2 cups shredded sharp Cheddar cheese (8 ounces)

2 tablespoons chopped fresh parsley

2 tablespoons chopped onion

1 teaspoon salt

1/2 teaspoon Worcestershire sauce

1/8 teaspoon pepper

Dash of ground red pepper (cayenne)

4 eggs

2 1/2 cups milk

BETTY'S TIP

For a relaxing brunch, prepare this strata the night before and pop it in the oven the next day, about 1 1/2 hours before you'd like to serve it. While it's baking, cut up slices of fresh fruit and microwave some strips of bacon.

Stacked Enchilada Bake

PREP 10 min **BAKE** 20 min **SERVINGS** 6

- 12 corn tortillas (5 or 6 inches in diameter), torn into bite-size pieces
- 2 cans (15 to 16 ounces each) chili beans in sauce, undrained
- 1 can (10 ounces) enchilada sauce
- 11/2 cups shredded Monterey Jack cheese (6 ounces)
- 3 medium green onions, sliced (3 tablespoons)

1. Heat oven to 400°. Spray 2-quart casserole with cooking spray.
2. Place half of the tortilla pieces in casserole; top with 1 can of beans. Repeat layers. Pour enchilada sauce over beans and tortilla pieces. Sprinkle with cheese and onions.
3. Bake uncovered about 20 minutes or until bubbly around edge.

1 SERVING Calories 300 (Calories from Fat 90) | Fat 10g (Saturated 6g) | Cholesterol 25mg | Sodium 910mg | Carbohydrate 45g (Dietary Fiber 8g) | Protein 16g % DAILY VALUE Vitamin A 26% | Vitamin C 14% | Calcium 32% | Iron 22% EXCHANGES 3 Starch, 1 Lean Meat CARBOHYDRATE CHOICES 2 1/2

Easy Cheesy Manicotti

PREP 25 min **BAKE** 1 hr 20 min **SERVINGS** 7

1 jar (28 ounces) chunky-style spaghetti sauce

2 packages (10 ounces each) frozen chopped spinach, thawed and squeezed to drain

1 container (12 ounces) small curd creamed cottage cheese (1 1/2 cups)

1/8 cup grated Parmesan cheese

1 teaspoon dried oregano leaves, crumbled

1/4 teaspoon pepper

1 package (8 ounces) manicotti shells (14 shells)

2 cups shredded mozzarella cheese (8 ounces)

1. Heat oven to 350°. Spread about one-third of the spaghetti sauce in ungreased rectangular baking dish, 13 × 9 × 2 inches.
2. Mix spinach, cottage cheese, Parmesan cheese, oregano and pepper. Fill manicotti shells with spinach mixture; place on spaghetti sauce in baking dish.
3. Pour remaining spaghetti sauce evenly over shells, covering completely. Cover and bake 1 hour. Sprinkle with mozzarella cheese. Cover and bake 15 to 20 minutes longer or until shells are tender.

2 SHELLS Calories 425 (Calories from Fat 115) | Fat 13g (Saturated 6g) | Cholesterol 25mg | Sodium 1060mg | Carbohydrate 54g (Dietary Fiber 4g) | Protein 23g % DAILY VALUE Vitamin A 100% | Vitamin C 20% | Calcium 40% | Iron 16% EXCHANGES 3 Starch, 2 Vegetable, 1 1/2 Medium-Fat Meat, 1/2 Fat CARBOHYDRATE CHOICES 3 1/2

BETTY'S TIP

Try using a baby spoon to fill the manicotti shells—it works great! Or fill a resealable plastic food-storage bag with the spinach mixture, snip off a corner and pipe the mixture into the shells.

Satisfying Slow Cooker Suppers

Hearty Beef Chili 200
Italian Beef Stew 201
Old-Fashioned Beef Stew 202
Cajun Pot Roast with Maque Choux 203
Garlic-Braised Beef and Potatoes 204
Mexicali Round Steak 205
Savory Pot Roast 207
Beef Steak Chili 208
Swiss Steak Supper 209
Ginger-Orange Beef Pita Sandwiches 210
Lime-Garlic Chicken with Rice 212
Chunky Chicken Chili 213
Smothered Buttermilk Chicken with Peas 214
Turkey Chili Verde 215
Turkey Breast with Wild Rice Stuffing 216
Dill-Turkey Chowder 217
Hearty Turkey Dinner 218
Italian Turkey-Rice Dinner 219
Turkey and Sweet Potatoes 220
Harvest Sausage and Vegetable Casserole 221
Corn, Ham and Potato Scallop 222
Honey-Dijon Ham 223
Ravioli with Sausage and Peppers 224
Curried Pork and Veggie Stew 225
Porketta with Two Potatoes 226
Southwestern Pork Stew 227
Barbecued Pork Chops 229
Pork Chops with Spiced Fruit Stuffing 230
Pork Chops with Apple-Cherry Stuffing 231
Savory Barbecued Ribs 232
Smoky-Flavored Barbecued Ribs 235
Honey-Barbecue-Glazed Pork Roast with Carrots and Corn 236
Easy Pork Chili 237
Easy Bean and Kielbasa Soup 238
Moroccan Lamb and Rice 239
French Onion Soup 240
Ratatouille Bean Stew 241
Squash and Apple Bisque 242
Peach and Cherry Chutney 245

Hearty Beef Chili

PREP 10 min COOK 9 hr SERVINGS 10

- 2 pounds beef stew meat
- 1 envelope (1 ounce) onion soup mix (from 2-ounce package)
- 5 teaspoons chili powder
- 1 teaspoon ground cumin
- 1 can (15.5 ounces) kidney beans, rinsed and drained
- 2 cans (10 ounces each) diced tomatoes and mild green chilies, undrained
- 1 can (15 ounces) tomato sauce
- 1 can (14.5 ounces) diced tomatoes, undrained

1. Place all ingredients in order listed in 3 1/2- to 4-quart slow cooker.
2. Cover and cook on Low heat setting 8 to 9 hours.
3. Stir gently to mix before serving.

1 SERVING Calories 255 (Calories from Fat 100) | Fat 11g (Saturated 4g) | Cholesterol 55mg | Sodium 820mg | Carbohydrate 20g (Dietary Fiber 5g) | Protein 24g % DAILY VALUE Vitamin A 22% | Vitamin C 22% | Calcium 6% | Iron 24% EXCHANGES 1 Starch, 1 Vegetable, 2 1/2 Lean Meat CARBOHYDRATE CHOICES 1

BETTY'S TIP

To create a fun chili fest, set out bowls of your family's favorite toppings so that each member can create their own personalized "bowl of red." Shredded Cheddar cheese, chopped onion, sour cream, guacamole and pickled sliced jalapeño chilies are all tasty options.

Italian Beef Stew

PREP 15 min **COOK** 12 hr 15 min **SERVINGS** 6

1. Place beef, beef base, carrots, celery, garlic, onion, pepper, cannellini beans, tomatoes and gravy in order listed in 3 1/2- to 4-quart slow cooker.
2. Cover and cook on Low heat setting 10 to 12 hours.
3. Stir in Italian seasoning, sugar and frozen green beans. Increase heat setting to High. Cover and cook about 15 minutes or until green beans are tender.

1 SERVING Calories 340 (Calories from Fat 100) | Fat 11g (Saturated 4g) | Cholesterol 50mg | Sodium 800mg | Carbohydrate 41g (Dietary Fiber 10g) | Protein 29g % DAILY VALUE Vitamin A 100% | Vitamin C 22% | Calcium 16% | Iron 38% EXCHANGES 2 Starch, 2 Vegetable, 2 1/2 Lean Meat CARBOHYDRATE CHOICES 3

1 pound beef stew meat

1 teaspoon beef base

3 large carrots, cut into 1-inch pieces (2 cups)

2 medium stalks celery, cut into 1-inch pieces (1 1/2 cups)

2 cloves garlic, finely chopped

1 medium onion, coarsely chopped (1 1/2 cups)

1/4 teaspoon pepper

1 can (19 ounces) cannellini beans, rinsed and drained

1 can (28 ounces) crushed tomatoes in puree, undrained

1 jar (12 ounces) beef gravy

2 teaspoons Italian seasoning

1 teaspoon sugar

2 cups frozen cut green beans (from 1-pound bag)

BETTY'S TIP

Edible bowls are a fun and delicious way to serve up stew, chili or soup. To make chewy bread bowls, cut off the tops of small, round bread loaves and scoop out the bread, leaving a 1-inch-thick wall. Fill the loaves with the stew, chili or soup, and replace the top of the bread.

Old-Fashioned Beef Stew

PREP 20 min COOK 10 hr SERVINGS 5

- 1 1/2 pounds beef stew meat, cut into 3/4-inch cubes
- 4 medium carrots, cut into 1/2-inch slices
- 3 medium unpeeled potatoes, cut into 1/2-inch cubes
- 1 large onion, cut into 1-inch pieces
- 3 cups vegetable juice cocktail
- 3 tablespoons quick-cooking tapioca
- 3 teaspoons beef bouillon granules
- 2 teaspoons Worcestershire sauce
- 1/4 teaspoon pepper

1. Mix all ingredients in 3 1/2- to 4-quart slow cooker.
2. Cover and cook on Low heat setting 9 to 10 hours.

1 SERVING Calories 390 (Calories from Fat 145) | Fat 16g (Saturated 6g) | Cholesterol 85mg | Sodium 1260mg | Carbohydrate 36g (Dietary Fiber 5g) | Protein 31g % DAILY VALUE Vitamin A 100% | Vitamin C 46% | Calcium 6% | Iron 30% EXCHANGES 2 Starch, 1 Vegetable, 3 Lean Meat, 1 Fat CARBOHYDRATE CHOICES 2 1/2

BETTY'S TIP

You may be tempted to stir this hearty family meal as it cooks, but there's no need. Beef stew meat becomes flavorful and tender after long, moist cooking at a low temperature—which is exactly what a slow cooker does.

Cajun Pot Roast with Maque Choux

PREP 10 min COOK 10 hr SERVINGS 6

- 2- to 2 1/2-pound beef boneless chuck roast
- 1 tablespoon Cajun seasoning
- 1 package (10 ounces) frozen whole kernel corn
- 1 medium onion, chopped (1/2 cup)
- 1/2 cup chopped green bell pepper
- 1 can (14.5 ounces) diced tomatoes, undrained
- 1/8 teaspoon pepper
- 1/2 teaspoon red pepper sauce

1. Rub both sides of beef with Cajun seasoning. Place beef in 3 1/2- to 4-quart slow cooker. Top with corn, onion and bell pepper.
2. Mix tomatoes, pepper and pepper sauce. Pour over vegetables in slow cooker.
3. Cover and cook on Low heat setting 8 to 10 hours.
4. Remove beef and vegetables from slow cooker with slotted spoon. Slice beef. To serve, spoon beef juices from slow cooker over beef and vegetables.

1 SERVING Calories 270 (Calories from Fat 80) | Fat 9g (Saturated 3g) | Cholesterol 105mg | Sodium 590mg | Carbohydrate 12g (Dietary Fiber 2g) | Protein 36g % DAILY VALUE Vitamin A 24% | Vitamin C 4% | Calcium 6% | Iron 32% EXCHANGES 1 Starch, 4 1/2 Very Lean Meat, 1 Fat CARBOHYDRATE CHOICES 1

BETTY'S TIP

Cajun cuisine is hearty, country-style food influenced by French and Southern cooking. Maque choux (pronounced MOCK shoo) means "smothered corn" in Cajun country. The corn is loaded with tomatoes, peppers and onions.

Garlic-Braised Beef and Potatoes

PREP 15 min COOK 9 hr 15 min SERVINGS 8

- 3-pound beef boneless bottom round roast
- 8 small red potatoes (about 1 1/2 pounds), cut in half
- 8 cloves garlic, peeled
- 1 envelope garlic-and-herb dry soup mix (from 2.4-ounce package)
- 1 can (10 3/4 ounces) condensed beefy mushroom soup
- 2 cups frozen broccoli flowerets (from 1-pound bag)

1. Trim fat from beef. Place potatoes and garlic in 4- to 5-quart slow cooker. Place beef on potatoes. Sprinkle dry soup mix over beef; pour mushroom soup evenly over top.
2. Cover and cook on Low heat setting 8 to 9 hours.
3. Remove beef and vegetables from slow cooker with slotted spoon. Slice beef. Arrange beef and vegetables on serving platter. Cover and keep warm.
4. Place frozen broccoli in slow cooker with remaining sauce. Increase heat setting to High. Cover and cook about 15 minutes or until broccoli is tender. Serve with beef and potatoes.

1 SERVING Calories 335 (Calories from Fat 70) | Fat 8g (Saturated 2g) | Cholesterol 90mg | Sodium 500mg | Carbohydrate 28g (Dietary Fiber 3g) | Protein 38g % DAILY VALUE Vitamin A 10% | Vitamin C 18% | Calcium 4% | Iron 26% EXCHANGES 1 1/2 Starch, 1 Vegetable, 4 1/2 Very Lean Meat, 1 Fat CARBOHYDRATE CHOICES 2

BETTY'S TIP

The garlic cloves you toss in at the start of this recipe become soft and sweet as they slow roast along with the beef and veggies. Fish the cloves out with a slotted spoon at the end of the cooking time—they taste great spread on buttered rolls.

Mexicali Round Steak

PREP **15 min** COOK **9 hr** SERVINGS **6**

1. Trim fat from beef. Cut beef into 6 serving pieces. Place beef in 3 1/2- to 6-quart slow cooker.
2. Mix remaining ingredients except cheese; pour over beef.
3. Cover and cook on Low heat setting 8 to 9 hours. Sprinkle cheese over beef mixture.

1 SERVING Calories 250 (Calories from Fat 35) | Fat 4g (Saturated 1g) | Cholesterol 60mg | Sodium 830mg | Carbohydrate 31g (Dietary Fiber 8g) | Protein 31g % DAILY VALUE Vitamin A 20% | Vitamin C 16% | Calcium 10% | Iron 28% EXCHANGES 2 Starch, 3 Very Lean Meat CARBOHYDRATE CHOICES 2

1 1/2 pounds beef boneless round steak

1 cup frozen whole kernel corn (from 1-pound bag), thawed and drained

1 cup chopped fresh cilantro

1/2 cup beef broth

3 medium stalks celery, thinly sliced (1 1/2 cups)

1 large onion, sliced

1 jar (20 ounces) salsa

1 can (15 ounces) black beans, rinsed and drained

1 cup shredded Monterey Jack cheese with jalapeño peppers (4 ounces), if desired

BETTY'S TIP

Give this round steak a flavor twist by using pinto beans instead of the black beans and sprinkling with Cheddar cheese in place of the Monterey Jack cheese.

Savory Pot Roast

PREP 20 min **COOK** 8 to 9 hr **FINISH TIME** 15 min **SERVINGS** 6

- 2- to 2 1/2-pound beef bottom round roast
- 2 teaspoons olive or vegetable oil
- 2 or 3 medium potatoes, cut into 2-inch pieces
- 2 1/2 cups baby-cut carrots
- 2 cups sliced mushrooms (about 5 ounces)
- 1 medium stalk celery, sliced (1/2 cup)
- 1 medium onion, chopped (1/2 cup)
- 1 teaspoon salt
- 1/2 teaspoon pepper
- 1/2 teaspoon dried thyme leaves
- 1 can (14 1/2 ounces) diced tomatoes, undrained
- 1 can (10 1/2 ounces) condensed beef consommé or broth
- 1 can (5 1/2 ounces) eight-vegetable juice
- 1/4 cup all-purpose flour

1. Trim excess fat from beef. Heat oil in 10-inch skillet over medium-high heat. Cook beef in oil about 10 minutes, turning occasionally, until brown on all sides.
2. Place potatoes, carrots, mushrooms, celery and onion in 4- to 6-quart slow cooker. Sprinkle with salt, pepper and thyme. Place beef on vegetables. Pour tomatoes, consommé and vegetable juice over beef.
3. Cover and cook on Low heat setting 8 to 10 hours or until beef and vegetables are tender.
4. Remove beef and vegetables from cooker, using slotted spoon; place on serving platter and keep warm.
5. Skim fat from beef juices in cooker if desired. Remove 1/2 cup of the juices from the cooker; mix with flour until smooth. Gradually stir flour mixture into remaining juices in cooker. Cook on High heat setting about 15 minutes or until thickened. Serve sauce with beef and vegetables.

1 SERVING Calories 270 (Calories from Fat 55) | Fat 6g (Saturated 2g) | Cholesterol 75mg | Sodium 880mg | Carbohydrate 26g (Dietary Fiber 4g) | Protein 32g
% DAILY VALUE Vitamin A 90% | Vitamin C 24% | Calcium 6% | Iron 26%
EXCHANGES 1 Starch, 2 Vegetable, 3 Lean Meat CARBOHYDRATE CHOICES 2

BETTY'S TIP

If you just have tomato juice in your cupboard, go ahead and use it instead of the eight-vegetable juice. Regular-size carrots, cut into 2-inch pieces, can be used if you are out of baby-cut carrots. And a drained 4-ounce can of sliced mushrooms can be used instead of the fresh mushrooms.

Beef Steak Chili

PREP 15 min COOK 7 hr 15 min SERVINGS 8

- 1 pound beef boneless round steak, cut into 1/2-inch pieces
- 1 large onion, chopped (1 cup)
- 2 medium stalks celery, cut into 1/2-inch pieces (1 cup)
- 2 cans (14 1/2 ounces each) diced tomatoes, undrained
- 1 can (15 ounces) tomato sauce
- 3 teaspoons chili powder
- 2 teaspoons ground cumin
- 1/4 teaspoon dried oregano leaves
- 1/4 teaspoon ground cinnamon
- 1 medium bell pepper, cut into 1-inch pieces (1 cup)
- 1 can (15 to 16 ounces) kidney beans, rinsed and drained
- Shredded Cheddar cheese, if desired

1. Mix all ingredients except bell pepper, beans and cheese in 3 1/2- to 4-quart slow cooker.
2. Cover and cook on Low heat setting 6 to 7 hours.
3. Stir in bell pepper and beans. Increase heat setting to High. Cook uncovered about 15 minutes or until slightly thickened. Serve with cheese.

1 SERVING Calories 170 (Calories from Fat 25) | Fat 3g (Saturated 1g) | Cholesterol 30mg | Sodium 660mg | Carbohydrate 24g (Dietary Fiber 6g) | Protein 18g % DAILY VALUE Vitamin A 16% | Vitamin C 30% | Calcium 6% | Iron 20% EXCHANGES 1 Starch, 2 Vegetable, 1 Lean Meat CARBOHYDRATE CHOICES 1 1/2

BETTY'S TIP

You also can use a 28-ounce can of whole tomatoes instead of the diced tomatoes. Use a spoon to break up the whole tomatoes in the slow cooker.

Swiss Steak Supper

PREP 15 min COOK 8 hr SERVINGS 6

1 1/2 pounds beef boneless round steak, cut into 6 serving pieces

1/2 teaspoon peppered seasoned salt

6 to 8 new potatoes, cut into fourths

1 1/2 cups baby-cut carrots

1 medium onion, sliced

1 can (14 1/2 ounces) diced tomatoes with basil, garlic and oregano, undrained

1 jar (12 ounces) home-style beef gravy

Chopped fresh parsley, if desired

1. Spray 12-inch skillet with cooking spray; heat over medium-high heat. Sprinkle beef with seasoned salt. Cook beef in skillet 6 to 8 minutes, turning once, until brown.
2. Layer potatoes, carrots, beef and onion in 4- to 5-quart slow cooker. Mix tomatoes and gravy; spoon over mixture in slow cooker.
3. Cover and cook on Low heat setting 7 to 8 hours. Sprinkle with parsley.

1 SERVING Calories 220 (Calories from Fat 45) | Fat 5g (Saturated 2g) | Cholesterol 60mg | Sodium 680mg | Carbohydrate 20g (Dietary Fiber 3g) | Protein 27g % DAILY VALUE Vitamin A 50% | Vitamin C 15% | Calcium 4% | Iron 20% EXCHANGES 1 Starch, 1 Vegetable, 3 Very Lean Meat CARBOHYDRATE CHOICES 1

BETTY'S TIP

Peppered seasoned salt is one of the newer varieties of seasoned salt available in the supermarket. If you have trouble finding it, use regular seasoned salt and sprinkle the beef with pepper, or you can just use salt and pepper.

Ginger-Orange Beef Pita Sandwiches

PREP 25 min COOK 4 to 6 hr FINISH TIME 15 min SERVINGS 6

- 1 pound beef boneless round steak
- 1 medium red onion, cut into eighths
- 1 medium orange bell pepper, cut into 1-inch pieces (1 1/2 cups)
- 1 medium jicama, peeled and cut into julienne strips (1 1/2 cups)
- 1 tablespoon grated orange peel
- 1/3 cup orange juice
- 1 teaspoon finely chopped gingerroot
- 1/2 teaspoon salt
- 1 package (6 ounces) frozen snap pea pods, thawed
- 3 pita breads (6 inches in diameter), cut in half to form pockets
- Peach Cherry Chutney (page 245) or other chutney, if desired

1. Trim excess fat from beef. Cut beef lengthwise into 2-inch strips. Cut strips crosswise into 1/8-inch slices.
2. Place beef, onion, bell pepper and jicama in 3 1/2- to 6-quart slow cooker. Mix orange peel, orange juice, gingerroot and salt; pour over beef and vegetables.
3. Cover and cook on Low heat setting 4 to 6 hours or until beef is tender.
4. Stir in snap pea pods. Cover and cook on Low heat setting about 15 minutes or until pea pods are crisp-tender.
5. Spoon beef mixture into pita breads. Serve with Golden Fruit Chutney.

1 SERVING Calories 195 (Calories from Fat 25) | Fat 3g (Saturated 1g) | Cholesterol 35mg | Sodium 370mg | Carbohydrate 31g (Dietary Fiber 7g) | Protein 18g % DAILY VALUE Vitamin A 2% | Vitamin C 80% | Calcium 6% | Iron 18% EXCHANGES 2 Fruit, 2 1/2 Very Lean Meat CARBOHYDRATE CHOICES 1 1/2

BETTY'S TIP

To peel or not to peel gingerroot—that is the question. The great thing is, you can do either! Plus, if you would rather not spend the extra couple of minutes finely chopping the gingerroot, use a grater instead. Grate against the fibrous strings on the narrow ends of the gingerroot instead of the wider flat side. You can also see the fibers when you slice off a piece of gingerroot.

Lime-Garlic Chicken with Rice

PREP 10 min COOK 10 hr SERVINGS 6

- 1 1/4 pounds bone-in, skinless chicken thighs
- 1/4 cup fresh lime juice (2 limes)
- 1 1/2 cups chicken broth
- 2 cloves garlic, finely chopped
- 1/2 teaspoon dried thyme leaves
- 1/4 teaspoon pepper
- 2 tablespoons butter or margarine
- 1 cup uncooked instant rice

1. Place chicken in 3- to 4-quart slow cooker. Add remaining ingredients except rice.
2. Cover and cook on Low heat setting 8 to 10 hours. During last 15 minutes of cooking, stir in rice.
3. Remove chicken from slow cooker. Place cooked rice on each serving plate. Top with chicken. Spoon any remaining juices over chicken.

1 SERVING Calories 215 (Calories from Fat 80) | Fat 9g (Saturated 4g) | Cholesterol 50mg | Sodium 320mg | Carbohydrate 17g (Dietary Fiber 0g) | Protein 16g % DAILY VALUE Vitamin A 4% | Vitamin C 2% | Calcium 2% | Iron 10% EXCHANGES 1 Starch, 2 Lean Meat, 1 Fat CARBOHYDRATE CHOICES 1

BETTY'S TIP

For a picture-perfect presentation, garnish individual plates with chopped fresh parsley and fresh lime wedges.

Chunky Chicken Chili

PREP 5 min **COOK** 9 hr 15 min **SERVINGS** 6

2 pounds boneless, skinless chicken thighs

2 cans (14 1/2 ounces each) diced tomatoes with green chilies, undrained

1 can (15 ounces) tomato sauce

1 envelope (1 1/4 ounces) mild chili seasoning mix

2 cans (15 1/2 ounces each) hominy

Sour cream, if desired

Cilantro, if desired

1. Place chicken in 3 1/2- to 4-quart slow cooker. Mix tomatoes, tomato sauce and chili seasoning; pour over chicken.
2. Cover and cook on Low heat setting 7 to 9 hours.
3. Stir to break up chicken. Stir in hominy. Cover and cook on Low heat setting about 15 minutes or until thoroughly heated. Serve chili with sour cream and cilantro.

1 SERVING Calories 390 (Calories from Fat 125) | Fat 14g (Saturated 4g) | Cholesterol 95mg | Sodium 1230mg | Carbohydrate 36g (Dietary Fiber 6g) | Protein 36g % DAILY VALUE Vitamin A 18% | Vitamin C 22% | Calcium 10% | Iron 26% EXCHANGES 2 Starch, 1 Vegetable, 4 Lean Meat CARBOHYDRATE CHOICES 2 1/2

BETTY'S TIP

To add some kick to this chunky chili, use hot chili seasoning instead of the mild and add a 4.5-ounce can of chopped green chiles with the tomatoes.

Smothered Buttermilk Chicken with Peas

PREP 30 min COOK 8 hr 15 min SERVINGS 5

- 1 pound boneless, skinless chicken thighs, cut into 3/4-inch pieces
- 3 medium carrots, sliced (1 1/2 cups)
- 1 small onion, chopped (1/3 cup)
- 1/2 cup water
- 2 tablespoons butter or margarine, melted
- 1/4 teaspoon salt
- 1/4 teaspoon pepper
- 1 dried bay leaf
- 1 package (1.2 ounces) roasted chicken gravy mix
- 1/3 cup buttermilk
- 2 teaspoons all-purpose flour
- 1 cup frozen green peas (from 1-pound bag), thawed and drained
- 1 can (10.2 ounces) refrigerated buttermilk biscuits (5 biscuits)

1. Mix chicken, carrots, onion, water, butter, salt, pepper and bay leaf in 4- to 6–quart slow cooker.
2. Cover and cook on Low heat setting 6 to 8 hours. During last 20 minutes of cooking, stir in gravy mix.
3. Remove bay leaf. Mix buttermilk and flour. Stir flour mixture and peas into chicken mixture. Increase heat setting to High. Cover and cook 10 to 15 minutes or until peas are hot.
4. While chicken mixture is cooking, make biscuits as directed on can. Split biscuits; serve chicken mixture over biscuits.

1 SERVING Calories 470 (Calories from Fat 200) | Fat 22g (Saturated 6g) | Cholesterol 60mg | Sodium 1380mg | Carbohydrate 42g (Dietary Fiber 4g) | Protein 26g % DAILY VALUE Vitamin A 100% | Vitamin C 6% | Calcium 8% | Iron 20% EXCHANGES 2 1/2 Starch, 1 Vegetable, 2 Medium-Fat Meat, 2 Fat CARBOHYDRATE CHOICES 3

BETTY'S TIP

If you don't have buttermilk on hand, you can use 3 tablespoons of sour cream or yogurt mixed with 2 tablespoons of milk instead.

Turkey Chili Verde

PREP 15 min COOK 10 hr SERVINGS 6

- 2 1/2-pound boneless turkey breast half
- 1 jar (16 ounces) mild green salsa
- 1 medium onion, chopped (1/2 cup)
- 1 medium potato, chopped (3/4 cup)
- 4 cloves garlic, finely chopped
- 1/2 cup chicken broth
- 1 teaspoon ground cumin
- 6 flour tortillas (8 to 10 inches in diameter), warmed
- Fresh cilantro leaves, if desired
- Sour cream, if desired

1. Place turkey in 3 1/2- to 4-quart slow cooker. Mix salsa, onion, potato, garlic, broth and cumin; pour over turkey.
2. Cover and cook on Low heat setting 8 to 10 hours.
3. Remove turkey from slow cooker. Slice turkey. Serve turkey and sauce in tortillas with cilantro and sour cream.

1 SERVING Calories 375 (Calories from Fat 45) | Fat 5g (Saturated 1g) | Cholesterol 125mg | Sodium 700mg | Carbohydrate 35g (Dietary Fiber 3g) | Protein 50g % DAILY VALUE Vitamin A 10% | Vitamin C 10% | Calcium 10% | Iron 26% EXCHANGES 2 Starch, 1 Vegetable, 6 Very Lean Meat CARBOHYDRATE CHOICES 2

Chicken Chili Verde Substitute boneless, skinless chicken thighs for the turkey breast, cooking until tender enough to be shredded into the sauce.

BETTY'S TIP

To warm tortillas in the oven before serving, wrap in aluminum foil and heat at 325° for about 15 minutes. Or place them on a paper towel and microwave on High for 30 seconds.

Turkey Breast with Wild Rice Stuffing

PREP 15 min COOK 9 hr SERVINGS 12

- 4 cups cooked wild rice
- 1 large onion, finely chopped (3/4 cup)
- 1/2 cup dried cranberries
- 1/3 cup slivered almonds
- 2 medium peeled or unpeeled cooking apples, coarsely chopped (2 cups)
- 4- to 5-pound boneless whole turkey breast, thawed if frozen

1. Mix all ingredients except turkey.
2. Place turkey in 3 1/2- to 6-quart slow cooker. Place wild rice mixture around edge of cooker.
3. Cover and cook on Low heat setting 8 to 9 hours.

1 SERVING Calories 310 (Calories from Fat 80) | Fat 9g (Saturated 3g) | Cholesterol 85mg | Sodium 70mg | Carbohydrate 21g (Dietary Fiber 2g) | Protein 34g % DAILY VALUE Vitamin A 2% | Vitamin C 2% | Calcium 2% | Iron 8% EXCHANGES 1 1/2 Starch, 4 Very Lean Meat, 1 Fat CARBOHYDRATE CHOICES 1 1/2

BETTY'S TIP

Cooking apples have a crisp or slightly crisp texture and hold their shape well. Braeburn, Cortland, Empire and Greening are all good cooking apple choices.

Dill-Turkey Chowder

PREP 15 min COOK 8 hr 20 min SERVINGS 6

1 pound uncooked turkey breast slices, cut into 1-inch pieces

3/4 teaspoon garlic pepper

1/2 teaspoon salt

6 to 8 new potatoes, cut into 1-inch pieces

1 medium onion, chopped (1/2 cup)

2 medium carrots, sliced (1 cup)

2 teaspoons dried dill weed

2 1/2 cups chicken broth

1 can (15 1/4 ounces) whole kernel corn, drained

1 cup half-and-half

3 tablespoons cornstarch

1. Place turkey in 4- to 5-quart slow cooker; sprinkle with garlic pepper and salt. Stir in remaining ingredients except half-and-half and cornstarch.
2. Cover and cook on Low heat setting 6 to 8 hours.
3. Mix half-and-half and cornstarch; gradually stir into chowder until blended. Increase heat setting to High. Cover and cook about 20 minutes, stirring occasionally, until thickened.

1 SERVING Calories 265 (Calories from Fat 65) | Fat 7g (Saturated 3g) | Cholesterol 55mg | Sodium 840mg | Carbohydrate 33g (Dietary Fiber 3g) | Protein 21g % DAILY VALUE Vitamin A 36% | Vitamin C 12% | Calcium 8% | Iron 14% EXCHANGES 2 Starch, 1 Vegetable, 1 1/2 Very Lean Meat CARBOHYDRATE CHOICES 2

BETTY'S TIP

Using a jar is a quick way to mix the cornstarch with the liquid. Screw the lid on tight, and shake the jar until the mixture is smooth. This is faster than trying to stir until all the cornstarch is dissolved.

Hearty Turkey Dinner

PREP 15 min COOK 10 hr SERVINGS 4

- 6 small red potatoes (about 2 1/2 inches in diameter), cut into fourths
- 4 medium carrots, sliced (2 cups)
- 4 turkey thighs (about 2 pounds), skin removed
- 1/4 cup all-purpose flour
- 2 tablespoons onion soup mix (dry)
- 1 can (10 3/4 ounces) condensed cream of mushroom soup
- 1/3 cup chicken broth

1. Place potatoes and carrots in 3 1/2- to 4-quart slow cooker. Place turkey on vegetables.
2. Mix remaining ingredients; pour over turkey.
3. Cover and cook on Low heat setting 8 to 10 hours.

1 SERVING Calories 570 (Calories from Fat 125) | Fat 14g (Saturated 4g) | Cholesterol 5mg | Sodium 1110mg | Carbohydrate 52g (Dietary Fiber 6g) | Protein 65g % DAILY VALUE Vitamin A 100% | Vitamin C 20% | Calcium 14% | Iron 42% EXCHANGES 3 Starch, 1 Vegetable, 7 Very Lean Meat, 1 Fat CARBOHYDRATE CHOICES 3 1/2

BETTY'S TIP

If you find you're out of chicken broth, use water instead.

Italian Turkey-Rice Dinner

PREP **20 min** COOK **8 hr** SERVINGS **4**

3 medium carrots, shredded (2 cups)

2 medium stalks celery, sliced (1 cup)

1 small red bell pepper, chopped (1/2 cup)

1/2 teaspoon dried basil leaves

1/3 cup water

4 turkey thighs (8 to 12 ounces each), skin removed

1 teaspoon salt

1/4 teaspoon pepper

1/2 cup uncooked regular long-grain rice

1 teaspoon dried oregano leaves

1/2 cup shredded Italian-style six-cheese blend or mozzarella cheese (2 ounces)

1. Mix carrots, celery, bell pepper, basil and water in 3 1/2- to 4-quart slow cooker. Sprinkle turkey with salt and pepper; place on vegetable mixture.
2. Cover and cook on Low heat setting 6 to 7 hours.
3. Remove turkey from slow cooker. Stir rice and oregano into vegetable mixture; return turkey to slow cooker. Cover and cook on Low heat setting about 1 hour or until rice is tender.
4. Remove turkey from slow cooker. Stir cheese into rice mixture until melted. Serve with turkey.

1 SERVING Calories 370 (Calories from Fat 80) | Fat 9g (Saturated 4g) | Cholesterol 165mg | Sodium 810mg | Carbohydrate 27g (Dietary Fiber 2g) | Protein 47g % DAILY VALUE Vitamin A 100% | Vitamin C 34% | Calcium 16% | Iron 26% EXCHANGES 1 1/2 Starch, 1 Vegetable, 6 Very Lean Meat, 1/2 Fat CARBOHYDRATE CHOICES 2

BETTY'S TIP

Get a jump start by preparing the vegetables for this dinner ahead of time. Cut them as directed and refrigerate them in a plastic storage container or resealable bag until you're ready to make the recipe.

Turkey and Sweet Potatoes

PREP 15 min COOK 8 hr SERVINGS 6

- 3 medium sweet potatoes, peeled and cut into 2-inch pieces
- 3 turkey thighs, skin removed (about 1 1/2 pounds)
- 1 jar (12 ounces) home-style turkey gravy
- 2 tablespoons all-purpose flour
- 1 teaspoon parsley flakes
- 1/2 teaspoon dried rosemary leaves, crumbled
- 1/8 teaspoon pepper
- 1 package (10 ounces) frozen cut green beans

1. Layer sweet potatoes and turkey in 4- to 5-quart slow cooker. Mix remaining ingredients except beans until smooth. Pour over mixture in slow cooker.
2. Cover and cook on High heat setting 1 hour. Reduce heat setting to Low. Cover and cook 5 hours. Stir in beans. Cover and cook 1 to 2 hours.
3. Remove turkey and vegetables from slow cooker with slotted spoon. Stir sauce and serve with turkey and vegetables.

1 SERVING Calories 360 (Calories from Fat 80) | Fat 9g (Saturated 3g) | Cholesterol 155mg | Sodium 460mg | Carbohydrate 26g (Dietary Fiber 4g) | Protein 44g % DAILY VALUE Vitamin A 100% | Vitamin C 16% | Calcium 8% | Iron 24% EXCHANGES 1 1/2 Starch, 1 Vegetable, 5 Very Lean Meat, 1 Fat CARBOHYDRATE CHOICES 2

BETTY'S TIP

If you're not a fan of sweet potatoes, it's perfectly fine to use regular potatoes instead. There's no need to peel them—just cut the potatoes into 2-inch pieces.

Harvest Sausage and Vegetable Casserole

PREP 20 min **COOK** 8 hr **SERVINGS** 4 to 6

3 tablespoons zesty Italian dressing

1 tablespoon Dijon mustard

2 medium unpeeled potatoes, cut into 1-inch slices (2 cups)

2 medium onions, sliced

2 medium carrots, cut into 1-inch pieces (1 cup)

2 cups chopped green cabbage

1 ring (1 pound) fully cooked smoked turkey or chicken sausage, cut into 1-inch slices

1 can (14 1/2 ounces) diced tomatoes with green pepper, celery and onion, undrained

1. Mix dressing and mustard. Arrange potatoes in even layer in 3 1/2- to 4-quart slow cooker; drizzle with one-third of the dressing mixture. Arrange onions on potatoes; drizzle with one-third of the dressing mixture. Top with carrots and cabbage; drizzle with remaining dressing mixture.
2. Arrange sausage on vegetables. Pour tomatoes in even layer over sausage.
3. Cover and cook on Low heat setting 7 to 8 hours or until vegetables are tender.

1 SERVING Calories 335 (Calories from Fat 135) | Fat 15g (Saturated 3g) | Cholesterol 60mg | Sodium 1630mg | Carbohydrate 34g (Dietary Fiber 5g) | Protein 21g % DAILY VALUE Vitamin A 100% | Vitamin C 32% | Calcium 10% | Iron 14% EXCHANGES 2 Starch, 1 Vegetable, 2 Medium-Fat Meat CARBOHYDRATE CHOICES 2

BETTY'S TIP

If you use preshredded coleslaw mix from the produce department, you can skip slicing the carrots and chopping the cabbage.

Corn, Ham and Potato Scallop

PREP 10 min COOK 9 hr SERVINGS 6

- 6 cups 1-inch cubes peeled baking potatoes
- 1 1/2 cups cubed fully cooked ham
- 1 can (15 1/4 ounces) whole kernel corn, drained
- 1/4 cup chopped green bell pepper
- 2 teaspoons instant minced onion
- 1 can (10 3/4 ounces) condensed Cheddar cheese soup
- 1/2 cup milk
- 2 tablespoons all-purpose flour

1. Mix potatoes, ham, corn, bell pepper and onion in 3 1/2- to 4-quart slow cooker.
2. Mix soup, milk and flour in small bowl; beat with wire whisk until smooth. Pour soup mixture over potato mixture; stir gently to mix.
3. Cover and cook on Low heat setting 7 to 9 hours.

1 SERVING Calories 335 (Calories from Fat 70) | Fat 8g (Saturated 3g) | Cholesterol 30mg | Sodium 1130mg | Carbohydrate 51g (Dietary Fiber 4g) | Protein 15g % DAILY VALUE Vitamin A 22% | Vitamin C 18% | Calcium 8% | Iron 10% EXCHANGES 3 1/2 Starch, 1/2 Lean Meat, 1 Fat CARBOHYDRATE CHOICES 3 1/2

Corn, Roast Beef and Potato Scallop Substitute cooked roast beef for the ham.

BETTY'S TIP

Potatoes cook more quickly when cut into small pieces, so cubed potatoes will cook faster than quartered potatoes. The 1-inch chunks of potato in our recipe work well because they won't get too soft during the long cooking time.

Honey-Dijon Ham

PREP 15 min COOK 6 to 8 hrs SERVINGS 6

5-pound bone-in fully cooked smoked ham

1/3 cup apple juice

1/4 cup packed brown sugar

1 tablespoon honey

1 tablespoon Dijon mustard

1. Place ham in 4- to 6-quart slow cooker. Add apple juice. Mix brown sugar, honey and mustard; spread over ham.
2. Cover and cook on Low heat setting 6 to 8 hours or until ham is hot and glazed.
3. Remove ham from cooker; place on cutting board. Cut ham in half; reserve one half. Cut remaining half of ham into slices; place on serving platter to serve.
4. Cut reserved ham into 1/2-inch cubes. Place cubes in resealable plastic food-storage bags. Seal and save for a great addition to any omelet, frittata, soup or salad. Refrigerate up to 3 days or freeze up to 1 month for later use. If frozen, thaw in refrigerator before using.

1 SERVING Calories 155 (Calories from Fat 45) | Fat 5g (Saturated 2g) | Cholesterol 50mg | Sodium 1130mg | Carbohydrate 8g (Dietary Fiber 0g) | Protein 19g % DAILY VALUE Vitamin A 0% | Vitamin C 0% | Calcium 0% | Iron 8% EXCHANGES 1/2 Starch, 2 1/2 Lean Meat CARBOHYDRATE CHOICES 1/2

BETTY'S TIP

Many types of mustard are delicious with ham. If you prefer the taste of country-style mustard, a coarsely ground mustard or all-American yellow mustard, go ahead and use it—but then you may want to alter the name of the recipe as well!

Ravioli with Sausage and Peppers

PREP 5 min COOK 6 hr SERVINGS 4

- 1/2 package (25-ounce size) frozen cheese-filled ravioli
- 2 cups frozen stir-fry bell peppers and onions (from 1-pound bag)
- 1 jar (26 ounces) chunky spaghetti sauce
- 8 ounces fully cooked smoked sausage, sliced
- 1/4 cup freshly shredded Parmesan cheese (1 ounce)

Photo on page 198.

1. Mix all ingredients except cheese in 3 1/2- to 4-quart slow cooker.
2. Cover and cook on Low heat setting 5 to 6 hours.
3. Sprinkle individual servings with cheese.

1 SERVING Calories 635 (Calories from Fat 305) | Fat 34g (Saturated 12g) | Cholesterol 140mg | Sodium 2500g | Carbohydrate 55g (Dietary Fiber 4g) | Protein 27g % DAILY VALUE Vitamin A 32% | Vitamin C 50% | Calcium 34% | Iron 18% EXCHANGES 3 Starch, 2 Vegetable, 2 High-Fat Meat, 3 Fat CARBOHYDRATE CHOICES 3 1/2

BETTY'S TIP

If you'd prefer to use 2 cups of fresh veggies in this ravioli dish, go right ahead. Slice the sweet bell peppers and cut an onion into wedges.

Curried Pork and Veggie Stew

PREP 20 min COOK 10 hr SERVINGS 6

3 tablespoons all-purpose flour

2 tablespoons curry powder

1/2 teaspoon salt

1 pound pork boneless center-cut loin, cut into 1-inch pieces

1 tablespoon olive or vegetable oil

1 medium onion, chopped (1/2 cup)

1 pound small red potatoes, cut into fourths (3 cups)

1 can (14 1/2 ounces) whole tomatoes, undrained

1/2 cup apple juice

2 1/2 cups cauliflowerets

1. Mix flour, 1 tablespoon curry powder and salt in resealable plastic food-storage bag. Add pork; toss to coat. Heat oil in 10-inch skillet over medium-high heat. Cook pork in oil, stirring occasionally, until brown.
2. Place onion and potatoes in 3 1/2- to 4-quart slow cooker. Top with pork and tomatoes. Mix apple juice and remaining 1 tablespoon curry powder; pour mixture over pork.
3. Cover and cook on Low heat setting 8 to 9 hours.
4. Stir in cauliflowerets. Cover and cook on Low heat setting about 1 hour or until cauliflower is tender.

1 SERVING Calories 360 (Calories from Fat 110) | Fat 12g (Saturated 4g) | Cholesterol 70mg | Sodium 420mg | Carbohydrate 38g (Dietary Fiber 5g) | Protein 30g % DAILY VALUE Vitamin A 6% | Vitamin C 46% | Calcium 6% | Iron 20% EXCHANGES 2 Starch, 2 Vegetable, 3 Lean Meat CARBOHYDRATE CHOICES 2 1/2

BETTY'S TIP

Play up the Indian-inspired flavor of this stew by serving it over basmati rice with yogurt, mango chutney and cilantro or in pita folds or Indian naan bread.

Porketta with Two Potatoes

PREP 15 min COOK 10 hr SERVINGS 6

- 2 medium dark–orange sweet potatoes, peeled and cut into 1/2-inch cubes (about 2 1/2 cups)
- 2 medium Yukon gold potatoes, cut into 1/2-inch cubes (about 2 1/2 cups)
- 2 teaspoons fennel seed, crushed
- 1 teaspoon dried oregano leaves
- 1 teaspoon paprika
- 1/2 teaspoon garlic powder
- 1/2 teaspoon salt
- 1/4 teaspoon pepper
- 2-pound pork boneless loin roast
- 1 cup chicken broth

1. Place potatoes in 3 1/2- to 4-quart slow cooker. Mix fennel seed, oregano, paprika, garlic powder, salt and pepper. Rub herb mixture into pork. Place pork on potatoes. Pour broth over pork and potatoes.
2. Cover and cook on Low heat setting 8 to 10 hours.
3. Remove pork from slow cooker; place on serving platter. Slice pork. Serve pork with potatoes.

1 SERVING Calories 340 (Calories from Fat 110) | Fat 12g (Saturated 4g) | Cholesterol 95mg | Sodium 430mg | Carbohydrate 21g (Dietary Fiber 3g) | Protein 36g % DAILY VALUE Vitamin A 100% | Vitamin C 14% | Calcium 2% | Iron 12% EXCHANGES 1/1 2 Starch, 4 Lean Meat CARBOHYDRATE CHOICES 1 1/2

BETTY'S TIP

Some pork roasts come wrapped in netting. If this is the case with yours, carefully remove the netting before seasoning the roast and retie it with twine after you're done seasoning.

Southwestern Pork Stew

PREP **20 min** COOK **10 hr 30 min** SERVINGS **8**

1. Place onion and garlic in 3 1/2- to 4-quart slow cooker. Top with pork. Mix cornmeal, cumin, oregano and salt; sprinkle over pork and mix well. Add beans, tomatoes and broth; mix well.
2. Cover and cook on Low heat setting 8 to 10 hours.
3. Stir in corn. Cover and cook on Low heat setting about 30 minutes or until corn is tender.

1 SERVING Calories 290 (Calories from Fat 90) | Fat 10g (Saturated 3g) | Cholesterol 70mg | Sodium 770mg | Carbohydrate 23g (Dietary Fiber 4g) | Protein 31g % DAILY VALUE Vitamin A 8% | Vitamin C 16% | Calcium 4% | Iron 14% EXCHANGES 1 1/2 Starch, 4 Very Lean Meat, 1 Fat CARBOHYDRATE CHOICES 1 1/2

1 medium onion, chopped (1/2 cup)

3 large cloves garlic, finely chopped

2 pounds pork boneless top loin, trimmed of fat and cut into 1 1/2-inch pieces

1/4 cup cornmeal

2 teaspoons ground cumin

1/2 teaspoon dried oregano leaves

1/2 teaspoon salt

1 can (15 to 16 ounces) chili beans in sauce, undrained

1 can (14 1/2 ounces) diced tomatoes and mild chilies, undrained

1 cup chicken broth

2 cups frozen whole kernel corn (from 1-pound bag), thawed and drained

BETTY'S TIP

When you're in a hurry, use 1 tablespoon ready-to-use minced garlic. You'll find it in jars in the produce department of the supermarket.

Barbecued Pork Chops

PREP 15 min COOK 5 to 6 hr FINISH TIME 2 min SERVINGS 4

- 4 pork boneless loin chops, 1 inch thick (about 3/4 pound), trimmed of fat
- 4 slices onion
- 1 clove garlic, finely chopped
- 3/4 cup barbecue sauce
- 1 tablespoon water
- 2 teaspoons cornstarch

1. Place pork chops in 3 1/2- to 4-quart slow cooker. Top each chop with onion slice and sprinkle with garlic. Pour barbecue sauce over chops.
2. Cover and cook on Low heat setting 5 to 6 hours.
3. About 5 minutes before serving, remove pork from cooker; place on serving platter and cover to keep warm.
4. Mix water and cornstarch in 2-cup glass measuring cup or small microwavable bowl until smooth. Pour 1 cup of the juices from cooker into cornstarch mixture; mix well. Microwave uncovered on High 1 to 2 minutes, stirring once halfway through cooking, until mixture boils and thickens slightly. Serve sauce with pork.

1 SERVING Calories 240 (Calories from Fat 70) | Fat 8g (Saturated 3g) | Cholesterol 65mg | Sodium 510mg | Carbohydrate 19g (Dietary Fiber 1g) | Protein 23g % DAILY VALUE Vitamin A 2% | Vitamin C 2% | Calcium 2% | Iron 6% EXCHANGES 1 Starch, 3 Lean Meat CARBOHYDRATE CHOICES 1

BETTY'S TIP

If you happen to have bone-in chops in your freezer, you can use them in place of boneless chops—just make sure you thaw them in the refrigerator first.

Pork Chops with Spiced Fruit Stuffing

PREP **10 min** COOK **6 hr** SERVINGS **4**

- 1 cup diced dried fruit and raisin mixture
- 1 cup chicken broth
- 1/2 cup apple juice
- 3 tablespoons butter or margarine
- 1/4 teaspoon ground cinnamon
- 1/8 teaspoon ground nutmeg
- 1 package (6 ounces) herb stuffing mix
- 4 pork boneless loin chops, about 1/2 inch thick (about 1 pound)
- 1/8 teaspoon salt
- 1/8 teaspoon pepper

1. Mix dried fruit, broth, 1/4 cup apple juice, the butter, cinnamon and nutmeg in 3-quart saucepan. Heat to boiling. Stir in stuffing mix; remove saucepan from heat.
2. Arrange pork in 3 1/2- to 4-quart slow cooker. Pour remaining 1/4 cup apple juice over pork. Sprinkle with salt and pepper. Top with stuffing mixture.
3. Cover and cook on Low heat setting 5 to 6 hours.
4. Remove stuffing from slow cooker; place in serving bowl. Stir gently. Serve pork with stuffing.

1 SERVING Calories 505 (Calories from Fat 160) | Fat 18g (Saturated 4g) | Cholesterol 65mg | Sodium 1170mg | Carbohydrate 55g (Dietary Fiber 4g) | Protein 28g % DAILY VALUE Vitamin A 14% | Vitamin C 0% | Calcium 6% | Iron 18% EXCHANGES 3 Starch, 1 Fruit, 2 1/2 Lean Meat, 1 1/2 Fat CARBOHYDRATE CHOICES 3 1/2

BETTY'S TIP

One cup of your favorite chopped dried fruit, such as apples or apricots, can be used in place of the dried fruit and raisin mixture.

Pork Chops with Apple-Cherry Stuffing

PREP 15 min COOK 8 hr SERVINGS 6

1 package (6 ounces) herb stuffing mix

2 medium stalks celery, chopped (1 cup)

1 medium tart cooking apple, peeled and chopped

1 medium onion, chopped (1/2 cup)

1 cup dried cherries

1/4 cup butter or margarine, melted

1 cup chicken broth

6 pork boneless loin chops, about 1/2 inch thick

1. Spray inside of 4- to 5-quart slow cooker with cooking spray. Mix all ingredients except pork. Place half of the stuffing mixture in slow cooker; top with pork. Spoon remaining stuffing over pork.
2. Cover and cook on Low heat setting 6 to 8 hours.

1 SERVING Calories 365 (Calories from Fat 155) | Fat 17g (Saturated 4g) | Cholesterol 65mg | Sodium 500mg | Carbohydrate 35g (Dietary Fiber 8g) | Protein 26g % DAILY VALUE Vitamin A 12% | Vitamin C 20% | Calcium 4% | Iron 10% EXCHANGES 1 1/2 Starch, 1 Fruit, 3 Lean Meat, 1/2 Fat CARBOHYDRATE CHOICES 2

Pork Chops with Apple-Cranberry Stuffing Substitute dried cranberries for the cooking apple.

BETTY'S TIP

Steamed green beans and baked sweet potatoes are tasty accompaniments for the pork chops.

Savory Barbecued Ribs

PREP 10 min COOK 8 to 9 hr FINISH TIME 1 hr SERVINGS 4

- 3 1/2 pounds pork spareribs or loin back ribs
- 1/4 cup packed brown sugar
- 1/2 teaspoon hickory smoked salt
- 1/4 teaspoon pepper
- 1/2 cup cola
- 1 1/4 cups barbecue sauce

1. Spray inside of 4 1/2- to 6-quart slow cooker with cooking spray.
2. Trim excess fat and remove membranes from ribs. Mix brown sugar, hickory salt and pepper; rub mixture into ribs. Cut ribs into 2- or 3-rib portions. Place ribs in slow cooker; pour cola around ribs.
3. Cover and cook on Low heat setting 8 to 9 hours or until ribs are tender.
4. Remove ribs from cooker; place in shallow baking pan. Drain liquid from cooker and discard. Brush both sides of ribs with barbecue sauce. Return ribs to cooker. Pour any remaining sauce over ribs. Cover and cook on Low heat setting about 1 hour until ribs are glazed and sauce is desired consistency. Cut into single-rib servings if desired.

1 SERVING Calories 780 (Calories from Fat 425) | Fat 47g (Saturated 17g) | Cholesterol 185mg | Sodium 1100mg | Carbohydrate 44g (Dietary Fiber 0g) | Protein 45g % DAILY VALUE Vitamin A 4% | Vitamin C 2% | Calcium 10% | Iron 20% EXCHANGES 3 Starch, 4 High-Fat Meat, 1 Fat CARBOHYDRATE CHOICES 3

BETTY'S TIP

For a comforting homemade dinner, serve mashed potatoes and hot-from-the-oven corn bread. Don't forget to pass the butter to top off the potatoes and corn bread!

Smoky-Flavored Barbecued Ribs

PREP 15 min COOK 8 to 9 hr FINISH TIME 1 hr SERVINGS 4

- 3 1/2 pounds pork loin back ribs
- 1/4 cup packed brown sugar
- 1/2 teaspoon pepper
- 3 tablespoons liquid smoke
- 2 cloves garlic, finely chopped
- 1 teaspoon salt
- 1 medium onion, sliced
- 1/2 cup cola
- 1 1/2 cups barbecue sauce

1. Spray inside of 5- to 6-quart slow cooker with cooking spray.
2. Remove inner skin from ribs. Mix brown sugar, pepper, liquid smoke, garlic and salt; rub mixture into ribs. Cut ribs into about 4-inch pieces. Layer ribs and onion in slow cooker. Pour cola over ribs.
3. Cover and cook on Low heat setting 8 to 9 hours or until ribs are tender. Remove ribs from cooker. Drain liquid from cooker and discard.
4. Pour barbecue sauce into shallow bowl. Dip ribs into sauce. Place ribs in cooker. Pour any remaining sauce over ribs. Cover and cook on Low heat setting 1 hour.

1 SERVING 890 (Calories from Fat 540) | Fat 60g (Saturated 22g) | Cholesterol 230mg | Sodium 1540mg | Carbohydrate 32g (Dietary Fiber 2g) | Protein 58g
% DAILY VALUE Vitamin A 8% | Vitamin C 6% | Calcium 12% | Iron 26%
EXCHANGES 2 Starch, 7 High-Fat Meat CARBOHYDRATE CHOICES 2

BETTY'S TIP

Cola adds a wonderful sweetness to the ribs, but you can use water instead if you don't have any cola on hand. Pork ribs are by far the most popular choice for barbecued ribs, but try beef short ribs for a change. Trim any excess fat from the short ribs before adding them to the cooker.

Honey-Barbecue-Glazed Pork Roast with Carrots and Corn

PREP **15 min** COOK **10 hr 20 min** SERVINGS **6**

- 3-pound pork boneless shoulder roast
- 1 bag (1 pound) baby-cut carrots
- 1/2 cup barbecue sauce
- 1/4 cup honey
- 3 tablespoons balsamic vinegar
- 1 teaspoon seasoned salt
- 2/3 cup barbecue sauce
- 1/4 cup all-purpose flour
- 1 cup frozen whole kernel corn (from 1-pound bag)

1. Remove fat from pork. Place pork in 3 1/2- to 4-quart slow cooker. Arrange carrots around and on top of pork. Mix 1/2 cup barbecue sauce, the honey, vinegar and seasoned salt in small bowl; pour over pork and carrots.
2. Cover and cook on Low heat setting 8 to 10 hours.
3. Remove pork and vegetables from slow cooker; place on serving platter. Cover to keep warm. Mix 2/3 cup barbecue sauce and the flour; gradually stir into juices in slow cooker. Increase heat setting to High. Cover and cook about 15 minutes, stirring occasionally, until thickened.
4. Stir corn into mixture in slow cooker. Cover and cook on High heat setting 5 minutes. Serve sauce over pork and vegetables.

1 SERVING Calories 635 (Calories from Fat 250) | Fat 27g (Saturated 10g) | Cholesterol 145mg | Sodium 890mg | Carbohydrate 46g (Dietary Fiber 3g) | Protein 51g % DAILY VALUE Vitamin A 100% | Vitamin C 8% | Calcium 4% | Iron 16% EXCHANGES 3 Starch, 5 1/2 Medium-Fat Meat CARBOHYDRATE CHOICES 3

BETTY'S TIP

The flavor of the sauce for this roast depends on purchased barbecue sauce, so use your family's favorite brand.

Easy Pork Chili

PREP 10 min **COOK** 10 hr 5 min **SERVINGS** 6

1 pound pork boneless shoulder, cut into 1-inch pieces

1 medium onion, chopped (1/2 cup)

1 jar (16 ounces) salsa

1 can (15 ounces) chunky tomato sauce with onions, celery and green bell peppers

1 teaspoon Mexican seasoning

1 can (4.5 ounces) chopped green chiles, drained

1 can (15 ounces) black beans, rinsed and drained

1. Mix all ingredients except beans in 3 1/2- to 4-quart slow cooker.
2. Cover and cook on Low heat setting 8 to 10 hours.
3. Stir in beans. Cover and cook about 5 minutes or until hot.

1 SERVING Calories 275 (Calories from Fat 90) | Fat 10g (Saturated 3g) | Cholesterol 50mg | Sodium 960mg | Carbohydrate 30g (Dietary Fiber 8g) | Protein 24g % DAILY VALUE Vitamin A 12% | Vitamin C 32% | Calcium 10% | Iron 20% EXCHANGES 2 Starch, 2 1/2 Very Lean Meat, 1 Fat CARBOHYDRATE CHOICES 2

Easy Steak Chili Substitute beef round steak for the pork.

BETTY'S TIP

If you like your chili with a little less heat, use mild salsa and omit the Mexican seasoning. If you'd like to kick the spice up a notch, use medium-spicy salsa and 1 teaspoon Mexican seasoning.

Easy Bean and Kielbasa Soup

PREP **25 min** COOK **11 hr** SERVINGS **8**

- 1/2 package (20-ounce size) 15- or 16-dried bean soup mix, sorted and rinsed
- 5 cans (14 ounces each) chicken broth
- 1 package (16 ounces) kielbasa sausage, cut lengthwise in half, then sliced
- 1 can (14 1/2 ounces) diced tomatoes, undrained
- 4 medium carrots, chopped (2 cups)
- 3 medium stalks celery, chopped (1 1/2 cups)
- 1 large onion, chopped (1 cup)
- 2 tablespoons tomato paste
- 1 teaspoon dried thyme leaves
- 1/2 teaspoon salt
- 1/2 teaspoon pepper

1. Heat bean soup mix and broth to boiling in 4-quart saucepan; reduce heat. Cover and simmer 1 hour.
2. Pour bean mixture into 5- to 6-quart slow cooker. Stir in remaining ingredients.
3. Cover and cook on Low heat setting 8 to 10 hours.

1 SERVING Calories 310 (Calories from Fat 165) | Fat 17g (Saturated 6g) | Cholesterol 30mg | Sodium 1330mg | Carbohydrate 27g (Dietary Fiber 7g) | Protein 17g % DAILY VALUE Vitamin A 54% | Vitamin C 12% | Calcium 10% | Iron 20% EXCHANGES 1 Starch, 2 Vegetable, 1 1/2 High-Fat Meat, 1 Fat CARBOHYDRATE CHOICES 2

Easy Bean Soup Omit the kielbasa.

BETTY'S TIP

To add a touch of color and flavor, stir 1/4 cup of chopped fresh parsley into the soup just before serving.

Moroccan Lamb and Rice

PREP **10 min** COOK **9 hr** SERVINGS **4**

1 pound boneless lamb, cut into 1-inch pieces, or 1 pound lamb stew meat

1 small apple, shredded

1 package (6.9 ounces) rice and vermicelli mix with chicken seasonings

1 1/2 cups chicken broth

1 teaspoon curry powder

1/4 cup raisins

1/4 cup slivered almonds

1. Mix lamb, apple, seasoning packet from rice mix, broth and curry powder in 3 1/2- to 4-quart slow cooker.
2. Cover and cook on Low heat setting 7 to 9 hours. During last 25 minutes of cooking, stir in rice and raisins. Increase heat setting to High. Cover and cook 20 minutes or until rice is tender.
3. Sprinkle almonds over individual servings.

1 SERVING Calories 305 (Calories from Fat 100) | Fat 11g (Saturated 3g) | Cholesterol 65mg | Sodium 630mg | Carbohydrate 26g (Dietary Fiber 2g) | Protein 25g % DAILY VALUE Vitamin A 0% | Vitamin C 0% | Calcium 4% | Iron 14% EXCHANGES 1 Starch, 1/2 Fruit, 3 Lean Meat, 1 1/2 Fat CARBOHYDRATE CHOICES 2

BETTY'S TIP

Use the largest holes on a kitchen grater to shred the apple for this stew. Large holes produce less juice and the bigger shreds mean the job is done faster.

French Onion Soup

PREP 15 min COOK 5 hr 35 min SERVINGS 8

- 3 large onions, sliced
- 3 tablespoons butter or margarine, melted
- 4 cans (14 ounces each) beef broth
- 3 tablespoons all-purpose flour
- 1 tablespoon Worcestershire sauce
- 1 teaspoon sugar
- 1/4 teaspoon pepper
- Cheesy Broiled French Bread (below left)

1. Mix onions and butter in 5- to 6-quart slow cooker. Cover and cook on High heat setting 4 to 5 hours or until onions begin to brown slightly around edges.
2. Mix 1/4 cup of the broth, the flour, Worcestershire sauce, sugar and pepper in small bowl. Stir flour mixture and remaining broth into onions. Cover and cook on High heat setting 30 to 35 minutes or until hot.
3. Make Cheesy Broiled French Bread. Place 1 slice bread on each bowl of soup.

Cheesy Broiled French Bread

8 slices French bread, 1 inch thick

3/4 cup shredded mozzarella cheese (3 ounces)

2 tablespoons grated or shredded Parmesan cheese

Set oven control to broil. Place bread slices on ungreased cookie sheet. Sprinkle with cheeses. Broil with tops 5 to 6 inches from heat 1 to 2 minutes or until cheeses are melted.

1 SERVING Calories 295 (Calories from Fat 80) | Fat 9g (Saturated 5g) | Cholesterol 20mg | Sodium 1410mg | Carbohydrate 40g (Dietary Fiber 3g) | Protein 13g % DAILY VALUE Vitamin A 6% | Vitamin C 2% | Calcium 18% | Iron 14% EXCHANGES 2 1/2 Starch, 1 Vegetable, 1 1/2 Fat CARBOHYDRATE CHOICES 2 1/2

BETTY'S TIP

Top this soup with large crouton cubes instead of making the cheesy bread, and simply sprinkle soup with shredded Parmesan or mozzarella cheese before serving.

Ratatouille Bean Stew

PREP 10 min COOK 12 hr SERVINGS 5

1 cup dried garbanzo beans

1 medium onion, chopped (1/2 cup)

2 cloves garlic, finely chopped

1 can (14 ounces) chicken broth

1 jar (4 1/2 ounces) sliced mushrooms, drained

1/4 teaspoon salt

1 large zucchini, sliced

1 medium red or green bell pepper, cut into pieces

1 teaspoon Italian seasoning

1 can (14.5 ounces) diced tomatoes with Italian-style herbs, undrained

1. Soak and drain beans as directed on package.
2. Mix beans, onion, garlic, broth, mushrooms and salt in 3 1/2- to 4-quart slow cooker.
3. Cover and cook on Low heat setting 10 to 12 hours. During last 35 minutes of cooking, stir in zucchini, bell pepper, Italian seasoning and tomatoes. Increase heat setting to High. Cover and cook 30 to 35 minutes or until vegetables are tender.

1 SERVING Calories 220 (Calories from Fat 25) | Fat 3g (Saturated 0g) | Cholesterol 0mg | Sodium 85mg | Carbohydrate 35g (Dietary Fiber 9g) | Protein 11g % DAILY VALUE Vitamin A 40% | Vitamin C 52% | Calcium 8% | Iron 20% EXCHANGES 2 Starch, 1 Vegetable, 1/2 Very Lean Meat, 1/2 Fat CARBOHYDRATE CHOICES 2

BETTY'S TIP

It's easy to make this recipe vegetarian; simply use vegetable broth in place of the chicken broth.

Squash-and-Apple Bisque

PREP 15 min COOK 8 to 10 hr COOK 3 to 5 hr
FINISH TIME 15 min SERVINGS 8

- 1 butternut squash (2 pounds), peeled and cubed
- 1 medium onion, chopped (1/2 cup)
- 1 can (14 1/2 ounces) ready-to-serve chicken broth
- 2 cups applesauce
- 1/2 teaspoon ground ginger
- 1/4 teaspoon salt
- 1 cup sour cream

1. Mix all ingredients except sour cream in 3 1/2- to 6-quart slow cooker.
2. Cover and cook on Low heat setting 8 to 10 hours (or High heat setting 3 to 5 hours) or until squash is tender.
3. Place one-third to one-half of the mixture at a time in blender or food processor. Cover and blend on high speed until smooth. Return mixture to cooker.
4. Stir in sour cream. Cover and cook on Low heat setting 15 minutes or just until soup is hot; stir.
5. Garnish each serving with a dollop of sour cream.

1 SERVING Calories 140 (Calories from Fat 55) | Fat 6g (Saturated 4g) | Cholesterol 20mg | Sodium 330mg | Carbohydrate 19g (Dietary Fiber 2g) | Protein 3g % DAILY VALUE Vitamin A 70% | Vitamin C 12% | Calcium 6% | Iron 4% EXCHANGES 1 Starch, 1 Vegetable, 1 Fat CARBOHYDRATE CHOICES 1

BETTY'S TIP

For a delightful taste treat, serve this bisque thoroughly chilled. Garnish with thin slices of Granny Smith apples and a sprinkling of finely chopped crystallized ginger.

Peach Cherry Chutney

PREP 15 min COOK 6 to 8 hr SERVINGS 6

2 cans (15 1/4 ounces each) sliced peaches, well drained and chopped

1/2 cup sugar

1/3 cup dried cherries

1/3 cup cider vinegar

2 teaspoons finely chopped jalapeño chili

1 teaspoon grated gingerroot

1/2 teaspoon ground allspice

1/2 cup chopped red onion

1. Mix all ingredients in 2- to 3 1/2-quart slow cooker.
2. Cover and cook on Low heat setting 6 to 8 hours or until very thick. Cool about 2 hours.
3. Spoon chutney into container. Cover and store in refrigerator up to 3 weeks.

1 TABLESPOON Calories 20 (Calories from Fat 0) | Fat 0g (Saturated 0g) | Cholesterol 0mg | Sodium 0mg | Carbohydrate 6g (Dietary Fiber 1g) | Protein 0g % DAILY VALUE Vitamin A 0% | Vitamin C 2% | Calcium 0% | Iron 0% EXCHANGES 1 Vegetable CARBOHYDRATE CHOICES 1/2

BETTY'S TIP

If you prefer, use a teaspoon of ground ginger in place of the grated fresh gingerroot. Also, you can use dried cranberries or raisins if dried cherries aren't available.

Pizzas with Pizzazz

Salsa Pizza with Cheese Crust 248

Taco Pizza 249

Cheeseburger Pizza 250

Sloppy Joe Pizza 251

Easy Philly Cheesesteak Pizza 253

Thai Chicken Pizzas 254

Double-Cheese, Spinach and Chicken Pizza 257

Hawaiian Pizza 259

Chicken, Artichoke and Red Onion Pizza 260

Chicken Pizza Mexicana 261

Chicken French-Bread Pizza 263

Chicken Gyro Pizza 265

Turkey Gyro Pizzas 266

Deep-Dish Turkey Pizza 267

Double-Cheese Pepperoni Pizza 268

Breakfast Pizza 269

Sausage Pizza Pie 270

Classic Pizza 271

Shrimp-Pesto Pizzas 273

Sun-Dried Tomato and Herb Pizza 274

Greek Pita Pizzas 275

Four-Cheese Pesto Pizza 276

Mini White Pizza 277

Salsa Pizza with Cheese Crust

PREP 15 min COOK 10 min BAKE 28 min SERVINGS 8

- 1 pound lean ground beef
- 1 1/4 cups thick-and-chunky salsa
- 2 cups Original Bisquick mix
- 1/4 cup mild salsa-flavored or jalapeño-flavored process cheese sauce
- 1/4 cup hot water
- 8 medium green onions, sliced (1/2 cup)
- 1 cup shredded Colby-Monterey Jack cheese (4 ounces)

1. Heat oven to 375°. Spray large cookie sheet with cooking spray. Cook beef in 10-inch skillet over medium heat 8 to 10 minutes, stirring occasionally, until brown; drain. Stir in salsa; remove from heat.
2. Stir Bisquick mix, cheese sauce and water in medium bowl until soft dough forms; beat vigorously 20 strokes. Place dough on surface dusted with Bisquick mix; gently roll in Bisquick mix to coat. Shape into ball; knead about 5 times or until smooth. Roll dough into 14-inch circle; place on cookie sheet. Spread beef mixture over dough to within 2 inches of edge. Sprinkle with onions. Fold edge of dough over beef mixture. Sprinkle cheese over beef mixture.
3. Bake 25 to 28 minutes or until crust is golden brown and cheese is melted.

1 SERVING Calories 315 (Calories from Fat 160) | Fat 18g (Saturated 8g) | Cholesterol 50mg | Sodium 750mg | Carbohydrate 22g (Dietary Fiber 1g) | Protein 17g % DAILY VALUE Vitamin A 12% | Vitamin C 6% | Calcium 16% | Iron 14% EXCHANGES 1 Starch, 1 Vegetable, 2 High-Fat Meat CARBOHYDRATE CHOICES 1 1/2

Salsa Pork Pizza with Cheese Crust Substitute 1 pound of bulk pork sausage for the ground beef.

BETTY'S TIP

Garnish this Mexican-style pizza with chopped tomato, shredded lettuce and sliced ripe olives. A dollop of guacamole or sour cream makes a tasty topping.

Taco Pizza

PREP 20 min BAKE 12 min SERVINGS 4

1 round focaccia bread or 1 package (14 ounces) ready-to-serve original Italian pizza crust (12 inches in diameter)

3/4 pound extra-lean ground beef

2 tablespoons taco seasoning mix (from 1 1/4-ounce envelope)

1 can (10 ounces) diced tomatoes and green chilies, drained

1/2 cup shredded reduced-fat Cheddar cheese (2 ounces)

Shredded lettuce, if desired

Reduced-fat sour cream, if desired

Chopped tomatoes, if desired

1. Heat oven to 425°. Place bread on 12-inch pizza pan or cookie sheet.
2. Cook beef in 10-inch nonstick skillet over medium heat 8 to 10 minutes, stirring occasionally, until brown; drain. Stir in taco seasoning mix; stir in half the amount of water as directed on package. Reduce heat to low. Simmer uncovered 5 minutes.
3. Spoon beef mixture over bread. Top with tomatoes. Sprinkle with cheese. Bake about 12 minutes or until tomatoes are hot and cheese is melted. Serve topped with lettuce, sour cream and tomatoes.

1 SERVING Calories 585 (Calories from Fat 180) | Fat 20g (Saturated 5g) | Cholesterol 50mg | Sodium 1600mg | Carbohydrate 73g (Dietary Fiber 4g) | Protein 32g % DAILY VALUE Vitamin A 18% | Vitamin C 10% | Calcium 16% | Iron 36% EXCHANGES 5 Starch, 2 Lean Meat, 2 Fat CARBOHYDRATE CHOICES 5

BETTY'S TIP

A pizza crust by any other name. . . . When you're looking for ready-to-serve pizza crusts, keep in mind they have many names, including "Italian flatbread" and "Italian bread shell."

Cheeseburger Pizza

PREP 20 min BAKE 28 min STAND 5 min SERVINGS 8

- 1 pound lean ground beef
- 1/2 cup process cheese sauce
- 2 cups Original Bisquick mix
- 1/4 cup process cheese sauce
- 1/4 cup hot water
- 1/4 cup shredded Colby-Monterey Jack cheese (1 ounce)
- 1 roma (plum) tomato, chopped (1/3 cup)

1. Heat oven to 375°. Spray large cookie sheet with cooking spray. Cook beef in 10-inch skillet over medium-high heat 5 to 7 minutes, stirring occasionally, until brown; drain. Stir in 1/2 cup cheese sauce until cheese is melted.
2. Stir Bisquick mix, 1/4 cup cheese sauce and the hot water until soft dough forms; beat vigorously 20 strokes. Place dough on surface dusted with Bisquick mix; gently roll in Bisquick mix to coat. Shape into ball; knead about 5 times or until smooth. Roll dough into 14-inch circle; place on cookie sheet. Spoon beef mixture over dough to within 2 inches of edge. Fold edge of dough over beef mixture.
3. Bake 25 to 28 minutes or until crust is golden brown. Sprinkle with cheese and tomato. Let stand 5 minutes before cutting.

1 SERVING Calories 455 (Calories from Fat 250) | Fat 28g (Saturated 13g) | Cholesterol 75mg | Sodium 990mg | Carbohydrate 29g (Dietary Fiber 1g) | Protein 22g % DAILY VALUE Vitamin A 12% | Vitamin C 2% | Calcium 18% | Iron 16% EXCHANGES 2 Starch, 2 High-Fat Meat, 2 Fat CARBOHYDRATE CHOICES 2

Turkey Burger Pizza Substitute 1 pound ground turkey for the ground beef.

BETTY'S TIP

Cheeseburger lovers will want to top this pizza with all their favorite fixin's—chopped onion, pickle relish, chopped tomato, ketchup and mustard.

Sloppy Joe Pizza

PREP **10 min** BAKE **10 min** SERVINGS **6**

1. Heat oven to 425°. Cook beef in 10-inch nonstick skillet over medium heat 8 to 10 minutes, stirring occasionally, until brown; drain. Stir in taco seasoning mix.
2. Place pizza crust on ungreased cookie sheet. Spread evenly with bean dip. Spoon beef over bean layer. Sprinkle with cheese.
3. Bake 8 to 10 minutes or until cheese is melted. Serve with salsa and guacamole.

1 SERVING Calories 515 (Calories from Fat 190) | Fat 21g (Saturated 9g) | Cholesterol 65mg | Sodium 660mg | Carbohydrate 55g (Dietary Fiber 3g) | Protein 27g % DAILY VALUE Vitamin A 16% | Vitamin C 0% | Calcium 18% | Iron 26% EXCHANGES 3 1/2 Starch, 2 1/2 High-Fat Meat CARBOHYDRATE CHOICES 3 1/2

1 pound lean ground beef

3 tablespoons taco seasoning mix (from 1 1/4-ounce envelope)

1 package (14 ounces) ready-to-serve original Italian pizza crust or other 12-inch ready-to-serve pizza crust

1/3 cup purchased black bean dip

1 cup shredded Monterey Jack cheese with jalapeño peppers (4 ounces)

Salsa and guacamole, if desired

BETTY'S TIP

Using purchased black bean dip makes this easy recipe even easier. You may find a variety of flavors, so feel free to experiment to find your family's favorite.

Easy Philly Cheesesteak Pizza

PREP **10 min** BAKE **10 min** SERVINGS **6**

1 can (13.8 ounces) refrigerated pizza crust dough

2 cups frozen stir-fry bell peppers and onions (from 1-pound bag)

2 tablespoons Dijon-mayonnaise blend

8 ounces thinly sliced cooked deli roast beef

2 cups shredded process American cheese (8 ounces)

1. Heat oven to 425°. Spray 12-inch pizza pan with cooking spray. Press pizza crust dough in pan. Bake 8 minutes.
2. While crust is baking, spray 10-inch nonstick skillet with cooking spray; heat over medium-high heat. Cook frozen bell pepper mixture in skillet 4 to 5 minutes, stirring frequently, until crisp-tender.
3. Spread Dijon-mayonnaise blend over partially baked crust. Top with roast beef, bell pepper mixture and cheese. Bake 8 to 10 minutes or until crust is golden brown.

1 SERVING Calories 370 (Calories from Fat 160) | Fat 18g (Saturated 9g) | Cholesterol 50mg | Sodium 830mg | Carbohydrate 28g (Dietary Fiber 2g) | Protein 24g % DAILY VALUE Vitamin A 12% | Vitamin C 20% | Calcium 20% | Iron 16% EXCHANGES 2 Starch, 2 1/2 Medium-Fat Meat, 1/2 Fat CARBOHYDRATE CHOICES 2

BETTY'S TIP

Here's a quick take on the cheesesteak sandwich made famous in Philadelphia in the 1930s. Turning it into a hearty pizza means it can serve the whole family super-fast.

Thai Chicken Pizzas

PREP **5 min** BAKE **20 min** SERVINGS **6**

- 6 flour tortillas (8 to 10 inches in diameter)
- 1/2 cup peanut butter
- 1/4 cup soy sauce
- 2 tablespoons seasoned rice vinegar
- 2 teaspoons sugar
- 2 cups shredded mozzarella cheese (8 ounces)
- 2 cups chopped cooked chicken breast
- 1 bag (1 pound) frozen stir-fry vegetables, thawed and drained

1. Heat oven to 400°. Place tortillas on ungreased cookie sheet. Bake about 5 minutes or until crisp.
2. Mix peanut butter, soy sauce, vinegar and sugar; spread over tortillas. Top each with 1/4 cup of the cheese. Spread chicken and vegetables evenly over tortillas. Sprinkle with remaining 1/2 cup cheese.
3. Bake 10 to 15 minutes or until pizzas are hot and cheese is melted.

1 SERVING Calories 490 (Calories from Fat 215) | Fat 24g (Saturated 10g) | Cholesterol 60mg | Sodium 1330mg | Carbohydrate 37g (Dietary Fiber 5g) | Protein 36g % DAILY VALUE Vitamin A 20% | Vitamin C 22% | Calcium 36% | Iron 18% EXCHANGES 2 Starch, 1 Vegetable, 4 Lean Meat, 2 Fat CARBOHYDRATE CHOICES 2 1/2

BETTY'S TIP

Peanut sauce, found in the Asian foods section of your grocery store, can be used in place of the peanut butter, soy sauce, vinegar and sugar. Use slightly less than 1 cup.

Double-Cheese, Spinach and Chicken Pizza

PREP 5 min **BAKE** 10 min **SERVINGS** 6

1 package (14 ounces) ready-to-serve original Italian pizza crust or other 12-inch ready-to-serve pizza crust

1 cup shredded Havarti cheese (4 ounces)

2 cups washed fresh baby spinach leaves (from 10-ounce bag)

1 cup diced cooked chicken

1/4 cup chopped drained roasted red bell peppers (from 7-ounce jar)

1/2 teaspoon garlic salt

1 cup shredded Cheddar cheese (4 ounces)

1. Heat oven to 425°. Place pizza crust on ungreased 12-inch pizza pan.
2. Top with Havarti cheese, spinach, chicken, bell peppers, garlic salt and Cheddar cheese.
3. Bake 8 to 10 minutes or until crust is golden brown.

1 SERVING Calories 450 (Calories from Fat 160) | Fat 18g (Saturated 9g) | Cholesterol 60mg | Sodium 750mg | Carbohydrate 51g (Dietary Fiber 2g) | Protein 23g % DAILY VALUE Vitamin A 36% | Vitamin C 12% | Calcium 22% | Iron 22% EXCHANGES 3 Starch, 1 Vegetable, 2 Medium-Fat Meat, 1 Fat CARBOHYDRATE CHOICES 3 1/2

BETTY'S TIP

To make shredding cheese a breeze, shred it right from the refrigerator or put it in the freezer for 30 minutes.

Hawaiian Pizza

PREP 5 min BAKE 10 min SERVINGS 6

1 package (14 ounces) ready-to-serve original Italian pizza crust or other 12-inch ready-to-serve pizza crust

1 can (8 ounces) tomato sauce

2 cups cubed cooked chicken

1 can (8 ounces) pineapple tidbits, well drained

1 cup shredded mozzarella cheese (4 ounces)

1. Heat oven to 400°. Place pizza crust on ungreased cookie sheet.
2. Spread tomato sauce over pizza crust. Top with chicken and pineapple. Sprinkle with cheese.
3. Bake 8 to 10 minutes or until pizza is hot and cheese is melted.

1 SERVING Calories 375 (Calories from Fat 80) | Fat 9g (Saturated 4g) | Cholesterol 50mg | Sodium 830mg | Carbohydrate 47g (Dietary Fiber 3g) | Protein 26g % DAILY VALUE Vitamin A 8% | Vitamin C 6% | Calcium 20% | Iron 18% EXCHANGES 3 Starch, 2 1/2 Lean Meat CARBOHYDRATE CHOICES 3

BETTY'S TIP

Crushed pineapple, very well drained, can be substituted for the pineapple tidbits.

Chicken, Artichoke and Red Onion Pizza

PREP **5 min** BAKE **10 min** SERVINGS **4**

- 2 teaspoons butter or margarine
- 1 large red onion, sliced (2 cups)
- 1 package (14 ounces) ready-to-serve original Italian pizza crust or other 12-inch ready-to-serve pizza crust
- 1 cup cubed cooked chicken or turkey
- 1 jar (6 to 7 ounces) marinated artichoke hearts, drained and sliced
- 3 tablespoons sliced drained roasted red bell peppers (from 7-ounce jar)
- 1 cup shredded sharp Cheddar cheese (4 ounces)

1. Heat oven to 400°. Melt butter in 8-inch skillet over medium heat. Cook onion in butter 3 to 5 minutes, stirring occasionally, until crisp-tender.
2. Place pizza crust on ungreased cookie sheet. Spread onion over pizza crust. Top with chicken, artichoke hearts, bell peppers and cheese.
3. Bake 8 to 10 minutes or until cheese is melted.

1 SERVING Calories 560 (Calories from Fat 170) | Fat 19g (Saturated 10g) | Cholesterol 65mg | Sodium 1015mg | Carbohydrate 68g (Dietary Fiber 7g) | Protein 29g % DAILY VALUE Vitamin A 20% | Vitamin C 18% | Calcium 28% | Iron 26% EXCHANGES 4 Starch, 1 Vegetable, 2 High-Fat Meat, 1/2 Fat CARBOHYDRATE CHOICES 4 1/2

BETTY'S TIP

Artichoke hearts add a distinctive flavor to this easy pizza. Serve the pizza for a light supper, or cut it into small squares for a great appetizer. If you don't have roasted red bell peppers, use jarred pimientos.

Chicken Pizza Mexicana

PREP 10 min **GRILL** 10 min **SERVINGS** 4

2 cups shredded taco-seasoned cheese (8 ounces)

1 package (14 ounces) ready-to-serve original Italian pizza crust or other 12-inch ready-to-serve pizza crust

1 1/2 cups chopped cooked chicken

2 roma (plum) tomatoes, thinly sliced

1 small jalapeño chili, seeded and finely chopped

1. Heat coals or gas grill for direct heat. Sprinkle cheese evenly over pizza crust. Top with remaining ingredients.
2. Cover and grill pizza 4 to 6 inches from medium heat 8 to 10 minutes or until crust is crisp and cheese is melted. (If crust browns too quickly, place a piece of aluminum foil between crust and grill.)

1 SERVING Calories 640 (Calories from Fat 245) | Fat 27g (Saturated 14g) | Cholesterol 105mg | Sodium 890mg | Carbohydrate 59g (Dietary Fiber 3g) | Protein 39g % DAILY VALUE Vitamin A 16% | Vitamin C 10% | Calcium 32% | Iron 26% EXCHANGES 4 Starch, 4 Lean Meat, 2 Fat CARBOHYDRATE CHOICES 4

BETTY'S TIP

For individual pizzas, use two 6-inch Italian pizza crusts and just divide the ingredients equally between them. The grilling time should be about the same.

Chicken French-Bread Pizza

PREP 10 min GRILL 12 min SERVINGS 6

1 loaf (1 pound) unsliced French bread

1 can (8 ounces) pizza sauce

2 cups cubed cooked chicken

1 can (2 1/4 ounces) sliced ripe olives, drained

1 cup shredded reduced-fat mozzarella cheese (4 ounces)

1. Heat oven to 425°. Split bread horizontally in half. Place bread, cut sides up, on cookie sheet.
2. Spread pizza sauce over bread. Top with chicken and olives. Sprinkle with cheese. Bake about 12 minutes or until cheese is melted and chicken is heated through.

1 SERVING Calories 375 (Calories from Fat 110) | Fat 12g (Saturated 4g) | Cholesterol 50mg | Sodium 820mg | Carbohydrate 42g (Dietary Fiber 3g) | Protein 25g % DAILY VALUE Vitamin A 6% | Vitamin C 6% | Calcium 22% | Iron 18% EXCHANGES 3 Starch, 2 Medium-Fat Meat CARBOHYDRATE CHOICES 3

BETTY'S TIP

At your next party, cut thin slices of this chicken- and olive-laden pizza to serve as appetizers.

Chicken Gyro Pizza

PREP 20 min GRILL 25 min SERVINGS 6

- 2 cups Original Bisquick mix
- 1/4 teaspoon dried oregano leaves
- 1/2 cup cold water
- 6 slices chicken breast, cut into strips
- 1 can (2 1/4 ounces) sliced ripe olives, drained
- 1/2 cup crumbled feta cheese (2 ounces)
- 1 1/2 cups shredded mozzarella cheese (6 ounces)
- 1 small tomato, chopped (1/2 cup)
- 1/2 cup chopped cucumber

1. Move oven rack to lowest position. Heat oven to 425°. Spray 12-inch pizza pan with cooking spray. Stir Bisquick mix, oregano and water; beat vigorously with spoon 20 strokes until soft dough forms. Press dough in pizza pan, using fingers dipped in Bisquick mix; pinch edge to form 1/2-inch rim. Bake about 15 minutes or until golden brown.
2. Top crust with chicken and olives; sprinkle with feta and mozzarella cheeses.
3. Bake about 10 minutes or until cheese is melted. Sprinkle with tomato and cucumber.

1 SERVING Calories 310 (Calories from Fat 125) | Fat 14g (Saturated 6g) | Cholesterol 40mg | Sodium 910mg | Carbohydrate 27g (Dietary Fiber 1g) | Protein 18g % DAILY VALUE Vitamin A 8% | Vitamin C 2% | Calcium 34% | Iron 10% EXCHANGES 2 Starch, 2 Medium-Fat Meat CARBOHYDRATE CHOICES 2

BETTY'S TIP

The Mediterranean flavors and ingredients typical of a gyro—roasted meat with grilled vegetables and cucumber-yogurt sauce, rolled in pita bread—are transformed into a pizza the whole family will enjoy. If you prefer, mint leaves can be used in place of the oregano.

Turkey Gyro Pizzas

PREP 10 min BAKE 10 min SERVINGS 4

- 4 pita breads (6 inches in diameter)
- 1/2 cup sour cream
- 1 1/2 teaspoons chopped fresh or 1/2 teaspoon dried mint leaves
- 1 1/2 cups shredded mozzarella cheese (6 ounces)
- 1/2 pound sliced cooked deli turkey breast, cut into strips
- 1/2 cup chopped cucumber
- 1 small tomato, chopped (1/2 cup)
- 1 cup crumbled feta cheese (4 ounces)

1. Heat oven to 400°. Place pita breads on ungreased cookie sheet.
2. Mix sour cream and mint; spread evenly over pitas. Sprinkle each pita with 1/4 cup of the mozzarella cheese. Top with turkey, cucumber, tomato and feta cheese. Sprinkle with remaining 1/2 cup mozzarella cheese.
3. Bake about 10 minutes or until pizzas are hot and cheese is melted.

1 SERVING Calories 475 (Calories from Fat 205) | Fat 23g (Saturated 14g) | Cholesterol 100mg | Sodium 1500mg | Carbohydrate 35g (Dietary Fiber 1g) | Protein 33g % DAILY VALUE Vitamin A 16% | Vitamin C 4% | Calcium 58% | Iron 12% EXCHANGES 2 Starch, 1 Vegetable, 3 Lean Meat, 3 Fat CARBOHYDRATE CHOICES 2

BETTY'S TIP

Look to your deli to jump-start your dinner. Cooked turkey, chicken or roast beef—or whatever you have on hand—works great in this recipe.

Deep-Dish Turkey Pizza

PREP 20 min **BAKE** 1 hr 7 min **SERVINGS** 6

1 1/3 cups Original Bisquick mix

1/3 cup Italian dressing

1 can (15 ounces) cannellini beans, drained, rinsed and mashed

1 1/2 cups diced cooked turkey or chicken

1 package (10 ounces) frozen chopped spinach, thawed and squeezed to drain

1 cup (4 ounces) shredded mozzarella cheese

3 eggs, slightly beaten

1 1/4 cups milk

1/3 cup slivered almonds

1. Heat oven to 375°F. Mix Bisquick mix, dressing and beans. Spread in bottom and 2 inches up side of springform pan, 9 × 3 inches. Bake 10 to 12 minutes or until set.
2. Layer with turkey, spinach and cheese. Mix eggs and milk; pour over cheese. Sprinkle evenly with almonds.
3. Bake 50 to 55 minutes or until golden brown and knife inserted near center comes out clean. Let stand 10 minutes. Loosen edge from side of pan; remove side of pan.

1 SERVING Calories 460 (Calories from Fat 210) | Fat 23g (Saturated 6g) | Cholesterol 150mg | Sodium 710mg | Carbohydrate 38g (Dietary Fiber 6g) | Protein 30g % DAILY VALUE Vitamin A 60% | Vitamin C 4% | Calcium 40% | Iron 25% EXCHANGES 3 Lean Meat, 2 1/2 Fat CARBOHYDRATE CHOICES 2

BETTY'S TIP

A potato masher makes quick work of smashing the cannellini beans.

Double-Cheese Pepperoni Pizza

PREP 20 min STAND 8 min BAKE 17 min SERVINGS 8

- 3 cups Original Bisquick mix
- 2/3 cup very hot water
- 2 tablespoons vegetable oil
- 4 smoked string cheese pieces (from 4-ounce package), cut lengthwise in half
- 1/4 cup Italian-style tomato paste
- 1 small onion, cut lengthwise in half, then cut crosswise into thin slices
- 1/2 medium bell pepper, thinly sliced
- 1 can (4 ounces) mushroom pieces and stems, drained
- 1/2 package (3 1/4-ounce size) sliced pepperoni
- 1 can (2 1/4 ounces) sliced ripe olives, drained, if desired
- 2 cups shredded mozzarella cheese (8 ounces)

1. Stir Bisquick mix, water and oil until soft dough forms; beat vigorously 20 strokes. Let stand 8 minutes.
2. Move oven rack to lowest position. Heat oven to 450°. Spray 12-inch pizza pan with cooking spray. Press dough on bottom and 1 inch over side of pizza pan. Place string cheese along edge of dough. Fold 1 inch edge of dough over and around cheese; press to seal. Bake 7 minutes.
3. Spread tomato paste over crust. Top with onion, bell pepper, mushrooms, pepperoni and olives. Sprinkle with mozzarella cheese. Bake 8 to 10 minutes or until crust is golden brown and cheese is melted.

1 SERVING Calories 360 (Calories from Fat 170) | Fat 19g (Saturated 7g) | Cholesterol 25mg | Sodium 1150mg | Carbohydrate 32g (Dietary Fiber 2g) | Protein 15g % DAILY VALUE Vitamin A 10% | Vitamin C 8% | Calcium 34% | Iron 12% EXCHANGES 2 Starch, 1 1/2 High-Fat Meat, 1 Fat CARBOHYDRATE CHOICES 2

BETTY'S TIP

Short on time? Omit the string cheese, and press the dough just on the bottom of the pizza pan, not over the side.

Breakfast Pizza

PREP **25 min** COOK **20 min** BAKE **20 min** SERVINGS **4**

1/3 cup mayonnaise or salad dressing

1/3 cup sour cream

1 1/2 teaspoons dried fines herbes

1/2 pound bulk pork sausage

1 can (3.8 ounces) refrigerated pizza crust dough

4 eggs

1/2 cup milk

1/4 teaspoon salt

1/8 teaspoon pepper

1 medium zucchini, cut lengthwise in half and sliced

1 medium onion, chopped (1/2 cup)

1 cup shredded Swiss cheese (4 ounces)

1. Heat oven to 425°. Spray cookie sheet with cooking spray. Mix mayonnaise, sour cream and fines herbes; set aside. Cook sausage in 10-inch skillet over medium heat 8 to 10 minutes, stirring occasionally, until no longer pink. Drain and remove sausage, reserving 1 tablespoon drippings in skillet; set aside.
2. Pat crust dough into 10 × 12-inch circle on cookie sheet, building up edge slightly. Bake about 8 minutes or until light brown. Beat eggs, milk, salt and pepper with wire whisk.
3. Heat reserved drippings in skillet over medium heat until hot. Cook zucchini and onion in drippings, stirring frequently, until tender. Pour egg mixture into skillet. As mixture begins to set at bottom and side, gently lift cooked portions with spatula so that thin, uncooked portion can flow to bottom. Avoid constant stirring. Cook 3 to 4 minutes or until eggs are set throughout but still moist; remove from heat.
4. Spread mayonnaise mixture over crust. Top with sausage and egg mixture. Sprinkle with cheese. Bake about 10 minutes or until cheese is melted and crust edge is light brown.

1 SERVING Calories 720 (Calories from Fat 390) | Fat 43g (Saturated Fat 15g) | Cholesterol 285mg | Sodium 1460mg | Carbohydrate 54g (Dietary Fiber 2g) | Protein 30g % DAILY VALUE Vitamin A 25% | Vitamin C 6% | Calcium 40% | Iron 25% EXCHANGES 2 1/2 High-Fat Meat, 4 Fat CARBOHYDRATE CHOICES 3 1/2

BETTY'S TIP

Serve this hearty pizza with some mixed fruit and a beverage, and you'll have a great breakfast or brunch.

Sausage Pizza Pie

PREP 15 min COOK 10 min BAKE 25 min SERVINGS 8 to 10

- 1 pound bulk pork sausage
- 1 can (8 ounces) pizza sauce
- 1/2 teaspoon dried oregano leaves
- 1 3/4 cups all-purpose flour
- 1/2 cup process cheese spread (room temperature)
- 1/4 cup water
- Green and red bell pepper rings
- 1 cup shredded mozzarella cheese (4 ounces)

1. Heat oven to 375°. Spray large cookie sheet with cooking spray. Cook sausage in 10-inch skillet over medium heat 8 to 10 minutes, stirring frequently, until no longer pink; drain. Stir in pizza sauce and oregano; set aside.
2. Mix flour, cheese spread and water until soft dough forms. Shape into ball. Roll into 14-inch circle on lightly floured surface. Place dough on cookie sheet. Spread sausage mixture over dough to within 3 inches of edge. Fold dough over edge of mixture. Top sausage with bell pepper rings; sprinkle with cheese.
3. Bake 23 to 25 minutes or until crust is light golden brown and cheese is melted.

1 SERVING Calories 230 (Calories from Fat 110) | Fat 12g (Saturated 5g) | Cholesterol 30mg | Sodium 530mg | Carbohydrate 20g (Dietary Fiber 1g) | Protein 11g % DAILY VALUE Vitamin A 6% | Vitamin C 10% | Calcium 12% | Iron 8% EXCHANGES 1 Starch, 1 Vegetable, 1 High-Fat Meat, 1/2 Fat CARBOHYDRATE CHOICES 1

BETTY'S TIP

If you think you can take the heat, try using hot pork sausage and process cheese with jalapeños.

Classic Pizza

PREP 10 min COOK 10 min BAKE 18 min SERVINGS 8

1 pound bulk Italian sausage

1 medium onion, chopped (1/2 cup)

1 can (10 ounces) refrigerated pizza crust dough

1/2 cup pizza sauce

1 cup shredded mozzarella cheese (4 ounces)

1/2 cup shredded provolone cheese (2 ounces)

1/4 cup chopped fresh basil leaves

1/2 cup chopped prosciutto

1. Heat oven to 425°. Cook sausage and onion in 10-inch skillet over medium heat 8 to 10 minutes, stirring occasionally, until sausage is no longer pink; drain.
2. Spray cookie sheet with cooking spray. Press pizza crust dough into 12-inch circle on cookie sheet. Press dough from center to edge so edge is slightly thicker than center.
3. Spread pizza sauce over dough to within 1/2 inch of edge. Mix cheeses; sprinkle over sauce. Spoon sausage mixture over cheeses. Sprinkle with basil and prosciutto.
4. Bake about 18 minutes or until crust is golden brown and cheeses are melted and lightly browned.

1 SERVING Calories 295 (Calories from Fat 155) | Fat 17g (Saturated 7g) | Cholesterol 50mg | Sodium 850mg | Carbohydrate 18g (Dietary Fiber 1g) | Protein 18g % DAILY VALUE Vitamin A 4% | Vitamin C 4% | Calcium 16% | Iron 10% EXCHANGES 1 Starch, 2 High-Fat Meat CARBOHYDRATE CHOICES 1

BETTY'S TIP

These days, it's highly likely your local deli stocks prosciutto, but if you're having a tough time tracking down this Italian-seasoned, salt-cured ham, use about 4 ounces of fully cooked smoked ham instead.

Shrimp-Pesto Pizzas

PREP 10 min **STAND** 3 min **BAKE** 12 min **SERVINGS** 4

1. Heat oven to 425°. Pour boiling water over sun-dried tomatoes. Let stand 3 minutes; drain.
2. Place breads on cookie sheet. Spread pesto over breads. Top with shrimp and tomatoes. Sprinkle with cheese.
3. Bake about 12 minutes or until cheese is melted and shrimp are thoroughly heated. Sprinkle with basil.

1 SERVING Calories 315 (Calories from Fat 115) | Fat 13g (Saturated 4g) | Cholesterol 175mg | Sodium 700mg | Carbohydrate 23g (Dietary Fiber 2g) | Protein 27g % DAILY VALUE Vitamin A 12% | Vitamin C 2% | Calcium 22% | Iron 24% EXCHANGES 1 1/2 Starch, 3 Lean Meat, 1 Fat CARBOHYDRATE CHOICES 1 1/2

1/4 cup finely chopped sun-dried tomatoes (not in oil)

4 rounds focaccia bread or 2 packages (10 ounces each) ready-to-serve Italian pizza crusts (6 inches in diameter)

1/4 cup basil pesto

3/4 pound cooked peeled deveined medium shrimp, thawed if frozen and tails peeled

1/2 cup shredded reduced-fat mozzarella cheese (2 ounces)

Chopped fresh basil leaves, if desired

BETTY'S TIP

Instead of chopping the basil, you may want to chiffonade it instead. Those thin strips of fresh basil you see in restaurants are a lot easier to make than you might think: Roll up a basil leaf so you have a tiny tube, then slice it into thin strips.

Sun-Dried Tomato and Herb Pizza

PREP 10 min BAKE 10 min SERVINGS 6

- 1 package (14 ounces) ready-to-serve original Italian pizza crust or other 12-inch ready-to-serve pizza crust
- 1/4 cup soft cream cheese with chives and onions
- 1/2 cup sun-dried tomatoes in oil, drained and sliced
- 2 tablespoons chopped fresh or 2 teaspoons dried oregano leaves
- 2 tablespoons chopped fresh or 2 teaspoons dried basil leaves
- 1 cup shredded mozzarella cheese (4 ounces)
- 1/4 cup shredded Cheddar cheese (1 ounce)

1. Heat oven to 425°. Place pizza crust on ungreased cookie sheet. Spread with cream cheese. Top with tomatoes, oregano and basil. Sprinkle with cheeses.
2. Bake 8 to 10 minutes or until cheese is melted. Cut into wedges.

1 SERVING Calories 305 (Calories from Fat 90) | Fat 10g (Saturated 5g) | Cholesterol 25mg | Sodium 510mg | Carbohydrate 43g (Dietary Fiber 2g) | Protein 13g % DAILY VALUE Vitamin A 8% | Vitamin C 8% | Calcium 18% | Iron 18% EXCHANGES 2 Starch, 3 Vegetable, 2 Fat CARBOHYDRATE CHOICES 3

Sun-Dried Tomato, Herb and Mushroom Pizza Add 1/2 cup thinly sliced mushrooms to the pizza when topping with the tomatoes and use 1 1/4 cups shredded provolone cheese (5 ounces) instead of the mozzarella and Cheddar cheeses.

BETTY'S TIP

A salad of romaine lettuce, sunflower nuts and crumbled feta cheese drizzled with champagne vinaigrette makes a delicious side dish to this flavorful pizza.

Greek Pita Pizzas

PREP 10 min **BAKE** 10 min **SERVINGS** 4

- 4 pita breads (6 inches in diameter)
- 1/2 cup roasted garlic–flavored or regular hummus
- 1 cup crumbled feta cheese (4 ounces)
- 1 small onion, sliced
- 2 cups shredded spinach
- 1 large tomato, seeded and chopped (1 cup)
- 1/4 cup sliced ripe or Kalamata olives

1. Heat oven to 400°. Place pita breads in ungreased jelly roll pan, 15 1/2 × 10 1/2 × 1 inch.
2. Spread hummus on each pita bread. Sprinkle with cheese.
3. Bake 8 to 10 minutes or until cheese is melted. Top each pizza with onion, spinach, tomato and olives.

1 SERVING Calories 335 (Calories from Fat 115) | Fat 13g (Saturated 6g) | Cholesterol 35mg | Sodium 930mg | Carbohydrate 44g (Dietary Fiber 5g) | Protein 15g % DAILY VALUE Vitamin A 20% | Vitamin C 12% | Calcium 28% | Iron 20% EXCHANGES 2 Starch, 3 Vegetable, 2 Fat CARBOHYDRATE CHOICES 3

Greek Pita Pizzas with Chicken Sprinkle 1 or 2 tablespoons of chopped cooked chicken over the hummus for each pita.

BETTY'S TIP

You can use 4 ready-to-serve Italian pizza crusts (6 inches in diameter) instead of the pita breads.

Four-Cheese Pesto Pizza

PREP 10 min BAKE 12 min SERVINGS 6

- 6 whole wheat or white pita breads (6 inches in diameter)
- 1 package (8 ounces) reduced-fat cream cheese (Neufchâtel) or regular cream cheese, softened
- 2 tablespoons milk
- 6 tablespoons basil pesto
- 1 can (2 1/4 ounces) sliced ripe olives, drained
- 1/2 cup shredded part-skim mozzarella cheese (3 ounces)
- 1/2 cup shredded Fontina or provolone cheese (3 ounces)
- 2 tablespoons grated Parmesan cheese
- 2 tablespoons chopped fresh parsley

1. Heat oven to 425°. Place pita breads on ungreased large cookie sheet.
2. Mix cream cheese and milk until smooth. Spread on pita breads to within 1/4 inch of edge. Gently spread pesto over cream cheese. Top with olives. Sprinkle with cheeses and parsley.
3. Bake 7 to 12 minutes or until thoroughly heated and cheese is melted.

1 SERVING Calories 410 (Calories from Fat 215) | Fat 24g (Saturated 10g) | Cholesterol 45mg | Sodium 900mg | Carbohydrate 35g (Dietary Fiber 5g) | Protein 19g % DAILY VALUE Vitamin A 20% | Vitamin C 2% | Calcium 36% | Iron 16% EXCHANGES 2 Starch, 1 Vegetable, 1 1/2 High-Fat Meat, 2 Fat CARBOHYDRATE CHOICES 2

BETTY'S TIP

Pesto used to be available only in restaurants, or it had to be made from scratch. Today, there are a variety of pestos available on supermarket shelves. Try experimenting with different flavors to find your favorite in this recipe.

Mini White Pizzas

PREP **20 min** BAKE **11 min** SERVINGS **4**

1 1/2 cups Original Bisquick mix

1/3 cup boiling water

1/2 cup reduced-fat or regular Alfredo sauce

1/2 cup finely chopped cooked chicken

1/2 cup chopped fresh mushrooms

2 tablespoons chopped fresh or 1 teaspoon dried basil leaves

1 cup shredded mozzarella cheese (4 ounces)

Additional fresh basil leaves, if desired

Photo on page 246.

1. Heat oven to 450°. Spray large cookie sheet with cooking spray. Stir Bisquick mix and water until soft dough forms. Divide dough into fourths. Pat each part of dough into 6-inch circle on cookie sheet, using fingers dusted with Bisquick mix; pinch edge to form 1/2-inch rim.
2. Spread Alfredo sauce on dough. Top with chicken, mushrooms and chopped basil. Sprinkle with cheese.
3. Bake 9 to 11 minutes or until crusts are golden brown and cheese is bubbly. Garnish with additional basil leaves.

1 PIZZA Calories 340 (Calories from Fat 145) | Fat 16g (Saturated 7g) | Cholesterol 40mg | Sodium 940mg | Carbohydrate 31g (Dietary Fiber 1g) | Protein 18g % DAILY VALUE Vitamin A 8% | Vitamin C 0% | Calcium 34% | Iron 10% EXCHANGES 2 Starch, 2 Medium-Fat Meat, 1 Fat CARBOHYDRATE CHOICES 2

BETTY'S TIP

Using boiling water makes the pizza dough more chewy and flavorful. Keep it to one step by measuring 1/3 cup water in a small glass measuring cup and microwaving on High until full bubbles appear.

Main-Dish Salads

Steak Caesar Salad 280
Fajita Salad 281
Deli Beef and Bean Tossed Salad 283
Roast Beef and Tomato Salad 284
Southwestern Chicken BLT Salad 285
Caribbean Chicken Salad 287
Chicken-Curry-Couscous Salad 289
Chopped-Chicken Asian Salad 290
Meditteranean Chicken Salad 293
Greek Chicken Salad 294
Quick Garden Chicken Salad 295
Thai Chicken Salad 297
Raspberry Chicken Salad 298
Garden Vegetables, Chicken and Pasta Salad 301
Wild Rice Chicken Salad with Raspberry Vinaigrette 303
Chicken and Berries Salad 304
Turkey Tabbouleh Salad 305
Turkey Taco Salad 307
Turkey and Fruit Tossed Salad 308
Turkey Salad with Fruit 309
Turkey and Dried Cherry Salad 310
Ten-Minute Ham Salad 311
Ham and Slaw Salad 312
Asian Pork Salad 313
Antipasto Vegetable Salad 314
Italian Tortellini Salad 315
Spinach-Shrimp Salad with Hot Bacon Dressing 316
Caribbean Shrimp Salad 317
Three-Bean and Tuna Salad 318
Italian Tuna Toss 319
Chopped Vegetable and Crabmeat Salad 321
Summer Salmon Salad 322
Caesar Salad with Lobster 323
Tuscan Panzanella Salad 324
Spring Vegetable Paella 325
Fruited Taco Salad 327
Greek Pasta Salad 328
Warm Tuscan Bean Salad 331

Steak Caesar Salad

PREP 10 min GRILL 18 min SERVINGS 4

Caesar Dressing (below right)

1-pound beef boneless top sirloin steak, about 1 inch thick

1 tablespoon freshly ground pepper

1 bunch romaine, torn into bite-size pieces

1 cup garlic-flavored croutons

1/2 cup freshly shredded Parmesan cheese

Shredded Parmesan cheese, if desired

1. Make Caesar Dressing. Sprinkle beef with pepper. Heat coals or gas grill for direct heat.
2. Cover and grill beef 4 to 5 inches from medium heat 15 to 18 minutes for medium doneness, turning once. Cut beef across grain into thin slices.
3. Toss romaine, croutons, 1/2 cup Parmesan cheese and the dressing. Top with beef slices. Serve with additional shredded Parmesan cheese.

Caesar Dressing

1/4 cup olive or vegetable oil

1/4 cup fat-free cholesterol-free egg product

1 tablespoon lemon juice

1 teaspoon Dijon mustard

1 teaspoon anchovy paste

1 large clove garlic, finely chopped

Shake all ingredients in tightly covered container.

1 SERVING Calories 430 (Calories from Fat 70) | Fat 8g (Saturated 10g) | Cholesterol 75mg | Sodium 390mg | Carbohydrate 11g (Dietary Fiber 2g) | Protein 31g %DAILY VALUE Vitamin A 26% | Vitamin C 40% | Calcium 20% | Iron 26% EXCHANGES 2 Vegetable, 4 Medium-Fat Meat, 2 Fat CARBOHYDRATE CHOICES 1

BETTY'S TIP

Crunched for time? Pick up a bottle of your favorite Caesar dressing instead of making it from scratch. Or toss in pieces of leftover cooked chicken instead of grilling steak.

Fajita Salad

PREP 15 min COOK 6 min SERVINGS 4

- 3/4 pound lean beef boneless sirloin steak
- 1 tablespoon vegetable oil
- 2 medium bell peppers, cut into strips
- 1 small onion, thinly sliced
- 4 cups bite-size pieces salad greens
- 1/3 cup Italian dressing
- 1/4 cup plain yogurt

1. Cut beef with grain into 2-inch strips; cut strips across grain into 1/8-inch slices. Heat oil in 10-inch nonstick skillet over medium-high heat. Cook beef in oil about 3 minutes, stirring occasionally, until brown. Remove beef from skillet.
2. Cook bell peppers and onion in skillet about 3 minutes, stirring occasionally, until bell peppers are crisp-tender. Stir in beef.
3. Place salad greens on serving platter. Top with beef mixture. Mix dressing and yogurt; drizzle over salad.

1 SERVING Calories 230 (Calories from Fat 125) | Fat 14g (Saturated 3g) | Cholesterol 45mg | Sodium 230mg | Carbohydrate 12g (Dietary Fiber 3g) | Protein 17g %DAILY VALUE Vitamin A 8% | Vitamin C 68% | Calcium 4% | Iron 12% EXCHANGES 2 Vegetable, 2 Medium-Fat Meat, 1/2 Fat CARBOHYDRATE CHOICES 1

BETTY'S TIP

Check out the meat case of your local grocery store for the many precut meats now available. In addition to being a time-saving convenience, these precut meats often come in small, one-time-use portions.

Deli Beef and Bean Tossed Salad

PREP 10 min **SERVINGS** 6

1 bag (10 ounces) salad mix (about 8 cups)

1 pint (2 cups) deli three-bean salad or 1 can (15 to 17 ounces) three-bean salad, chilled

1/4 pound deli cooked lean beef, cut into julienne strips (3/4 cup)

1 cup shredded reduced-fat Cheddar or Swiss cheese (4 ounces)

12 cherry tomatoes, cut in half

Place all ingredients in large bowl; toss lightly to mix.

1 SERVING Calories 100 (Calories from Fat 20) | Fat 2g (Saturated 1g) | Cholesterol 15mg | Sodium 590mg | Carbohydrate 13g (Dietary Fiber 3g) | Protein 10g %DAILY VALUE Vitamin A 6% | Vitamin C 12% | Calcium 10% | Iron 8% EXCHANGES 1/2 Starch, 1 Vegetable, 1 Very Lean Meat CARBOHYDRATE CHOICES 1

Deli Ham and Bean Tossed Salad Substitute 1/4 pound deli cooked ham, cut into julienne strips (3/4 cup) for the beef.

BETTY'S TIP

For a colorful presentation, select a salad mix that contains lettuce, shredded carrot and shredded red cabbage.

Roast Beef and Tomato Salad

PREP **25 min** SERVINGS **4**

Sherry Vinaigrette (below right)

1 head Boston lettuce

1 bunch arugula, torn into bite-size pieces

1/2 pound thinly sliced cooked roast beef

1 small red onion, thinly sliced and separated into rings

1 medium tomato, thinly sliced

1 cup crumbled Gorgonzola or blue cheese (4 ounces)

1. Make Sherry Vinaigrette.
2. Place Boston lettuce leaves on serving platter. Sprinkle arugula over lettuce. Fold roast beef slices. Place roast beef, onion and tomato on greens. Sprinkle with cheese. Serve with vinaigrette.

Sherry Vinaigrette

1/4 cup olive or vegetable oil

4 teaspoons dry sherry or red wine vinegar

1 teaspoon Dijon mustard

1/8 teaspoon salt

Dash of pepper

1 small shallot, finely chopped

Shake all ingredients in tightly covered container.

1 SERVING Calories 350 (Calories from Fat 225) | Fat 25g (Saturated 8g) | Cholesterol 70mg | Sodium 550mg | Carbohydrate 6g (Dietary Fiber 2g) | Protein 25g %DAILY VALUE Vitamin A 20% | Vitamin C 18% | Calcium 18% | Iron 12% EXCHANGES 1 Vegetable, 3 Medium-Fat Meat, 2 Fat CARBOHYDRATE CHOICES 1/2

BETTY'S TIP

All this salad needs is some chewy European bread or slices of warm focaccia to complete the meal. A glass of red wine would also be a delicious accompaniment.

Southwestern Chicken BLT Salad

PREP 20 min **SERVINGS** 6

Salsa Bacon Dressing (below left)

1 bag (10 ounces) romaine and leaf lettuce mix

2 packages (6 ounces each) refrigerated cooked Southwest-flavor chicken breast strips

4 roma (plum) tomatoes, coarsely chopped

1/2 cup chopped cooked bacon

1/2 cup croutons

1. Make Salsa Bacon Dressing.
2. Mix remaining ingredients in large bowl. Add Salsa Bacon Dressing; toss until coated.

Salsa Bacon Dressing

1/2 cup thick-and-chunky salsa

1/2 cup refrigerated bacon-flavored dip

1 tablespoon chopped fresh parsley

Mix all ingredients in small bowl.

1 SERVING Calories 195 (Calories from Fat 80) | Fat 9g (Saturated 4g) | Cholesterol 60mg | Sodium 410mg | Carbohydrate 7g (Dietary Fiber 2g) | Protein 22g %DAILY VALUE Vitamin A 40% | Vitamin C 30% | Calcium 6% | Iron 10% EXCHANGES 1 Vegetable, 3 Lean Meat CARBOHYDRATE CHOICES 1/2

BETTY'S TIP

The bacon dip in the salad dressing blends nicely with the cooked bacon in the salad, but if you can't find it, refrigerated ranch dip works great, too.

Caribbean Chicken and Black Bean Salad

PREP 20 min SERVINGS 4

Spicy Lime Dressing (below left)

2 cups cut-up cooked chicken

1/4 cup chopped fresh cilantro

1 large tomato, chopped (1 cup)

1 medium avocado, chopped

1 small yellow summer squash, chopped

1 can (15 ounces) black beans, rinsed and drained

Leaf lettuce

Prepare Spicy Lime Dressing. Toss remaining ingredients except lettuce in large bowl. Pour dressing over salad; toss. Serve on lettuce.

Spicy Lime Dressing

1/4 cup lime juice

2 tablespoons olive or vegetable oil

1 tablespoon honey

1/2 teaspoon chili powder

1/4 teaspoon ground cumin

1/4 teaspoon salt

2 or 3 drops red pepper sauce

Shake all ingredients in tightly covered container.

1 SERVING Calories 445 (Calories from Fat 205) | Fat 23g (Saturated 5g) | Cholesterol 60mg | Sodium 630mg | Carbohydrate 40g (Dietary Fiber 10g) | Protein 29g %DAILY VALUE Vitamin A 10% | Vitamin C 32% | Calcium 10% | Iron 24% EXCHANGES 2 Starch, 2 1/2 Medium-Fat Meat, 2 Vegetable, 1 Fat CARBOHYDRATE CHOICES 2

BETTY'S TIP

Need help cutting a mango? Score the skin lengthwise into fourths with a knife, and peel like a banana. Cut the peeled mango lengthwise close to both sides of the seed, then dice.

Chicken-Curry-Couscous Salad

PREP 22 min CHILL 1 hr SERVINGS 4

Curry Dressing (below left)

2 cups cooked couscous

1 cup diced cooked chicken

1 cup raisins

1 medium red or yellow bell pepper, cut into thin strips

6 medium green onions, chopped (6 tablespoons)

1 can (15 to 16 ounces) garbanzo beans, rinsed and drained

1/2 cup chopped roasted almonds

1. Prepare Curry Dressing.
2. Place remaining ingredients except almonds in large bowl. Pour dressing over salad; toss until coated. Cover and refrigerate about 1 hour or until chilled. Top with almonds.

Curry Dressing

1/3 cup light olive or vegetable oil

1 tablespoon lemon juice

1 teaspoon sugar

1/2 teaspoon curry powder

1/4 teaspoon salt

1/8 teaspoon ground allspice

Shake all ingredients in tightly covered container.

1 SERVING Calories 710 (Calories from Fat 295) | Fat 33g (Saturated 4g) | Cholesterol 30mg | Sodium 540mg | Carbohydrate 89g (Dietary Fiber 14g) | Protein 28g % DAILY VALUE Vitamin A 18% | Vitamin C 100% | Calcium 14% | Iron 34% EXCHANGES 5 Starch, 2 Vegetable, 1 Lean Meat, 6 Fat CARBOHYDRATE CHOICES 5

BETTY'S TIP

Create a Middle Eastern luncheon by serving this salad with flatbread or pita breads.

Chopped-Chicken Asian Salad

PREP 30 min SERVINGS 4

Lime Dressing (below right)

2 cups chopped escarole

1 cup chopped cooked chicken

1 small jicama, peeled and chopped (1 cup)

1 large papaya, peeled and chopped (1 cup)

1 medium yellow or red bell pepper, chopped (1 cup)

1/2 cup dry-roasted peanuts

1/4 cup chopped cilantro

1. Prepare Lime Dressing.
2. Place remaining ingredients except peanuts and cilantro in large bowl. Pour dressing over salad; toss until coated. Top with peanuts and cilantro.

Lime Dressing

1/3 cup frozen (thawed) limeade

1/4 cup vegetable oil

1 tablespoon rice or white vinegar

1 teaspoon grated gingerroot

1/4 teaspoon salt

Shake all ingredients in tightly covered container.

1 SERVING Calories 410 (Calories from Fat 235) | Fat 26g (Saturated 4g) | Cholesterol 30mg | Sodium 340mg | Carbohydrate 36g (Dietary Fiber 9g) | Protein 17g % DAILY VALUE Vitamin A 30% | Vitamin C 100% | Calcium 6% | Iron 10% EXCHANGES 2 Vegetable, 1 Fruit, 2 Medium-Fat Meat, 2 1/2 Fat, 1/2 Other Carbohydrate CARBOHYDRATE CHOICES 2 1/2

BETTY'S TIP

Escarole is one of three main varieties of endive. It has broad, slightly curved, pale green leaves and is the mildest of the endive family. If you prefer, for an even milder flavor, you can use romaine in place of the escarole.

Mediterranean Chicken Salad

PREP 6 min **SERVINGS** 6

- 2 cups diced cooked chicken
- 1 bag (10 ounces) ready-to-eat Italian-blend salad greens
- 1 can (14 ounces) artichoke hearts, drained and chopped
- 1 can (4 1/4 ounces) chopped ripe olives, drained
- 1/4 cup tomato-and-herb Italian dressing

Mix all ingredients except dressing in large bowl. Toss with dressing until coated.

1 SERVING Calories 195 (Calories from Fat 100) | Fat 12g (Saturated 2g) | Cholesterol 40mg | Sodium 500mg | Carbohydrate 11g (Dietary Fiber 5g) | Protein 16g % DAILY VALUE Vitamin A 14% | Vitamin C 30% | Calcium 6% | Iron 14% EXCHANGES 2 Vegetable, 2 Medium-Fat Meat CARBOHYDRATE CHOICES 1/2

BETTY'S TIP

In keeping with the Mediterranean theme, try serving with pita bread triangles.

Greek Chicken Salad

PREP 25 min SERVINGS 4

Mint Vinaigrette (below right)

6 cups bite-size pieces assorted salad greens

2 cups cut-up cooked chicken

1/8 cup crumbled feta cheese

1 medium tomato, cut into wedges

1/2 medium cucumber, cut lengthwise in half, seeded and cut into 1/4-inch slices

1 small green bell pepper, coarsely chopped (1/2 cup)

4 medium green onions, sliced (1/4 cup)

12 Kalamata or large pitted ripe olives

1. Make Mint Vinaigrette.
2. Toss vinaigrette and remaining ingredients in large glass or plastic bowl.

Mint Vinaigrette

3 tablespoons lemon juice

1 1/2 teaspoons chopped fresh or 1/2 teaspoon dried mint leaves

1/2 teaspoon salt

1/8 teaspoon pepper

1 small clove garlic, finely chopped

Shake all ingredients in tightly covered container.

1 SERVING Calories 195 (Calories from Fat 70) | Fat 8g (Saturated 2g) | Cholesterol 65mg | Sodium 550mg | Carbohydrate 8g (Dietary Fiber 3g) | Protein 23g %DAILY VALUE Vitamin A 60% | Vitamin C 70% | Calcium 10% | Iron 14% EXCHANGES 1 1/2 Vegetable, 3 Lean Meat CARBOHYDRATE CHOICES 1/2

BETTY'S TIP

Try adding cut-up grilled chicken to this salad for a delicious charbroiled flavor. Or to save time, purchase cut-up grilled chicken from the refrigerated foods section of your supermarket.

Quick Garden Chicken Salad

PREP 10 min COOK 15 min SERVINGS 6

1 package (16 ounces) fusilli (corkscrew) pasta

2 cups cubed cooked chicken

1 small cucumber, chopped (1 cup)

1 medium yellow or red bell pepper, chopped (1 cup)

1 large tomato, chopped (1 cup)

3/4 cup spicy eight-vegetable juice

1/4 cup lemon juice

1/2 teaspoon freshly ground pepper

1/4 teaspoon salt

1 clove garlic, finely chopped

1. Cook pasta as directed on package; drain. Rinse with cold water; drain.
2. Mix pasta and remaining ingredients in large bowl. Serve immediately.

1 SERVING Calories 395 (Calories from Fat 45) | Fat 5g (Saturated 1g) | Cholesterol 40mg | Sodium 220mg | Carbohydrate 64g (Dietary Fiber 4g) | Protein 24g %DAILY VALUE Vitamin A 12% | Vitamin C 90% | Calcium 4% | Iron 20% EXCHANGES 4 Starch, 1 Vegetable, 1 1/2 Very Lean Meat CARBOHYDRATE CHOICES 4

BETTY'S TIP

Using fresh lemon juice will add a zip to this salad that purchased lemon juice can't beat! Keep in mind that it takes one lemon to get about 2 to 3 tablespoons of juice. To get the most juice out of a lemon, roll it back and forth on the counter several times with firm pressure.

Thai Chicken Salad

PREP 16 min **SERVINGS** 4

Honey Ginger Dressing (below left)

6 cups bite-size pieces assorted salad greens

1 1/2 cups shredded cooked chicken

1 medium carrot, shredded (3/4 cup)

1 can (14 to 15 ounces) baby corn nuggets, drained

1/3 cup flaked coconut, toasted*

1. Prepare Honey Ginger Dressing.
2. Place salad greens, chicken, carrot and corn in large bowl. Pour dressing over salad; toss until coated. Sprinkle with coconut.

Honey Ginger Dressing

1/4 cup vegetable oil

2 tablespoons balsamic or cider vinegar

2 tablespoons soy sauce

1 tablespoon honey

1 teaspoon grated gingerroot

Shake all ingredients in tightly covered container.

1 SERVING Calories 375 (Calories from Fat 190) | Fat 21g (Saturated 5g) | Cholesterol 45mg | Sodium 750mg | Carbohydrate 32g (Dietary Fiber 4g) | Protein 19g % DAILY VALUE Vitamin A 32% | Vitamin C 26% | Calcium 4% | Iron 14% EXCHANGES 1 Starch, 3 Vegetable, 1 1/2 Lean Meat, 3 Fat CARBOHYDRATE CHOICES 2

*To toast coconut, cook in ungreased heavy skillet over medium-low heat 6 to 14 minutes, stirring frequently until browning begins, then stirring constantly until golden brown. Or bake uncovered in ungreased shallow pan in 350° oven 5 to 7 minutes, stirring occasionally, until golden brown.

BETTY'S TIP

Go ahead and use packaged, assorted prewashed salad greens for this recipe to save time.

Raspberry Chicken Salad

PREP 15 min SERVINGS 4

Raspberry Dressing (below)

6 cups bite-size pieces mixed salad greens (such as Bibb, iceberg, romaine or spinach)

2 cups cut-up cooked chicken

1 cup fresh raspberries

1/3 cup thinly sliced celery

Freshly ground pepper, if desired

1. Prepare Raspberry Dressing.
2. Toss salad greens, chicken, raspberries and celery. Serve with dressing and pepper.

Raspberry Dressing

1 cup plain fat-free yogurt

1/2 cup fresh raspberries

1 tablespoon raspberry or red wine vinegar

2 teaspoons sugar

Place all ingredients into blender. Cover and blend on high speed about 15 seconds or until smooth.

1 SERVING Calories 195 (Calories from Fat 55) | Fat 6g (Saturated 2g) | Cholesterol 60mg | Sodium 135mg | Carbohydrate 15g (Dietary Fiber 5g) | Protein 25g % DAILY VALUE Vitamin A 52% | Vitamin C 44% | Calcium 18% | Iron 12% EXCHANGES 1 Vegetable, 1/2 Fruit, 2 1/2 Lean Meat CARBOHYDRATE CHOICES 1

BETTY'S TIP

Keep a bag of frozen loose-pack unsweetened raspberries in your freezer so you can make this salad when fresh raspberries aren't available.

Garden Vegetables, Chicken and Pasta Salad

PREP 15 min **CHILL** 10 min **SERVINGS** 4

- 1 bag (16 ounces) frozen garden herb vegetables with pasta
- 1 cup shredded cooked chicken
- 2 medium stalks celery, sliced (1 cup)
- 1/4 cup ranch dressing
- Freshly ground pepper, if desired

1. Cook vegetables as directed on package.
2. Stir in chicken, celery and dressing. Cover and refrigerate 10 minutes to cool. Sprinkle with pepper.

1 SERVING Calories 265 (Calories from Fat 90) | Fat 10g (Saturated 1g) | Cholesterol 35mg | Sodium 650mg | Carbohydrate 28g (Dietary Fiber 4g) | Protein 16g % DAILY VALUE Vitamin A 48% | Vitamin C 48% | Calcium 6% | Iron 10% EXCHANGES 1 Starch, 2 Vegetable, 1 1/2 Medium-Fat Meat, 1/2 Fat CARBOHYDRATE CHOICES 2

BETTY'S TIP

Want a twist on this main dish? Try using frozen creamy Cheddar vegetables with pasta, or garlic-seasoned vegetables with pasta.

Wild-Rice Chicken Salad with Raspberry Vinaigrette

PREP **10 min** CHILL **1 hr** SERVINGS **6**

3 cups cold cooked wild rice

1 1/2 cups cubed cooked chicken or turkey

4 medium green onions, chopped (1/4 cup)

1 medium green bell pepper, chopped (1 cup)

1 can (8 ounces) sliced water chestnuts, drained

1 package (6 ounces) diced dried fruits and raisins

1/3 cup raspberry vinegar

1/4 cup honey

2 tablespoons vegetable oil

1. Mix all ingredients except vinegar, honey and oil in large bowl.
2. Shake vinegar, honey and oil in tightly covered container. Pour over wild-rice mixture; toss. Cover and refrigerate 1 to 2 hours to blend flavors.

1 SERVING Calories 330 (Calories from Fat 70) | Fat 8g (Saturated 1g) | Cholesterol 30mg | Sodium 45mg | Carbohydrate 55g (Dietary Fiber 5g) | Protein 14g % DAILY VALUE Vitamin A 8% | Vitamin C 38% | Calcium 4% | Iron 12% EXCHANGES 2 Starch, 2 Vegetable, 1 Fruit, 1 Lean Meat CARBOHYDRATE CHOICES 3

BETTY'S TIP

Instead of diced dried fruits and raisins, try dried cherries or cranberries.

Chicken and Berries Salad

PREP 15 min SERVINGS 4

Fruity Yogurt Dressing (below right)

4 cups bite-size pieces mixed salad greens (iceberg, Bibb, romaine or spinach)

2 cups cut-up cooked chicken

1 cup raspberries

1/2 cup sliced strawberries

1/4 cup thinly sliced leek

1/4 cup sliced almonds, toasted

Freshly ground pepper

Photo on page 278.

1. Make Fruity Yogurt Dressing.
2. Toss salad greens, chicken, berries and leek in large bowl. Sprinkle with almonds. Serve with dressing. Sprinkle with pepper.

Fruity Yogurt Dressing

1 cup plain fat-free yogurt

1/4 cup raspberries

1/4 cup sliced strawberries

1 tablespoon raspberry or red wine vinegar

2 teaspoons sugar

Place all ingredients in blender or food processor. Cover and blend on high speed about 15 seconds or process until smooth.

1 SERVING Calories 265 (Calories from Fat 100) | Fat 11g (Saturated 2g) | Cholesterol 65mg | Sodium 140mg | Carbohydrate 16g (Dietary Fiber 5g) | Protein 26g % DAILY VALUE Vitamin A 36% | Vitamin C 60% | Calcium 18% | Iron 12% EXCHANGES 1 1/2 Vegetable, 1/2 Fruit, 3 1/2 Lean Meat CARBOHYDRATE CHOICES 1

BETTY'S TIP

If raspberries or strawberries aren't in season, use frozen unsweetened loose-pack raspberries or strawberries for the salad and dressing instead.

Turkey Tabbouleh Salad

PREP 10 min STAND 30 min CHILL 1 hr SERVINGS 4

- 3/4 cup uncooked cracked wheat or bulgur
- 1 1/2 cups chopped fresh parsley
- 1 cup cut-up cooked turkey breast
- 1 can (8 3/4 ounces) garbanzo beans, rinsed and drained
- 2 tablespoons chopped fresh mint leaves
- 3 medium tomatoes, chopped (2 1/4 cups)
- 4 medium green onions, chopped (1/4 cup)
- 1/4 cup olive or vegetable oil
- 1/4 cup lemon juice
- 1 teaspoon salt
- 1/4 teaspoon pepper

1. Cover cracked wheat with cold water. Let stand 30 minutes. Drain, pressing out as much water as possible.
2. Place cracked wheat, parsley, turkey, beans, mint, tomatoes and onions in large glass or plastic bowl. Mix remaining ingredients. Pour over wheat mixture; toss.
3. Cover and refrigerate at least 1 hour to blend flavors.

1 SERVING Calories 345 (Calories from Fat 155) | Fat 17g (Saturated 2g) | Cholesterol 25mg | Sodium 720mg | Carbohydrate 38g (Dietary Fiber 9g) | Protein 19g % DAILY VALUE Vitamin A 18% | Vitamin C 90% | Calcium 8% | Iron 24% EXCHANGES 2 1/2 Starch, 1 Very Lean Meat, 3 Fat CARBOHYDRATE CHOICES 2 1/2

BETTY'S TIP

If you'd prefer to serve this Middle Eastern salad as a side dish, just leave out the turkey. The flavors pair especially well with a grilled fish or chicken main dish.

Turkey Taco Salad

PREP 10 min COOK 12 min SERVINGS 4

1. Cook ground turkey in 10-inch nonstick skillet over medium heat, stirring occasionally, until no longer pink. (If turkey sticks to skillet, add up to 2 tablespoons water.) Stir in garlic, flour, beans, cumin, chili powder, onion salt and pepper. Cook about 5 minutes or until thickened and bubbly.
2. Divide lettuce among 4 plates. Top with turkey mixture, onion, bell pepper, tomatoes and cheese. Mix salsa and dressing; serve with salad. Top salad with sour cream.

1 SERVING Calories 410 (Calories from Fat 80) | Fat 8g (Saturated 2.5g) | Cholesterol 45mg | Sodium 1140mg | Carbohydrate 45g (Dietary Fiber 10g) | Protein 37g % DAILY VALUE Vitamin A 50% | Vitamin C 25% | Calcium 25% | Iron 25% EXCHANGES 1/2 Starch, 2 Vegetable, 3 1/2 Very Lean Meat, 1 Fat CARBOHYDRATE CHOICES 3

3/4 pound lean (99% fat free) ground turkey breast

1/4 teaspoon garlic powder

2 tablespoons all-purpose flour

1 can (15 ounces) chili beans, undrained

1 tablespoon ground cumin

1 1/2 teaspoons chili powder

1/2 teaspoon onion salt

1/8 teaspoon pepper

6 cups bite-size pieces iceberg lettuce

1 medium onion, chopped

1 medium green bell pepper, chopped

2 medium tomatoes, chopped

1/2 cup shredded reduced-fat Cheddar cheese (4 ounces)

2/3 cup salsa

1/3 cup reduced-calorie Catalina dressing

1 cup nonfat sour cream

BETTY'S TIP

To add more zip to this Mexican dish, use Monterey Jack cheese with jalapeño peppers or, as it's also known, pepper Jack cheese.

Turkey and Fruit Tossed Salad

PREP 10 min SERVINGS 6

- 1 bag (10 ounces) salad mix (about 8 cups)
- 2 1/2 cups cubed cooked turkey or chicken
- 1 package (6 ounces) diced dried fruits and raisins (about 1 1/4 cups)
- 1 medium stalk celery, sliced (1/2 cup)
- 1/2 cup fat-free sweet-spicy French dressing

Place salad mix, turkey, dried fruits and celery in large bowl. Pour dressing over mixture; toss lightly to coat.

1 SERVING Calories 210 (Calories from Fat 35) | Fat 4g (Saturated 1g) | Cholesterol 50mg | Sodium 280mg | Carbohydrate 26g (Dietary Fiber 3g) | Protein 18g % DAILY VALUE Vitamin A 36% | Vitamin C 36% | Calcium 20% | Iron 10% EXCHANGES 2 Vegetable, 1 Fruit, 2 Very Lean Meat, 1/2 Fat CARBOHYDRATE CHOICES 2

BETTY'S TIP

Although any assortment of greens will taste great in this salad, the slightly bitter tang of an Italian-style mix with romaine and radicchio is especially nice with the chicken, dried fruit and subtly sweet French dressing.

Turkey Salad with Fruit

PREP 20 min CHILL 2 hr SERVINGS 6

- 3 cups cut-up cooked turkey or chicken
- 3/4 cup seedless red grapes
- 1 can (11 ounces) mandarin orange segments, drained
- 1 can (8 ounces) sliced water chestnuts, drained
- 2 medium stalks celery, thinly sliced (1 cup)
- 2 medium green onions, thinly sliced (2 tablespoons)
- 1 container (6 ounces) peach, orange or lemon low-fat yogurt (2/3 cup)
- 2 tablespoons soy sauce
- Mixed salad greens

1. Mix turkey, grapes, orange segments, water chestnuts, celery and onions in large bowl.
2. Mix yogurt and soy sauce. Pour over turkey mixture; toss. Cover and refrigerate about 2 hours or until chilled. Serve on salad greens.

1 SERVING Calories 220 (Calories from Fat 45) | Fat 5g (Saturated 2g) | Cholesterol 55mg | Sodium 430mg | Carbohydrate 23g (Dietary Fiber 1g) | Protein 22g % DAILY VALUE Vitamin A 6% | Vitamin C 26% | Calcium 8% | Iron 10% EXCHANGES 1 Vegetable, 1 Fruit, 2 1/2 Lean Meat CARBOHYDRATE CHOICES 1 1/2

Grilled Chicken Salad with Fruit Substitute 3 cups chopped grilled chicken breast in place of the turkey.

BETTY'S TIP

When fruit is at its peak, serve this salad over wedges of fresh pineapple or in honeydew melon halves instead of on top of the greens.

Turkey and Dried Cherry Salad

PREP 20 min COOK 10 min SERVINGS 4

- 2 cups uncooked gemelli (twist) pasta (8 ounces)
- 1 1/2 cups cubed cooked turkey
- 1/2 cup dried cherries
- 1/4 cup slivered almonds, toasted
- 1 medium stalk celery, thinly sliced (1/2 cup)
- 3 or 4 medium green onions, chopped (about 1/4 cup)
- 3/4 cup refrigerated poppy seed dressing

1. Cook and drain pasta as directed on package.
2. Mix pasta and remaining ingredients except dressing in large bowl. Pour dressing over mixture; toss until coated. Serve immediately, or cover and refrigerate until serving.

1 SERVING Calories 650 (Calories from Fat 270) | Fat 30g (Saturated 5g) | Cholesterol 45mg | Sodium 60mg | Carbohydrate 70g (Dietary Fiber 4g) | Protein 24g % DAILY VALUE Vitamin A 4% | Vitamin C 14% | Calcium 6% | Iron 20% EXCHANGES 4 Starch, 1/2 Fruit, 2 Medium-Fat Meat, 3 Fat CARBOHYDRATE CHOICES 4 1/2

BETTY'S TIP

Toasting almonds is easy. Just place them in an ungreased shallow pan and bake at 350° for 6 to 10 minutes, stirring occasionally, until golden brown.

Ten-Minute Ham Salad

PREP 10 min SERVINGS 6

- 6 cups bite-size pieces salad greens
- 2 cups cubed fully cooked smoked ham
- 1/3 cup Italian dressing
- 2 tablespoons sesame seed, toasted
- 1 medium cucumber, thinly sliced
- 1 medium tomato, cut into thin wedges
- 2 green onions, thinly sliced (2 tablespoons)
- 1/2 cup shredded Monterey Jack cheese (2 ounces)

Toss all ingredients except cheese in large bowl. Toss with cheese.

1 SERVING Calories 205 (Calories from Fat 125) | Fat 14g (Saturated 4g) | Cholesterol 35mg | Sodium 860mg | Carbohydrate 5g (Dietary Fiber 3g) | Protein 15g % DAILY VALUE Vitamin A 40% | Vitamin C 26% | Calcium 12% | Iron 10% EXCHANGES 1 Vegetable, 2 Lean Meat, 1 1/2 Fat CARBOHYDRATE CHOICES 0

BETTY'S TIP

To toast sesame seed, cook in ungreased heavy skillet over medium heat about 2 minutes, stirring frequently until browning begins, then stirring constantly until golden brown.

Ham and Slaw Salad

PREP **15 min** SERVINGS **4**

- 1 pint (2 cups) deli coleslaw (creamy style)
- 2 cans (8 ounces each) tropical fruit salad, chilled and drained
- 1/2 cup golden raisins
- Lettuce leaves, if desired
- 1 1/2 cups cubed fully cooked fat-free ham

1. If coleslaw is very wet, drain off excess liquid. Mix coleslaw, fruit salad and raisins in large bowl.
2. Line salad plates with lettuce leaves. Spoon coleslaw mixture over lettuce. Make indentation in center of each mound of coleslaw mixture; fill with ham.

1 SERVING Calories 275 (Calories from Fat 115) | Fat 13g (Saturated 2g) | Cholesterol 25mg | Sodium 750mg | Carbohydrate 34g (Dietary Fiber 3g) | Protein 8g % DAILY VALUE Vitamin A 18% | Vitamin C 12% | Calcium 4% | Iron 8% EXCHANGES 1 Starch, 1 Fruit, 1 Very Lean Meat, 2 Fat CARBOHYDRATE CHOICES 2

BETTY'S TIP

This is a great salad to serve when the weather is hot and you don't want to heat up your kitchen. Pair it with slices of crusty French bread and tall glasses of lemonade or iced tea.

Asian Pork Salad

PREP 10 min COOK 5 min SERVINGS 4

- 2 tablespoons soy sauce
- 1 tablespoon chili puree with garlic
- 1 teaspoon sesame or vegetable oil
- 1/2 pound pork tenderloin, cut into 1 1/2 × 1/2-inch strips
- 3 cups coleslaw mix (8 ounces)
- 1 small red bell pepper, cut into 1/2-inch strips
- 1 can (15 ounces) black beans, rinsed and drained

1. Mix soy sauce, chili puree and oil. Mix pork and 1 tablespoon of the soy sauce mixture; reserve remaining soy sauce mixture.
2. Spray 10-inch nonstick skillet with cooking spray; heat over medium-high heat. Cook pork in skillet, stirring occasionally, until no longer pink.
3. Place pork in large bowl. Add remaining soy sauce mixture and remaining ingredients; toss.

1 SERVING Calories 240 (Calories from Fat 35) | Fat 4g (Saturated 1g) | Cholesterol 35mg | Sodium 950mg | Carbohydrate 35g (Dietary Fiber 9g) | Protein 24g % DAILY VALUE Vitamin A 2% | Vitamin C 32% | Calcium 10% | Iron 22% EXCHANGES 2 Starch, 1 Vegetable, 2 Very Lean Meat CARBOHYDRATE CHOICES 2

BETTY'S TIP

Look for packaged chopped coleslaw mix in the produce department of your supermarket. If it's unavailable, you can use 3 cups of shredded cabbage.

Antipasto Vegetable Salad

PREP **25 min** CHILL **2 hr** SERVINGS **6**

- 1/2 cup red wine vinegar
- 1/8 cup olive or vegetable oil
- 2 tablespoons lemon juice
- 1 pound broccoli, separated into flowerets (6 cups)
- 2 large bulbs fennel, cut into 1-inch pieces
- 4 ounces mozzarella cheese, cut into 1/2-inch cubes
- 1 stick (2 1/2 ounces) pepperoni, cut into 1/2-inch cubes
- 2 jars (6 ounces each) marinated artichoke hearts, drained
- 1 jar (12 ounces) marinated mushrooms, drained
- 6 ounces whole Kalamata olives, pitted and cut in half
- Freshly ground pepper

1. Mix vinegar, oil and lemon juice in large glass or plastic bowl. Add remaining ingredients, except pepper; toss.
2. Cover and refrigerate about 2 hours or until chilled. Toss before serving. Sprinkle with pepper.

1 SERVING Calories 365 (Calories from Fat 155) | Fat 17g (Saturated 5g) | Cholesterol 20mg | Sodium 1000mg | Carbohydrate 21g (Dietary Fiber 8g) | Protein 14g % DAILY VALUE Vitamin A 28% | Vitamin C 100% | Calcium 24% | Iron 16% EXCHANGES 4 Vegetable, 1 High-Fat Meat, 1 1/2 Fat CARBOHYDRATE CHOICES 1 1/2

BETTY'S TIP

Look for prewashed and cut-up broccoli flowerets at the salad bar or in plastic bags in the produce section of the supermarket.

Italian Tortellini Salad

PREP **20 min** COOK **5 min** SERVINGS **4**

1 package (9 ounces) refrigerated cheese-filled tortellini

3/4 cup garlic-and-onion-flavored marinara sauce (from 28-ounce jar)

1/4 cup Italian dressing

1 cup broccoli flowerets

1/2 cup matchstick-cut carrots (from 10-ounce bag)

1 medium red or green bell pepper, chopped (1 cup)

1 package (3.5 ounces) sliced pepperoni, cut in half

1. Cook tortellini as directed on package; drain. Rinse with cold water; drain.
2. Mix marinara sauce and dressing in large bowl. Add tortellini and remaining ingredients; toss to mix.

1 SERVING Calories 365 (Calories from Fat 215) | Fat 24g (Saturated 7g) | Cholesterol 75mg | Sodium 920mg | Carbohydrate 26g (Dietary Fiber 3g) | Protein 12g % DAILY VALUE Vitamin A 100% | Vitamin C 100% | Calcium 8% | Iron 10% EXCHANGES 1 Starch, 2 Vegetable, 1 High-Fat Meat, 3 1/2 Fat CARBOHYDRATE CHOICES 2

BETTY'S TIP

For a heartier salad, add one can of kidney or other beans, rinsed and drained, and cubes of mozzarella or mild Cheddar cheese.

Spinach-Shrimp Salad with Hot Bacon Dressing

PREP 10 min COOK 10 min SERVINGS 4

- 4 slices bacon, cut into 1-inch pieces
- 1/4 cup white vinegar
- 1 tablespoon sugar
- 1/4 teaspoon ground mustard
- 4 cups lightly packed bite-size pieces spinach leaves
- 1 cup sliced mushrooms (3 ounces)
- 1 cup crumbled feta cheese (4 ounces)
- 1/2 pound cooked peeled deveined medium shrimp, thawed if frozen and tails peeled

1. Cook bacon in 10-inch skillet over medium-high heat, stirring occasionally, until crisp. Stir in vinegar, sugar and mustard; continue stirring until sugar is dissolved.
2. Toss spinach, mushrooms, cheese and shrimp in large bowl. Drizzle hot bacon dressing over spinach mixture; toss. Serve immediately.

1 SERVING Calories 210 (Calories from Fat 100) | Fat 11g (Saturated 6g) | Cholesterol 140mg | Sodium 570mg | Carbohydrate 7g (Dietary Fiber 1g) | Protein 20g % DAILY VALUE Vitamin A 62% | Vitamin C 16% | Calcium 18% | Iron 16% EXCHANGES 1 Vegetable, 2 1/2 Medium-Fat Meat CARBOHYDRATE CHOICES 1/2

BETTY'S TIP

Instead of plain feta, try using crumbled feta flavored with sun-dried tomatoes or basil-and-tomato in this easy-to-fix salad recipe.

Caribbean Shrimp Salad

PREP 20 min SERVINGS 4

Honey-Lime Dressing (below left)

1 bag (5 ounces) spring greens salad blend

1 pound cooked peeled deveined medium shrimp, thawed if frozen and tails peeled

1 small red onion, thinly sliced

1 can (15 1/4 ounces) pineapple shapes, drained

1 cup snow (Chinese) pea pods, strings removed

1. Make Honey-Lime Dressing.
2. Mix remaining ingredients in large bowl. Add dressing; toss until coated.

Honey-Lime Dressing

3 tablespoons honey

1 teaspoon grated lime peel

2 tablespoons lime juice

1 tablespoon vegetable oil

1 to 2 teaspoons finely chopped jalapeño chili

1/4 teaspoon salt

Mix all ingredients.

1 SERVING Calories 285 (Calories from Fat 45) | Fat 5g (Saturated 1g) | Cholesterol 220mg | Sodium 410mg | Carbohydrate 34g (Dietary Fiber 2g) | Protein 26g % DAILY VALUE Vitamin A 30% | Vitamin C 48% | Calcium 8% | Iron 26% EXCHANGES 1 Starch, 1 Vegetable, 3 Very Lean Meat CARBOHYDRATE CHOICES 2

BETTY'S TIP

Pineapple shapes are a relatively new product and can be found with the canned fruit. The little shapes included in the can are stars, circles and half-moons. If you'd prefer, you can substitute pineapple tidbits instead.

Three-Bean and Tuna Salad

PREP 20 min SERVINGS 4

Lemon Vinaigrette (below right)

1 can (15 to 16 ounces) cannellini beans, rinsed and drained

1 can (15 to 16 ounces) kidney beans, rinsed and drained

1 can (15 to 16 ounces) cut green beans, rinsed and drained

1 large bell pepper, chopped (1 1/2 cups)

1 medium onion, chopped (1/2 cup)

1/4 cup chopped fresh parsley

Lettuce leaves

1 can (6 ounces) tuna in water, drained

Lemon wedges, if desired

1. Make Lemon Vinaigrette.
2. Mix beans, bell pepper, onion and parsley in large bowl. Pour vinaigrette over bean mixture; toss.
3. Line salad plates with lettuce leaves. Spoon bean mixture over lettuce. Top with tuna. Serve with lemon wedges.

Lemon Vinaigrette

1/4 cup olive or vegetable oil

2 tablespoons lemon juice

1/4 teaspoon red pepper sauce

Shake all ingredients in tightly covered container.

1 SERVING Calories 365 (Calories from Fat 135) | Fat 15g (Saturated 3g) | Cholesterol 10mg | Sodium 790mg | Carbohydrate 45g (Dietary Fiber 12g) | Protein 25g % DAILY VALUE Vitamin A 10% | Vitamin C 88% | Calcium 10% | Iron 32% EXCHANGES 2 1/2 Starch, 2 Vegetable, 2 Lean Meat CARBOHYDRATE CHOICES 3

Three-Bean and Caper Salad Omit the tuna and add 1/4 cup drained capers.

BETTY'S TIP

For a super shortcut, use 1/3 cup Italian dressing in place of the Lemon Vinaigrette.

Italian Tuna Toss

PREP 15 min **SERVINGS** 6 to 8

- 1 bag (10 ounces) salad mix (about 8 cups)
- 1 bag (16 ounces) fresh cauliflowerets
- 1 medium cucumber, sliced (1 1/2 cups)
- 2 cans (6 ounces each) tuna in water, drained
- 1 jar (2 ounces) sliced pimientos, drained (1/4 cup)
- 1/3 cup Italian dressing
- 1/4 cup bacon-flavor bits or chips

Toss all ingredients except dressing and bacon bits in large bowl. Add dressing and bacon bits; toss.

1 SERVING Calories 175 (Calories from Fat 65) | Fat 7g (Saturated 1g) | Cholesterol 20mg | Sodium 400mg | Carbohydrate 9g (Dietary Fiber 4g) | Protein 19g % DAILY VALUE Vitamin A 36% | Vitamin C 88% | Calcium 6% | Iron 12% EXCHANGES 2 Vegetable, 2 Very Lean Meat, 1 Fat CARBOHYDRATE CHOICES 1/2

Italian Salami Toss Substitute 1/4 pound diced salami (about 3/4 cup) for the tuna.

BETTY'S TIP

You can also separate a small head of cauliflower into flowerets instead of using the bag of flowerets. One small head will yield about 3 cups. Instead of the bag of greens, you can use a small bunch of curly endive or romaine, torn into bite-size pieces.

Chopped Vegetable and Crabmeat Salad

PREP 20 min SERVINGS 4

Lime Dressing (below left)

2 cups chopped escarole

2 cans (6 ounces each) crabmeat, drained and flaked, or 2 cups chopped cooked turkey or chicken

1 small jicama, peeled and chopped (1 cup)

1 large papaya, peeled, seeded and chopped (1 cup)

1 medium yellow or red bell pepper, chopped (1 cup)

1/2 cup dry-roasted peanuts

1/4 cup chopped fresh cilantro

1. Make Lime Dressing.
2. Place remaining ingredients except peanuts and cilantro in large bowl. Pour dressing over salad; toss. Top with peanuts and cilantro.

Lime Dressing

1/3 cup frozen (thawed) limeade concentrate

1/4 cup vegetable oil

1 tablespoon rice or white vinegar

1 teaspoon grated gingerroot

1/4 teaspoon salt

Shake all ingredients in tightly covered container.

1 SERVING Calories 430 (Calories from Fat 215) | Fat 24g (Saturated 4g) | Cholesterol 75mg | Sodium 590mg | Carbohydrate 37g (Dietary Fiber 9g) | Protein 25g % DAILY VALUE Vitamin A 38% | Vitamin C 100% | Calcium 14% | Iron 12% EXCHANGES 1 Vegetable, 2 Fruit, 3 High-Fat Meat CARBOHYDRATE CHOICES 2 1/2

BETTY'S TIP

To get a head start on dinner, chop the papaya and bell pepper, wrap separately and refrigerate. You can also make the dressing a day ahead and refrigerate it.

Summer Salmon Salad

PREP 30 min SERVINGS 4

Toasted Sesame Dressing (below right)

1 small zucchini, thinly sliced

1 small yellow summer squash, thinly sliced (1 1/2 cups)

4 roma (plum) tomatoes, thinly sliced

1 small onion, sliced and separated into rings

1 cup sliced mushrooms (3 ounces)

Lettuce leaves

1 can (14 3/4 ounces) salmon, chilled, drained and flaked

1. Make Toasted Sesame Dressing.
2. Toss zucchini, summer squash, tomatoes, onion and mushrooms.
3. Line salad plates with lettuce leaves. Spoon vegetable mixture onto lettuce leaves. Place salmon on center of vegetable mixture. Spoon dressing over salads.

Toasted Sesame Dressing

1 tablespoon sesame seed

1/8 cup white wine vinegar

1 tablespoon sugar

2 tablespoons olive or vegetable oil

1 teaspoon ground mustard

1/2 teaspoon salt

1 large clove garlic, finely chopped

To toast sesame seed, cook in ungreased heavy skillet over medium heat about 2 minutes, stirring frequently until browning begins, then stirring constantly until golden brown; cool. Shake sesame seed and remaining ingredients in tightly covered container.

1 SERVING Calories 270 (Calories from Fat 135) | Fat 15g (Saturated 3g) | Cholesterol 60mg | Sodium 880mg | Carbohydrate 11g (Dietary Fiber 2g) | Protein 23g % DAILY VALUE Vitamin A 16% | Vitamin C 32% | Calcium 24% | Iron 10% EXCHANGES 2 Vegetable, 3 Lean Meat, 1 Fat CARBOHYDRATE CHOICES 1

Summer Salmon-Pasta Salad Add 2 cups cooked farfalle (bow-tie) pasta and double the dressing. Toss with the vegetable mixture and salmon before spooning onto lettuce.

BETTY'S TIP

If you have sesame seed oil in your pantry, use it in place of the olive oil and omit the sesame seed.

Caesar Salad with Lobster

PREP **10 min** SERVINGS **4**

1 bag (10 ounces) salad mix (about 8 cups)

1 can (11 ounces) mandarin orange segments, chilled and drained

1 package (8 ounces) refrigerated imitation lobster chunks

1 small unpeeled cucumber, cut into 1/4-inch slices

1/3 cup fat-free Caesar or ranch dressing

Sliced almonds, if desired

Place all ingredients except almonds in large bowl; toss lightly to coat. Sprinkle with almonds.

1 SERVING Calories 120 (Calories from Fat 10) | Fat 1g (Saturated 0g) | Cholesterol 40mg | Sodium 480mg | Carbohydrate 17g (Dietary Fiber 2g) | Protein 13g % DAILY VALUE Vitamin A 4% | Vitamin C 18% | Calcium 6% | Iron 6% EXCHANGES 2 Vegetable, 1/2 Fruit, 1 Very Lean Meat CARBOHYDRATE CHOICES 1

Caesar Salad with Crabmeat Substitute imitation crabmeat chunks in place of the lobster chunks.

BETTY'S TIP

For an extra-special touch, use the tines of a fork to create stripes down the side of an unwaxed cucumber before you cut it into slices.

Tuscan Panzanella Salad

PREP **15 min** SERVINGS **6**

- 1 bag (10 ounces) romaine and leaf lettuce mix
- 1 can (19 ounces) cannellini beans, rinsed and drained
- 2 cups large croutons
- 1 cup sweet grape tomatoes
- 1/2 cup thinly sliced red onion
- 1/3 cup Kalamata olives, cut in half
- 1/3 cup balsamic vinaigrette

Mix all ingredients except vinaigrette in large bowl. Add vinaigrette; toss until coated.

1 SERVING Calories 250 (Calories from Fat 80) | Fat 9g (Saturated 1g) | Cholesterol 5mg | Sodium 360mg | Carbohydrate 36g (Dietary Fiber 8g) | Protein 12g % DAILY VALUE Vitamin A 26% | Vitamin C 30% | Calcium 14% | Iron 26% EXCHANGES 2 Starch, 1 Vegetable, 1/2 High-Fat Meat, 1/2 Fat CARBOHYDRATE CHOICES 2 1/2

BETTY'S TIP

Sweet grape tomatoes are small and very sweet. If they're not available, you can use cherry tomatoes instead and just cut them in half. Or try yellow pear tomatoes if they are available at your market.

Spring Vegetable Paella

PREP **15 min** COOK **15 min** SERVINGS **6**

1 pound asparagus, cut into 2-inch pieces

3 cups broccoli flowerets

2 teaspoons olive or vegetable oil

1 medium red bell pepper, chopped (1 cup)

2 small zucchini, chopped (1 1/4 cups)

1 medium onion, chopped (1/2 cup)

3/4 teaspoon salt

1/2 teaspoon saffron threads

4 cups cooked brown or white rice, cold

2 large tomatoes, seeded and chopped (2 cups)

2 cans (15 to 16 ounces each) garbanzo beans, rinsed and drained

1 package (10 ounces) frozen green peas, thawed and drained

1. Heat 1 inch water to boiling in 2-quart saucepan. Add asparagus and broccoli. Heat to boiling; boil about 4 minutes or until crisp-tender; drain.
2. Heat oil in 10-inch skillet over medium-high heat. Cook asparagus, broccoli, bell pepper, zucchini, onion, salt and saffron in oil about 5 minutes, stirring occasionally, until onion is crisp-tender.
3. Stir in remaining ingredients. Serve on platter or individual serving plates lined with lettuce.

1 SERVING Calories 425 (Calories from Fat 65) | Fat 7g (Saturated 1g) | Cholesterol 0mg | Sodium 560mg | Carbohydrate 86g (Dietary Fiber 19g) | Protein 22g % DAILY VALUE Vitamin A 60% | Vitamin C 100% | Calcium 14% | Iron 36% EXCHANGES 5 Starch, 2 Vegetable CARBOHYDRATE CHOICES 6

Spring Vegetable and Chicken Paella Omit 1 can of garbanzo beans. Add 1 1/2 cups chopped cooked chicken or turkey with remaining ingredients in step 3. Continue as directed.

BETTY'S TIP

Saffron, the dried stigmas of crocus, is a fragrant spice that gives food a pretty yellow color. Because it is expensive, you may prefer to use 1/4 teaspoon ground turmeric as an affordable substitute.

Fruited Taco Salad

PREP 15 min SERVINGS 4

- Lime Cumin Vinaigrette (below left)
- 6 cups bite-size pieces salad greens
- 2 cups coarsely shredded cooked chicken
- 1/2 cup julienne strips peeled jicama
- 1 medium mango, seeded and cut up
- 1 cup raspberries
- Lime wedges, if desired
- Tortilla chips, if desired

1. Prepare Lime Cumin Vinaigrette.
2. Toss salad greens, chicken, jicama, mango, raspberries and vinaigrette. Just before serving, lightly squeeze juice from lime wedges over salad. Serve with tortilla chips.

Lime Cumin Vinaigrette

- 1/4 cup olive or vegetable oil
- 3 tablespoons lime juice
- 1 tablespoon honey
- 1 1/2 tablespoons chopped fresh cilantro
- 3/4 teaspoon ground cumin
- 1/4 teaspoon salt
- 1/8 teaspoon pepper
- 1 to 2 cloves garlic, finely chopped

Shake all ingredients in tightly covered container.

1 SERVING Calories 390 (Calories from Fat 215) | Fat 24g (Saturated 4g) | Cholesterol 60mg | Sodium 240mg | Carbohydrate 28g (Dietary Fiber 5g) | Protein 21g % DAILY VALUE Vitamin A 30% | Vitamin C 100% | Calcium 6% | Iron 12% EXCHANGES 2 Fruit, 3 Medium-Fat Meat, 1 Fat CARBOHYDRATE CHOICES 1 1/2

BETTY'S TIP

Jicama is a large root vegetable with a thin brown skin and a crisp white flesh. This sweet, nutty vegetable is delicious raw or cooked. Be sure to peel the skin before using.

Greek Orzo Salad

PREP 20 min SERVINGS 4

- 4 cups cooked rosamarina (orzo) pasta
- 1 cup shredded cooked chicken
- 2 medium cucumbers, chopped (1 1/2 cups)
- 1 medium red or green bell pepper, chopped (1 cup)
- 1/3 cup balsamic vinaigrette
- 1/2 cup pitted Kalamata or Greek olives
- 1/4 cup crumbled feta cheese

Place pasta, chicken, cucumbers and bell pepper in large bowl. Pour vinaigrette over salad; toss until coated. Top with olives and cheese.

1 SERVING Calories 305 (Calories from Fat 65) | Fat 7g (Saturated 2g) | Cholesterol 40mg | Sodium 280mg | Carbohydrate 46g (Dietary Fiber 4g) | Protein 19g % DAILY VALUE Vitamin A 20% | Vitamin C 100% | Calcium 8% | Iron 18% EXCHANGES 2 Starch, 1 Lean Meat, 3 Vegetable, 1 Fat CARBOHYDRATE CHOICES 3

BETTY'S TIP

Feta cheese is bursting with sharp, tangy, salty flavor. This crumbly cheese is traditionally made from goat's or sheep's milk, but due to its popularity is often made with cow's milk. Crumbled blue cheese, in place of the feta, is also good on this salad.

Warm Tuscan Bean Salad

PREP 15 min **COOK** 12 min **SERVINGS** 15 min

1. Heat oil in 12-inch skillet over medium heat. Cook carrots and onion in oil 5 to 7 minutes, stirring occasionally, until vegetables are crisp-tender.
2. Stir in beans, 1/2 cup reserved liquid, the oregano and pepper. Cook 5 minutes, stirring occasionally.
3. Line large platter with spinach. Top with bean mixture. Pour vinaigrette over salad. Sprinkle with bacon bits.

1 SERVING Calories 385 (Calories from Fat 100) | Fat 11g (Saturated 2g) | Cholesterol 5mg | Sodium 230mg | Carbohydrate 63g (Dietary Fiber 16g) | Protein 24g % DAILY VALUE Vitamin A 72% | Vitamin C 22% | Calcium 24% | Iron 50% EXCHANGES 3 Starch, 3 Vegetable, 1 Medium-Fat Meat, 1 Fat CARBOHYDRATE CHOICES 3

1 tablespoon olive or vegetable oil

2 medium carrots, sliced (1 cup)

1 medium onion, chopped (1/2 cup)

2 cans (15 to 16 ounces each) cannellini beans, drained and 1/2 cup liquid reserved

1 1/2 teaspoons chopped fresh or 1/2 teaspoon dried oregano leaves

1/4 teaspoon pepper

4 cups bite-size pieces spinach leaves

1/4 cup red wine vinaigrette or Italian dressing

2 tablespoons bacon flavor bits

BETTY'S TIP

If you want to make Tuscan Bean and Chicken Salad, omit 1 can of cannellini beans and add 1 1/2 cups cubed cooked chicken or turkey with the beans in step 2.

One-Dish Grilling

Skewered Steak Dinner 334

Beef and Corn Kabobs 335

Vidalia-Topped Caesar Burgers 337

Minted-Smoked Lamb Chops 338

Spicy Southwest Chicken Kabobs 339

Cheddar-Stuffed Chicken Breasts 341

Paella on the Grill 342

Lemon Chicken with Fennel and Onions 343

Pesto Chicken Packets 345

Grilled Teriyaki Burgers 346

Blue Cheese Turkey Burgers 347

Grilled Texas Turkey Burgers 349

Tex-Mex Chicken Enchilada Packets 350

Honey-Cumin Barbecue Pork Packets 351

Grilled Kielbasa and Cabbage 352

Lemon and Herb Salmon Packets 353

Fisherman's Grilled Packet 354

Pineapple-Lime Shrimp Kabobs 355

Shrimp Kabobs 356

Pesto-Artichoke Pizza 357

Grilled Portabella and Bell-Pepper Sandwiches 359

Skewered Steak Dinner

PREP 15 min MARINATE 30 min COOK 15 min
GRILL 15 min SERVINGS 6

- 1 1/2 pounds beef boneless sirloin, cut into strips
- 1/2 cup fat-free Italian dressing
- 6 new potatoes (1/2 pound)
- 1 medium onion, cut into 6 wedges
- 6 small whole mushrooms
- 6 mini red bell peppers
- 6 mini pattypan squash

1. Mix beef and dressing in shallow glass or plastic dish. Cover and refrigerate, stirring occasionally, at least 30 minutes but no longer than 24 hours.
2. Heat 1 inch water to boiling in 1 1/2-quart saucepan. Add potatoes. Boil about 15 minutes or until almost tender; drain. Cool slightly.
3. Heat coals or gas grill for direct heat. Remove beef from marinade; reserve marinade. Thread beef, potatoes, onion, mushrooms, bell peppers and squash alternately on each of six 15-inch metal skewers, leaving about 1/4-inch space between each piece. Brush kabobs generously with marinade.
4. Cover and grill kabobs 4 to 6 inches from medium heat 12 to 15 minutes for medium beef doneness, turning frequently and brushing with marinade. Discard any remaining marinade.

1 SERVING Calories 185 (Calories from Fat 35) | Fat 4g (Saturated 1g) | Cholesterol 60mg | Sodium 230mg | Carbohydrate 13g (Dietary Fiber 2g) | Protein 24g % DAILY VALUE Vitamin A 18% | Vitamin C 32% | Calcium 2% | Iron 16% EXCHANGES 1/2 Starch, 1 Vegetable, 3 Very Lean Meat, 1/2 Fat CARBOHYDRATE CHOICES 1

BETTY'S TIP

The new mini red bell peppers and pattypan squash are fun and easy to use for kabobs. If they are unavailable, use 1 medium bell pepper and 1 medium yellow summer squash, each cut into 1-inch pieces.

Beef and Corn Kabobs

PREP **20 min** MARINATE **4 hr** GRILL **20 min** SERVINGS **6**

1/3 cup vegetable oil

1/4 cup red wine vinegar

1 tablespoon chopped fresh or 1 teaspoon dried thyme leaves

1/2 teaspoon ground red pepper (cayenne)

1 clove garlic, finely chopped

1 1/2 pounds beef boneless top round steak, cut into 1-inch cubes

4 small ears corn, husks removed

2 green or red bell peppers, cut into 1 1/2-inch pieces

1. Mix oil, vinegar, thyme, red pepper and garlic in medium nonmetal bowl or resealable plastic food-storage bag. Add beef; stir to coat with marinade. Cover dish or seal bag and refrigerate, stirring beef occasionally, at least 4 hours but no longer than 24 hours.
2. Heat coals or gas grill for direct heat. Cut each ear of corn into 3 pieces. Remove beef from marinade; reserve marinade. Thread beef, corn and bell peppers alternately on each of six 10- to 12-inch metal skewers, leaving about 1/4-inch space between each piece. Brush kabobs with marinade.
3. Cover and grill kabobs 4 to 5 inches from medium heat 15 to 20 minutes for medium beef doneness, turning frequently and brushing with marinade. Discard any remaining marinade.

1 SERVING Calories 280 (Calories from Fat 115) | Fat 13g (Saturated 3g) | Cholesterol 60mg | Sodium 55mg | Carbohydrate 18g (Dietary Fiber 2g) | Protein 25g % DAILY VALUE Vitamin A 6% | Vitamin C 30% | Calcium 2% | Iron 14% EXCHANGES 1 Starch, 1 Vegetable, 2 1/2 Medium-Fat Meat CARBOHYDRATE CHOICES 1

BETTY'S TIP

It's important to marinate food in a nonmetal dish. Acid-based marinades, such as those with lemon juice and vinegar, can react with some metals and give foods an off-flavor.

Vidalia-Topped Caesar Burgers

PREP 15 min GRILL 15 min SERVINGS 4

- 1 pound ground beef
- 2 tablespoons chopped fresh parsley
- 1/2 cup Caesar dressing
- 1/2 teaspoon peppered seasoned salt
- 1 small Vidalia onion, cut into 1/4- to 1/2-inch slices
- 1 1/2 cups shredded romaine
- 2 tablespoons freshly shredded Parmesan cheese
- 4 sandwich buns, split

1. Heat coals or gas grill for direct heat. Mix beef, parsley, 2 tablespoons of the dressing and the peppered seasoned salt. Shape mixture into 4 patties, about 1/2 inch thick.
2. Cover and grill patties 4 to 6 inches from medium heat 12 to 15 minutes, turning once, until patties are no longer pink in center and juice of beef is clear. Add onion slices to grill for last 8 to 10 minutes of grilling, brushing with 2 tablespoons of the dressing and turning once, until crisp-tender.
3. Toss romaine, remaining 1/4 cup dressing and the cheese. Layer romaine, burger and onion in each bun.

1 SERVING Calories 480 (Calories from Fat 260) | Fat 29g (Saturated 9g) | Cholesterol 70mg | Sodium 920mg | Carbohydrate 27g (Dietary Fiber 2g) | Protein 27g % DAILY VALUE Vitamin A 12% | Vitamin C 14% | Calcium 12% | Iron 20% EXCHANGES 1 1/2 Starch, 1 Vegetable, 3 High-Fat Meat, 1 Fat CARBOHYDRATE CHOICES 2

BETTY'S TIP

How do you make a perfect burger? Dampen your hands with water before forming patties so the meat won't stick to your hands. Avoid overmixing the ground beef mixture, or the cooked burgers will be dense and heavy. For the most flavor, don't press down on the hamburger patties with a spatula while they're grilling—you'll squeeze out the flavorful juices!

Mint-Smoked Lamb Chops

PREP 10 min GRILL 12 min SERVINGS 4

2 tablespoons dry white wine or chicken broth

2 tablespoons honey

1 tablespoon butter or margarine, melted

1 teaspoon chopped fresh mint leaves

1/4 teaspoon salt

1/8 teaspoon pepper

1 cup whole fresh mint leaves

8 lamb rib or loin chops, about 1 inch thick (about 2 pounds)

Photo on page 332.

1. Brush grill rack with vegetable oil. Heat coals or gas grill for direct heat.
2. Mix all ingredients except 1 cup mint and the lamb.
3. Sprinkle 1 cup mint over hot coals or lava rock. Immediately cover and grill lamb 4 to 5 inches from hot heat 6 minutes. Brush with wine mixture. Turn lamb; brush with wine mixture. Cover and grill about 6 minutes longer for medium doneness. Discard any remaining wine mixture.

1 SERVING Calories 390 (Calories from Fat 200) | Fat 22g (Saturated 9g) | Cholesterol 140mg | Sodium 260mg | Carbohydrate 6g (Dietary Fiber 0g) | Protein 41g % DAILY VALUE Vitamin A 2% | Vitamin C 0% | Calcium 2% | Iron 16% EXCHANGES 1/2 Fruit, 6 Lean Meat, 1 Fat CARBOHYDRATE CHOICES 1/2

BETTY'S TIP

Couscous goes wonderfully with lamb, with sliced cucumbers on the side. If you have extra fresh mint, sprinkle it over the cucumbers too.

Spicy Southwest Chicken Kabobs

PREP 10 min GRILL 20 min SERVINGS 6

1. Heat coals or gas grill for direct heat. Mix garlic pepper and oil. Cut each ear of corn into 3 pieces. Thread chicken, corn and bell peppers alternately on each of six 10- to 12-inch metal skewers, leaving 1/4-inch space between each piece. Brush kabobs with oil mixture.
2. Cover and grill kabobs 4 to 5 inches from medium heat 15 to 20 minutes, turning 2 or 3 times, until chicken is no longer pink in center.
3. Mix dressing and chili. Serve with kabobs.

1 SERVING Calories 390 (Calories from Fat 205) | Fat 23g (Saturated 3g) | Cholesterol 80mg | Sodium 430mg | Carbohydrate 19g (Dietary Fiber 2g) | Protein 28g % DAILY VALUE Vitamin A 6% | Vitamin C 64% | Calcium 6% | Iron 8% EXCHANGES 1 Starch, 1 Vegetable, 3 Lean Meat, 2 1/2 Fat CARBOHYDRATE CHOICES 1

1 tablespoon garlic pepper

2 tablespoons olive or vegetable oil

4 small ears corn, husks removed

1 1/2 pounds boneless, skinless chicken breasts, cut into 1-inch cubes

2 medium yellow or red bell peppers, cut into 1 1/2-inch pieces

3/4 cup ranch dressing

1 canned chipotle chili in adobo sauce, chopped

BETTY'S TIP

For quick and easy grilling, cut the chicken and vegetables the night before. Store in plastic food-storage bags in the refrigerator.

Cheddar-Stuffed Chicken Breasts

PREP 15 min GRILL 15 min SERVINGS 4

- 4 boneless, skinless chicken breast halves (about 1 1/4 pounds)
- 1/4 teaspoon salt
- 1/4 teaspoon pepper
- 3 ounces Cheddar cheese
- 1 tablespoon butter or margarine, melted
- 1/4 cup salsa

1. Heat coals or gas grill for direct heat. Flatten each chicken breast half to 1/4-inch thickness between sheets of plastic wrap or waxed paper. Sprinkle with salt and pepper.
2. Cut cheese into 4 slices, about 3 × 1 × 1/4 inch. Place 1 slice cheese on center of each chicken piece. Roll chicken around cheese, folding in sides. Brush rolls with butter.
3. Cover and grill chicken rolls, seam sides down, 4 to 5 inches from medium heat about 15 minutes, turning after 10 minutes, until juice of chicken is no longer pink in center. Serve with salsa.

1 SERVING Calories 250 (Calories from Fat 115) | Fat 13g (Saturated 7g) | Cholesterol 100mg | Sodium 400mg | Carbohydrate 1g (Dietary Fiber 0g) | Protein 32g % DAILY VALUE Vitamin A 8% | Vitamin C 2% | Calcium 12% | Iron 6% EXCHANGES 4 1/2 Lean Meat CARBOHYDRATE CHOICES 0

BETTY'S TIP

Enjoy these chicken rolls with deli coleslaw and hot cooked rice tossed with black beans.

Paella on the Grill

PREP **20 min** MARINATE **1 hr** GRILL **25 min** SERVINGS **6**

Saffron Marinade (below right)

1 pound boneless, skinless chicken breasts, cut into 1-inch pieces

1 pound uncooked medium shrimp in shells, thawed if frozen

1/2 pound chorizo sausage, cut into 1-inch pieces

8 roma (plum) tomatoes, cut into fourths

1 can (about 14 ounces) artichoke hearts, drained and cut in half

1 cup pitted Kalamata or Greek olives

Hot cooked rice, if desired

1. Make Saffron Marinade. Place remaining ingredients except rice in glass or plastic dish or resealable plastic food-storage bag. Pour marinade over mixture; stir to coat. Cover dish or seal bag and refrigerate 1 hour.
2. Heat coals or gas grill for direct heat. Remove chicken mixture from marinade; reserve marinade. Place chicken mixture in grill basket (grill "wok").
3. Cover and grill chicken mixture 4 inches from medium heat 20 to 25 minutes, stirring and brushing with marinade occasionally, until chicken is no longer pink in center. Discard any remaining marinade. Serve chicken mixture with rice.

Saffron Marinade

1 cup chicken broth

1/2 cup sherry wine vinegar

1/2 teaspoon salt

1/4 teaspoon curry powder

1/4 teaspoon crushed saffron threads or ground turmeric

2 cloves garlic, finely chopped

Mix all ingredients.

1 SERVING Calories 365 (Calories from Fat 180) | Fat 20g (Saturated 7g) | Cholesterol 150mg | Sodium 1280mg | Carbohydrate 14g (Dietary Fiber 5g) | Protein 37g % DAILY VALUE Vitamin A 26% | Vitamin C 18% | Calcium 8% | Iron 24% EXCHANGES 3 Vegetable, 4 1/2 Lean Meat, 1 Fat CARBOHYDRATE CHOICES 1

BETTY'S TIP

Chorizo sausage is a highly seasoned, coarsely ground pork sausage. If it is not available, use any smoked sausage.

Lemon Chicken with Fennel and Onions

PREP 20 min MARINATE 15 min GRILL 20 min SERVINGS 6

- 6 bone-in chicken breast halves (about 3 pounds)
- 1/3 cup olive or vegetable oil
- 1 teaspoon grated lemon peel
- 1/4 cup lemon juice
- 2 tablespoons chopped fresh or 2 teaspoons dried oregano leaves
- 1/2 teaspoon salt
- 2 medium bulbs fennel, cut into 1/2-inch slices
- 1 medium red onion, cut into 1/2-inch slices

1. Place chicken in shallow glass or plastic dish. Mix oil, lemon peel, lemon juice, oregano and salt; pour over chicken. Cover and let stand 15 minutes.
2. Heat coals or gas grill for direct heat. Remove chicken from marinade. Brush fennel and onion with marinade. Cover and grill chicken (skin sides down), fennel and onion 4 to 5 inches from medium heat 15 to 20 minutes, turning once and brushing frequently with marinade, until juice of chicken is no longer pink when centers of thickest pieces are cut. Discard any remaining marinade.

1 SERVING Calories 265 (Calories from Fat 135) | Fat 15g (Saturated 3g) | Cholesterol 75mg | Sodium 210mg | Carbohydrate 8g (Dietary Fiber 3g) | Protein 28g % DAILY VALUE Vitamin A 4% | Vitamin C 10% | Calcium 6% | Iron 8% EXCHANGES 1 Vegetable, 4 Lean Meat, 1 Fat CARBOHYDRATE CHOICES 1/2

BETTY'S TIP

For an easy summer meal, serve this lemony chicken with fresh tomato slices and angel hair pasta.

Pesto Chicken Packets

PREP 15 min GRILL 25 min SERVINGS 4

4 boneless, skinless chicken breast halves (about 1 1/4 pounds)

8 roma (plum) tomatoes, cut into 1/2 inch slices

4 small zucchini, cut into 1/2-inch slices

1/2 cup basil pesto

1. Heat coals or gas grill for direct heat. Cut four 18 × 12-inch sheets of heavy-duty aluminum foil. Place 1 chicken breast half, 2 sliced tomatoes and 1 sliced zucchini on one side of each foil sheet. Top each 2 tablespoons pesto.
2. Fold foil over chicken and vegetables so edges meet. Seal edges, making tight 1/2-inch fold; fold again. Allow space on sides for circulation and expansion.
3. Cover and grill packets 4 to 5 inches from medium heat 20 to 25 minutes or until juice of chicken is no longer pink when centers of thickest pieces are cut. Place packets on plates. Cut large X across top of each packet; fold back foil.

1 SERVING Calories 330 (Calories from Fat 180) | Fat 20g (Saturated 4g) | Cholesterol 75mg | Sodium 350mg | Carbohydrate 10g (Dietary Fiber 3g) | Protein 31g % DAILY VALUE Vitamin A 36% | Vitamin C 26% | Calcium 16% | Iron 14% EXCHANGES 2 Vegetable, 4 Very Lean Meat, 3 Fat CARBOHYDRATE CHOICES 1/2

BETTY'S TIP

Instead of using foil packets, try the new heavy-duty foil bags made especially for grilling.

Grilled Teriyaki Burgers

PREP 10 min COOL 15 min SERVINGS 4

- 1 pound ground beef
- 2 tablespoons soy sauce
- 1/4 teaspoon crushed gingerroot or 1/8 teaspoon ground ginger
- 1 clove garlic, crushed

1. Shape ground beef into 4 patties, each about 3/4 inch thick. Mix remaining ingredients; spoon onto patties. Turn patties; cover and refrigerate 10 minutes.
2. Spray grill rack with cooking spray. Heat coals or gas grill for direct heat. Grill patties about 4 inches from medium coals, turning once, until desired doneness, 5 to 7 minutes on each side from medium.

1 SERVING Calories 230 (Calories from Fat 145) | Fat 16g (Saturated 6g) | Cholesterol 65mg | Sodium 510mg | Carbohydrate 1g (Dietary Fiber 0g, Sugars 0g) | Protein 21g % DAILY VALUE Vitamin A 2% | Vitamin C 0% | Calcium 0% | Iron 10% EXCHANGES 3 Medium-Fat Meat CARBOHYDRATE CHOICES 0

BETTY'S TIP

You can also use the broiler for these patties. Prepare the patties as directed above and set the oven control to broil. Place patties on rack in broiler pan. Broil with tops about 3 inches from heat, turning once, until desired doneness, about 5 minutes on each side for medium.

Blue Cheese Turkey Burgers

PREP 10 min GRILL 20 min SERVINGS 6

- 1 1/2 pounds ground turkey
- 1/4 cup mayonnaise or salad dressing
- 4 ounces crumbled blue cheese
- 1 large red onion, sliced

1. Spray grill rack with cooking spray. Heat coals or gas grill for direct heat.
2. Mix turkey, mayonnaise and blue cheese. Shape mixture into 6 patties, about 3/4 inch thick.
3. Cover and grill patties 4 to 5 inches from medium heat 15 to 20 minutes, turning once, until turkey is no longer pink. Top with red onion slices.

1 SERVING Calories 290 (Calories from Fat 170) | Fat 19g (Saturated 6g) | Cholesterol 95mg | Sodium 390mg | Carbohydrate 1g (Dietary Fiber 0g, Sugars 1g) | Protein 29g % DAILY VALUE Vitamin A 2% | Vitamin C 0% | Calcium 10% | Iron 6% EXCHANGES 4 Medium-Fat Meat CARBOHYDRATE CHOICES 0

BETTY'S TIP

Make this flavorful burger into a sandwich and serve it on a hamburger bun. Toasted buns always add extra flavor—to toast buns, grill cut sides down about 4 minutes or until golden brown.

Grilled Texas Turkey Burgers

PREP 10 min GRILL 16 min SERVINGS 4

1 pound ground turkey

1/3 cup barbecue sauce

1 can (4 ounces) chopped green chilies, drained

4 slices (1 ounce each) Monterey Jack cheese with jalapeño peppers

1. Spray grill rack with cooking spray. Heat coals or gas grill for direct heat.
2. Mix turkey, barbecue sauce and chilies. Shape mixture into 4 patties, each about 3/4 inch thick.
3. Cover and grill patties 4 to 6 inches from medium heat 14 to 16 minutes, turning once, until no longer pink. About 1 minute before burgers are done, top each with cheese slice. Grill until cheese is melted.

1 SERVING Calories 300 (Calories from Fat 135) | Fat 15g (Saturated 7g) | Cholesterol 105mg | Sodium 570mg | Carbohydrate 9g (Dietary Fiber 1g, Sugars 7g) | Protein 32g % DAILY VALUE Vitamin A 10% | Vitamin C 8% | Calcium 22% | Iron 10% EXCHANGES 1/2 Starch, 1 Lean Meat, 1 Fat CARBOHYDRATE CHOICES 1/2

BETTY'S TIP

Turn up the heat by using 2 or 3 chopped fresh jalepeño chilies instead of the canned chilies. And, if you'd prefer a sandwich, serve the burgers on hamburger buns or grilled Texas toast.

Tex-Mex Chicken Enchilada Packets

PREP 20 min GRILL 12 min SERVINGS 4

- 1 cup diced cooked chicken
- 2 cups shredded Mexican cheese blend (8 ounces)
- 1 can (4.5 ounces) chopped green chiles
- 2 tablespoons finely chopped onion
- 1 container (8 ounces) sour cream
- 8 corn tortillas (6 inches in diameter)
- Cooking spray
- 1 can (10 ounces) enchilada sauce

1. Mix chicken, 1 1/2 cups of the cheese, the green chiles, onion and sour cream in medium bowl. Set aside.
2. If using charcoal grill, place drip pan directly under grilling area, and arrange coals around edge of firebox. Heat coals or gas grill for indirect heat. Spray both sides of each tortilla with cooking spray. Stack tortillas on microwavable plate; cover with microwavable paper towel. Microwave on High 30 seconds.
3. Cut four 18 × 12-inch sheets of heavy-duty aluminum foil. Spray with cooking spray. Spread 1/3 cup chicken mixture down center of each warm tortilla; roll up. Place 2 enchiladas, seam sides down, on one side of each foil sheet; drizzle each with about 1/4 cup enchilada sauce. Fold foil over enchiladas so edges meet. Seal edges, making tight 1/2-inch fold; fold again. Allow space on sides for circulation and expansion.
4. Place packets, seam sides up, over drip pan or over unheated side of gas grill and 4 to 6 inches from medium heat. Cover and grill packets 10 to 12 minutes or until enchiladas are hot. Carefully open packets to allow steam to escape. Place enchiladas on serving plates. Top with remaining 1/2 cup cheese.

1 SERVING Calories 600 (Calories from Fat 350) | Fat 39g (Saturated 21g) | Cholesterol 110mg | Sodium 920mg | Carbohydrate 33g (Dietary Fiber 4g) | Protein 28g % DAILY VALUE Vitamin A 30% | Vitamin C 10% | Calcium 60% | Iron 10% EXCHANGES 2 Starch, 3 High-Fat Meat, 3 Fat CARBOHYDRATE CHOICES 2

BETTY'S TIP

These enchilada packets are great for a casual backyard get-together. Serve with tortilla chips and salsa on the side, and wash it all down with a pitcher of margaritas or sangria.

Honey-Cumin Barbecue Pork Packets

PREP 20 min GRILL 20 min SERVINGS 4

1/2 cup barbecue sauce

1/4 cup honey

2 teaspoons ground cumin

4 pork boneless rib or loin chops, 3/4 to 1 inch thick (about 1 1/4 pounds)

2 large ears corn, each cut into 6 pieces

1 cup baby-cut carrots, cut lengthwise in half

2 cups refrigerated cooked new potato wedges (from 1-pound 4-ounce bag)

1 teaspoon salt

1. Heat coals or gas grill for direct heat. Cut four 18 × 12-inch sheets of heavy-duty aluminum foil. Spray with cooking spray.
2. Mix barbecue sauce, honey and cumin in small bowl. Place 1 pork chop on one side of each foil sheet. Top each with one-fourth of the corn, carrots and potatoes; sprinkle with 1/4 teaspoon salt. Spoon 3 tablespoons sauce mixture over each.
3. Fold foil over pork and vegetables so edges meet. Seal edges, making tight 1/2-inch fold; fold again. Allow space on sides for circulation and expansion.
4. Cover and grill packets 4 to 6 inches from medium heat 15 to 20 minutes, turning once, until pork is no longer pink in center. Place packets on plates. Cut large X across top of each packet; fold back foil.

1 SERVING Calories 385 (Calories from Fat 70) | Fat 8g (Saturated 3g) | Cholesterol 55mg | Sodium 960mg | Carbohydrate 59g (Dietary Fiber 4g) | Protein 23g % DAILY VALUE Vitamin A 100% | Vitamin C 14% | Calcium 4% | Iron 14% EXCHANGES 3 Starch, 2 Vegetable, 1 1/2 Very Lean Meat CARBOHYDRATE CHOICES 4

BETTY'S TIP

Look for the cooked potato wedges in the refrigerated section of the supermarket. If they are not available, cut 2 medium potatoes into wedges and place in a microwavable bowl. Cover and microwave on High for about 5 minutes or until crisp-tender. Place potatoes in packet and grill as directed.

Grilled Kielbasa and Cabbage

PREP 5 min GRILL 20 min SERVINGS 4

- 1 ring (1 pound) fully cooked kielbasa sausage
- 3 cups coleslaw mix (8 ounces)
- 1/2 medium green bell pepper, cut into 1-inch pieces
- 1/2 teaspoon celery seed
- 1/2 teaspoon salt
- 1/8 teaspoon pepper
- 1 tablespoon butter or margarine
- 3 tablespoons water
- Bratwurst buns, split, if desired

1. Heat coals or gas grill for direct heat. Place sausage in 8-inch square aluminum foil pan. Mix coleslaw mix, bell pepper, celery seed, salt and pepper. Mound cabbage mixture in center of sausage. Dot with butter; sprinkle with water. Cover with aluminum foil, sealing edges securely.
2. Cover and grill pan 4 to 6 inches from medium heat 15 to 20 minutes or until coleslaw mixture is crisp-tender and sausage is hot.
3. Cut sausage into 4 pieces. Serve sausage and coleslaw mixture on buns.

1 SERVING Calories 390 (Calories from Fat 305) | Fat 34g (Saturated 13g) | Cholesterol 70mg | Sodium 1380mg | Carbohydrate 8g (Dietary Fiber 1g) | Protein 14g % DAILY VALUE Vitamin A 4% | Vitamin C 24% | Calcium 4% | Iron 8% EXCHANGES 2 Vegetable, 1 1/2 High-Fat Meat | 4 Fat CARBOHYDRATE CHOICES 1/2

BETTY'S TIP

What exactly is kielbasa? Well, it's also known as Polish sausage, and it's usually made of pork, sometimes with beef added. It's generally sold smoked and precooked.

Lemon and Herb Salmon Packets

PREP **15 min** STAND **5 min** GRILL **14 min** SERVINGS **4**

- 2 cups uncooked instant rice
- 1 can (14 ounces) chicken broth
- 1 cup matchstick-cut carrots (from 10-ounce bag)
- 4 salmon fillets (4 to 6 ounces each)
- 1 teaspoon lemon pepper seasoning salt
- 1/2 teaspoon salt
- 1/3 cup chopped fresh chives
- 1 medium lemon, cut lengthwise in half, then cut crosswise into 1/4-inch slices

1. Heat coals or gas grill for direct heat. Cut four 18 × 12-inch sheets of heavy-duty aluminum foil. Spray with cooking spray. Mix rice and broth in medium bowl. Let stand about 5 minutes or until most of broth is absorbed. Stir in carrots.
2. Place salmon fillet on one side of each foil sheet. Sprinkle with lemon pepper seasoning salt and salt; top with chives. Arrange lemon slices over salmon. Spoon one-fourth of the rice mixture around each fillet.
3. Fold foil over salmon and rice so edges meet. Seal edges, making tight 1/2-inch fold; fold again. Allow space on sides for circulation and expansion.
4. Cover and grill packets 4 to 6 inches from low heat 11 to 14 minutes or until salmon flakes easily with fork. Place packets on plates. Cut large X across top of each packet; fold back foil.

1 SERVING Calories 400 (Calories from Fat 70) | Fat 8g (Saturated 2g) | Cholesterol 75mg | Sodium 1160mg | Carbohydrate 51g (Dietary Fiber 2g) | Protein 31g % DAILY VALUE Vitamin A 100% | Vitamin C 4% | Calcium 4% | Iron 18% EXCHANGES 3 1/2 Starch, 3 Very Lean Meat CARBOHYDRATE CHOICES 3 1/2

BETTY'S TIP

Use whatever fresh herbs you have on hand. Basil, parsley or thyme would all taste delicious with the salmon.

Fisherman's Grilled Packet

PREP **5 min** GRILL **30 min** SERVINGS **6**

- 1 can (14 1/2 ounces) stewed tomatoes, undrained
- 1 can (2 1/4 ounces) sliced ripe olives
- 1/4 cup basil pesto
- 1 whitefish fillet (about 2 pounds)
- 1/2 teaspoon salt
- 1/4 teaspoon pepper
- 2 tablespoons chopped fresh parsley

1. Heat coals or gas grill for direct heat. Cut 24 × 12-inch sheet of heavy-duty aluminum foil. Mix tomatoes, olives and pesto in nonmetal bowl.
2. Place fish on foil. Sprinkle with salt and pepper. Top with tomato mixture. Fold foil over fish and tomato mixture so edges meet. Seal edges, making tight 1/2-inch fold; fold again. Allow space on sides for circulation and expansion.
3. Cover and grill packet 4 to 6 inches from medium heat 20 to 30 minutes or until fish flakes easily with fork. Top with parsley.

1 SERVING Calories 275 (Calories from Fat 135) | Fat 15g (Saturated 3g) | Cholesterol 75mg | Sodium 630mg | Carbohydrate 6g (Dietary Fiber 1g) | Protein 29g % DAILY VALUE Vitamin A 10% | Vitamin C 8% | Calcium 8% | Iron 10% EXCHANGES 1 Vegetable, 4 Very Lean Meat, 1/2 Fat CARBOHYDRATE CHOICES 1/2

BETTY'S TIP

Other fish choices for this recipe include cod, haddock, halibut, perch, pollock and red snapper.

Pineapple-Lime Shrimp Kabobs

PREP 10 min MARINATE 15 min GRILL 7 min SERVINGS 4

Pineapple-Lime Marinade (below left)

3/4 pound uncooked peeled deveined large shrimp, thawed if frozen and tails peeled

1 can (8 ounces) pineapple chunks in juice, drained and 2 tablespoons juice reserved

1 orange bell pepper, cut into 12 pieces

4 medium green onions, cut into 1 1/2-inch pieces

1. Make Pineapple-Lime Marinade. Add shrimp, pineapple, bell pepper and onions to marinade; stir to coat. Cover dish or seal bag and refrigerate 15 to 30 minutes, turning once or twice.
2. Brush vegetable oil on grill rack. Heat coals or gas grill for direct heat. Thread shrimp, pineapple, bell pepper and onions alternately on each of four 12- to 14-inch metal skewers; reserve marinade.
3. Cover and grill kabobs 4 to 5 inches from medium heat 5 to 7 minutes, turning and brushing with marinade once, until shrimp are pink and firm and vegetables are tender. Discard any remaining marinade.

Pineapple-Lime Marinade

2 tablespoons olive or vegetable oil

1 teaspoon grated lime peel

2 tablespoons lime juice

2 tablespoons reserved pineapple juice

1/4 teaspoon salt

1/4 teaspoon red pepper sauce

2 cloves garlic, finely chopped

Mix all ingredients in large shallow glass or plastic dish or resealable plastic food-storage bag.

1 SERVING Calories 220 (Calories from Fat 70) | Fat 8g (Saturated 1g) | Cholesterol 185mg | Sodium 350mg | Carbohydrate 6g (Dietary Fiber 1g) | Protein 31g
% DAILY VALUE Vitamin A 100% | Vitamin C 6% | Calcium 12% | Iron 26%
EXCHANGES 1 Vegetable, 4 Lean Meat, 1 Fat CARBOHYDRATE CHOICES 1/2

BETTY'S TIP

Marinating for a little longer will intensify the flavor slightly, but don't leave it for more than 2 hours. The marinade will start to break down the tissues in the shrimp, and the bell peppers will not be as pretty.

Shrimp Kabobs

PREP 10 min MARINATE 30 min GRILL 8 min SERVINGS 4

- 1 pound uncooked peeled deveined large shrimp, thawed if frozen
- 1 cup fat-free Italian dressing
- 1 medium red onion, cut into 8 pieces
- 1 medium bell pepper, cut into 8 pieces
- 16 medium cherry tomatoes
- 16 small whole mushrooms

1. Place shrimp and dressing in shallow glass or plastic dish or heavy-duty resealable plastic food-storage bag. Cover dish or seal bag and refrigerate 30 minutes.
2. Heat coals or gas grill for direct heat. Remove shrimp from marinade; reserve marinade. Thread shrimp, onion, bell pepper, tomatoes and mushrooms alternately on each of four 15-inch metal skewers, leaving 1/4-inch space between each piece.
3. Grill kabobs uncovered 4 to 6 inches from medium heat 6 to 8 minutes, turning frequently and brushing several times with marinade, until shrimp are pink and firm. Discard any remaining marinade.

1 SERVING Calories 140 (Calories from Fat 10) | Fat 1 (Saturated 0g) | Cholesterol 160mg | Sodium 730mg | Carbohydrate 13g (Dietary 2g) | Protein 20g % DAILY VALUE Vitamin A 18% | Vitamin C 36% | Calcium 4% | Iron 20% EXCHANGES 2 1/2 Vegetable, 2 Very Lean Meat CARBOHYDRATE CHOICES 1

BETTY'S TIP

A large slice of watermelon makes a fun holder for these colorful kabobs.

Pesto-Artichoke Pizza

PREP **10 min** GRILL **10 min** SERVINGS **8**

- 2 packages (10 ounces each) ready-to-serve Italian pizza crusts (6 inches in diameter)
- 1 cup basil pesto
- 2 jars (6 to 7 ounces each) marinated artichoke hearts, drained and chopped
- 6 large roma (plum) tomatoes, sliced (2 cups)
- 2 cups shredded Monterey Jack cheese (8 ounces)

1. Heat coals or gas grill for direct heat. Grill pizza crusts, top sides down, 4 to 6 inches from medium heat 3 to 5 minutes or until light brown. Remove from grill.
2. Spread pesto over grilled side of crusts. Top with artichokes and tomatoes. Sprinkle with cheese.
3. Cover and grill about 5 minutes or until cheese is melted. Cut each pizza in half.

1 SERVING Calories 520 (Calories from Fat 280) | Fat 31g (Saturated 10g) | Cholesterol 30mg | Sodium 890mg | Carbohydrate 43g (Dietary Fiber 5g) | Protein 17g % DAILY VALUE Vitamin A 18% | Vitamin C 12% | Calcium 36% | Iron 22% EXCHANGES 2 1/2 Starch, 1 Vegetable, 1 High-Fat Meat, 4 1/2 Fat CARBOHYDRATE CHOICES 3

BETTY'S TIP

You can serve this easy grilled pizza as an appetizer, too. Simply cut each pizza into 8 wedges and serve.

Grilled Portabella and Bell-Pepper Sanwiches

PREP **15 min** GRILL **12 min** SERVINGS **6**

- 6 fresh medium portabella mushroom caps
- 1 large bell pepper, cut into 1/4-inch slices
- 1 large red onion, sliced
- 1 tablespoon olive or vegetable oil
- 1/2 teaspoon seasoned salt
- 1 round focaccia bread (8 or 9 inches in diameter)
- 1/4 cup mayonnaise or salad dressing
- 1/4 cup basil pesto
- 4 leaf lettuce leaves

1. Heat coals or gas grill for direct heat. Brush mushrooms, bell pepper and onion with oil. Sprinkle with seasoned salt. Place vegetables in grill basket.
2. Cover and grill vegetables 4 to 5 inches from medium heat 10 to 12 minutes, shaking grill basket occasionally to turn vegetables, until bell pepper and onion are crisp-tender and mushrooms are just tender.
3. Cut bread horizontally in half. Mix mayonnaise and pesto; spread over cut sides of bread. Layer lettuce and grilled vegetables on bottom half of bread. Add top of bread. Cut into 6 wedges.

1 SERVING Calories 290 (Calories from Fat 170) | Fat 19g (Saturated 3g) | Cholesterol 5mg | Sodium 690mg | Carbohydrate 26g (Dietary Fiber 2g) | Protein 5g % DAILY VALUE Vitamin A 10% | Vitamin C 24% | Calcium 4% | Iron 12% EXCHANGES 1 Starch, 2 Vegetable, 4 Fat CARBOHYDRATE CHOICES 2

BETTY'S TIP

It's easy to clean mushrooms just before using by wiping them off with a damp paper towel. If you find that the mushrooms are very water after cooking, pat dry before making sandwiches.

Helpful Nutrition and Cooking Information

Nutrition Guidelines

We provide nutrition information for each recipe that includes calories, fat, cholesterol, sodium, carbohydrate, fiber and protein. Individual food choices can be based on this information.

Recommended intake for a daily diet of 2,000 calories as set by the Food and Drug Administration

Total Fat	Less than 65g
Saturated Fat	Less than 20g
Cholesterol	Less than 300mg
Sodium	Less than 2,400mg
Total Carbohydrate	300g
Dietary Fiber	25g

Criteria Used for Calculating Nutrition Information

- The first ingredient was used wherever a choice is given (such as 1/3 cup sour cream or plain yogurt).
- The first ingredient amount was used wherever a range is given (such as 3- to 3 1/2-pound cut-up broiler-fryer chicken).
- The first serving number was used wherever a range is given (such as 4 to 6 servings).
- "If desired" ingredients and recipe variations were not included (such as sprinkle with brown sugar, if desired).
- Only the amount of a marinade or frying oil that is estimated to be absorbed by the food during preparation or cooking was calculated.

Ingredients Used in Recipe Testing and Nutrition Calculations

- Ingredients used for testing represent those that the majority of consumers use in their homes: large eggs, 2% milk, 80%-lean ground beef, canned ready-to-use chicken broth and vegetable oil spread containing not less than 65% fat.
- Fat-free, low-fat or low-sodium products were not used, unless otherwise indicated.
- Solid vegetable shortening (not butter, margarine, nonstick cooking sprays or vegetable oil spread as they can cause sticking problems) was used to grease pans, unless otherwise indicated.

Equipment Used in Recipe Testing

We use equipment for testing that the majority of consumers use in their homes. If a specific piece of equipment (such as a wire whisk) is necessary for recipe success, it is listed in the recipe.

- Cookware and bakeware without nonstick coatings were used, unless otherwise indicated.
- No dark-colored, black or insulated bakeware was used.
- When a pan is specified in a recipe, a metal pan was used; a baking dish or pie plate means ovenproof glass was used.
- An electric hand mixer was used for mixing only when mixer speeds are specified in the recipe directions. When a mixer speed is not given, a spoon or fork was used.

Cooking Terms Glossary

Beat: Mix ingredients vigorously with spoon, fork, wire whisk, hand beater or electric mixer until smooth and uniform.

Boil: Heat liquid until bubbles rise continuously and break on the surface and steam is given off. For rolling boil, the bubbles form rapidly.

Chop: Cut into coarse or fine irregular pieces with a knife, food chopper, blender or food processor.

Cube: Cut into squares 1/2 inch or larger.

Dice: Cut into squares smaller than 1/2 inch.

Grate: Cut into tiny particles using small rough holes of grater (citrus peel or chocolate).

Grease: Rub the inside surface of a pan with shortening, using pastry brush, piece of waxed paper or paper towel, to prevent food from sticking during baking (as for some casseroles).

Julienne: Cut into thin, matchlike strips, using knife or food processor (vegetables, fruits, meats).

Mix: Combine ingredients in any way that distributes them evenly.

Sauté: Cook foods in hot oil or margarine over medium-high heat with frequent tossing and turning motion.

Shred: Cut into long thin pieces by rubbing food across the holes of a shredder, as for cheese, or by using a knife to slice very thinly, as for cabbage.

Simmer: Cook in liquid just below the boiling point on top of the stove; usually after reducing heat from a boil. Bubbles will rise slowly and break just below the surface.

Stir: Mix ingredients until uniform consistency. Stir once in a while for stirring occasionally, often for stirring frequently and continuously for stirring constantly.

Toss: Tumble ingredients (such as green salad) lightly with a lifting motion, usually to coat evenly or mix with another food.

Metric Conversion Guide

Volume

U.S. UNITS	CANADIAN METRIC	AUSTRALIAN METRIC
1/4 teaspoon	1 mL	1 ml
1/2 teaspoon	2 mL	2 ml
1 teaspoon	5 mL	5 ml
1 tablespoon	15 mL	20 ml
1/4 cup	50 mL	60 ml
1/3 cup	75 mL	80 ml
1/2 cup	125 mL	125 ml
2/3 cup	150 mL	170 ml
3/4 cup	175 mL	190 ml
1 cup	250 mL	250 ml
1 quart	1 liter	1 liter
1 1/2 quarts	1.5 liters	1.5 liters
2 quarts	2 liters	2 liters
2 1/2 quarts	2.5 liters	2.5 liters
3 quarts	3 liters	3 liters
4 quarts	4 liters	4 liters

Weight

U.S. UNITS	CANADIAN METRIC	AUSTRALIAN METRIC
1 ounce	30 grams	30 grams
2 ounces	55 grams	60 grams
3 ounces	85 grams	90 grams
4 ounces (1/4 pound)	115 grams	125 grams
8 ounces (1/2 pound)	225 grams	225 grams
16 ounces (1 pound)	455 grams	500 grams
1 pound	455 grams	1/2 kilogram

NOTE: The recipes in this cookbook have not been developed or tested using metric measures. When converting recipes to metric, some variations in quality may be noted.

Measurements

INCHES	CENTIMETERS
1	2.5
2	5.0
3	7.5
4	10.0
5	12.5
6	15.0
7	17.5
8	20.5
9	23.0
10	25.5
11	28.0
12	30.5
13	33.0

Temperatures

FAHRENHEIT	CELSIUS
32°	0°
212°	100°
250°	120°
275°	140°
300°	150°
325°	160°
350°	180°
375°	190°
400°	200°
425°	220°
450°	230°
475°	240°
500°	260°

Index

Underscored page references indicate boxed text. **Boldfaced** page references indicate photographs.

A

Almonds, toasting, 310
Apples
  Pork Chops with Apple-Cherry Stuffing, 231
  Pork Chops with Apple-Cranberry Stuffing, 231
  Squash-and-Apple Bisque, 242, **243**
  Turkey Breast with Wild Rice Stuffing, 216
  varieties of, for cooking, 216
Artichokes
  Antipasto Vegetable Salad, 314
  Chicken, Artichoke and Red Onion Pizza, 260
  Mediterranean Chicken Salad, **292**, 293
  Paella on the Grill, 342
  Penne with Beef and Sun-Dried Tomatoes, **74**, 75
  Pesto-Artichoke Pizza, 357
Asian-style dishes
  Asian Pork Salad, 313
  Chicken and Cashew Bake, 155
  Chopped-Chicken Asian Salad, 290, **291**
  Ginger-Peanut-Shrimp Stir-Fry, 126
  Glazed Turkey and Pea Pods, **68**, 101
  Grilled Teriyaki Burgers, 346
  Halibut Asparagus Stir-Fry, **118**, 119
  Oriental Chicken Noodle Soup, 26
  Oriental Turkey and Rice, 104
  Polynesian Pork Stir-Fry, **114**, 115
  Smoked Turkey Lo Mein, 102
  Stir-Fried Beef and Broccoli, 76
  Szechuan Chicken and Pasta, **96**, 97
  Teriyaki Chicken Stir-Fry, 91
  Thai Chicken Pizzas, 254, **255**
  Thai Chicken Salad, **296**, 297
  Vegetable Chicken Stir-Fry, **98**, 99
Asparagus
  Asparagus-Dijon-Chicken Fettuccine, 83
  Chicken-and-Pasta Stir-Fry, **88**, 89
  Creamy Bow-Ties with Ham and Vegetables, **108**, 109
  Halibut Asparagus Stir-Fry, **118**, 119
  preparing for cooking, 109
  Spring Vegetable and Chicken Paella, 325
  Spring Vegetable Paella, 325

B

Bacon
  Salsa Bacon Dressing, 285
  Southwestern Chicken BLT Salad, 285
  Spinach-Shrimp Salad with Hot Bacon Dressing, 316
Barley
  Beef-Barley-Vegetable Stew, 48
  Hearty Turkey-Barley Soup, 27
  protein in, 27
Basil. *See also* Pesto
  Basil Rice Soup, 44, **45**
  Classic Pizza, 271
  Italian Chicken Linguine, 127
  Italian Shrimp Linguine, 127

Basil (*cont.*)
Shrimp-Pesto Pizzas, **272**, 273
slicing into chiffonade, 273
Three-Herb Chicken, 168
Beans. *See also* Green beans
Asian Pork Salad, 313
Beef Steak Chili, 208
Black Bean and Salsa Noodle Soup, **32**, 33
Black Bean Soup, **30**, 31
black-eyed peas, buying, 106
Buffalo-Chicken Chili, 64, **65**
Caribbean Chicken and Black Bean Salad, **286**, 287
Chicken-Curry-Couscous Salad, **288**, 289
Cincinnati-Style Chili, **62**, 63
Classic Chili, **62**, 63
Deep-Dish Turkey Pizza, 267
Deli Beef and Bean Tossed Salad, **282**, 283
Deli Ham and Bean Tossed Salad, 283
Easy Bean and Kielbasa Soup, 238
Easy Mexican Chicken and Beans, 94, **95**
Easy Pork Chili, 237
Easy Steak Chili, 237
Hearty Beef Chili, 200
Italian Beef Stew, 201
Lamb and Lentil Casserole, 181
Layered Chicken–Black Bean Enchiladas, 164
Meatless Black Bean Soup, 31
Mexicali Round Steak, 205
New England Baked Bean Stew, 52
Peppery Cajun Pork Pasta, 106
Pork and Lentil Casserole, 181
Ratatouille Bean Stew, 241
Southwestern Pork Stew, 227
Spring Vegetable Paella, 325
Stacked Enchilada Bake, **194**, 195
Three-Bean and Caper Salad, 318
Three-Bean and Tuna Salad, 318
Turkey Tabbouleh Salad, 305
Turkey Taco Salad, **306**, 307
Tuscan Bean and Chicken Salad, 331
Tuscan Panzanella Salad, 324
Vegetarian Chili, 61
Warm Tuscan Bean Salad, **330**, 331
White Chili, **66**, 67
Beef. *See also* Beef, ground
Beef and Corn Kabobs, 335
Beef-Barley-Vegetable Stew, 48
Beef Steak Chili, 208
Beef Stroganoff, 71
Cajun Pot Roast with Maque Choux, 203
Classic Beef Stew, 50
Corn, Roast Beef and Potato Scallop, 222
Deli Beef and Bean Tossed Salad, **282**, 283
Easy Philly Cheesesteak Pizza, **252**, 253
Easy Steak Chili, 237
Easy Weeknight Beef-Veggie Mix, 77
Fajita Salad, 281
Garlic-Braised Beef and Potatoes, 204
Ginger-Orange Beef Pita Sandwiches, 210, **211**
Greek Beef and Onion Stew, 51
Hearty Beef Chili, 200
as ingredient substitution, 266
Italian Beef Stew, 201
Mexicali Round Steak, 205
Old-Fashioned Beef Stew, 202
Penne with Beef and Sun-Dried Tomatoes, **74**, 75
Quick Beef and Vegetable Stew, 49
raw, slicing, 23
Roast Beef and Tomato Salad, 284
Savory Pot Roast, **206**, 207
short ribs, as ingredient substitution, 235
Skewered Steak Dinner, 334
Steak and Potato Soup, 23
Steak Caesar Salad, 280
Stir-Fried Beef and Broccoli, 76
Swiss Steak Supper, 209
trimming excess fat from, 13
Beef, ground
Beef, Carrot and Noodle Bake, 173
Beef and Bulgur Casserole, 149
Beef and Potatoes au Gratin, 148
Beef-Taco-Rice Skillet, 72
Cheeseburger Pizza, 250
Cheesy Lasagna Soup, 22
Cheesy Pizza Casserole, 150
Cincinnati-Style Chili, **62**, 63
Classic Chili, **62**, 63
Curried Beef Casserole, 144
Deep-Dish Spaghetti Pie, 151
Easy Taco Dinner, 73
Garlic Shepherd's Pie, 146, **147**
Grilled Teriyaki Burgers, 346
precooked, buying, 140
Quick Lasagna, **142**, 143
Salsa Pizza with Cheese Crust, 248
Skillet Beef Stew, 70
Sloppy Joe Pizza, 251
Spinach-Lasagna Casserole, 145

Taco Pizza, 249
Texas Tater Casserole, 141
Vidalia-Topped Caesar Burgers, **336**, 337
Western Beef Casserole au Gratin, 152
Wild Rice and Beef Casserole, 140
Bell peppers
Beef and Corn Kabobs, 335
Cheesy Lasagna Soup, 22
Chunky Vegetable Chowder, 47
Easy Philly Cheesesteak Pizza, **252**, 253
Fajita Salad, 281
Fettuccine Alfredo with Sausage, 107
Ginger-Orange Beef Pita Sandwiches, 210, **211**
Grilled Portabella and Bell-Pepper Sandwiches, **358**, 359
Lamb with Sweet Peppers and Garlic Sauce, 182, **183**
Mozzarella and Pesto Strata, 191
Quick Garden Chicken Salad, 295
Ratatouille Bean Stew, 241
Ravioli with Sausage and Peppers, **198**, 224
Sausage with Fettuccine, 107
Shrimp Kabobs, 356
Skewered Steak Dinner, 334
Spicy Southwest Chicken Kabobs, 339
Berries
Chicken and Berries Salad, **278**, 304
Fruited Taco Salad, **326**, 327
Fruity Yogurt Dressing, 304
Pork Chops with Apple-Cranberry Stuffing, 231
Raspberry Chicken Salad, 298, **299**
Raspberry Dressing, 298
Turkey and Corn Bread Stuffing Casserole, 174
Turkey Breast with Wild Rice Stuffing, 216
Bisquick mix
Cheeseburger Pizza, 250
Chicken Gyro Pizza, **264**, 265
Deep-Dish Turkey Pizza, 267
Double-Cheese Pepperoni Pizza, 268
Hot Chicken Salad with Sage Biscuits, **138**, 158
Mini White Pizzas, **246**, 277
Salsa Pizza with Cheese Crust, 248
Salsa Pork Pizza with Cheese Crust, 248
Turkey and Corn Bread Stuffing Casserole, 174
Turkey Burger Pizza, 250
Black-eyed peas
buying, 106
Peppery Cajun Pork Pasta, 106
Bok choy
Oriental Chicken Noodle Soup, 26
side salad, preparing, 26
Turkey-Ginger Tortellini Soup, 28
Bread. *See also* Tortillas
bread bowls, preparing, 201
Cheesy Broiled French Bread, 240
garlic bread, preparing, 107
Bread puddings. *See* Stratas
Broccoli
Antipasto Vegetable Salad, 314
Beef-Barley-Vegetable Stew, 48
Cheesy Turkey, Rice and Broccoli, 103
Chicken Stew with Potatoes, 53
Cream of Broccoli Soup, 39
cut-up flowerets, buying, 314
Garlic-Braised Beef and Potatoes, 204
Italian Chicken Linguine, 127
Italian Sausage and Mostaccioli Soup, 34, **35**
Italian Shrimp Linguine, 127
Italian Tortellini Salad, 315
Ranch Potatoes and Chicken Casserole, 160
Spring Vegetable and Chicken Paella, 325
Spring Vegetable Paella, 325
Stir-Fried Beef and Broccoli, 76
Tuna Primavera, 128
Turkey Divan, 171
vitamins in, 103
Bulgur
about, 149
Beef and Bulgur Casserole, 149
Turkey Tabbouleh Salad, 305
Burgers
Blue Cheese Turkey Burgers, 347
Grilled Teriyaki Burgers, 346
Grilled Texas Turkey Burgers, **348**, 349
preparing, tips for, 337
Vidalia-Topped Caesar Burgers, **336**, 337
Buttermilk, substitute for, 214

C

Cabbage. *See also* Bok choy
Asian Pork Salad, 313
coleslaw mix, buying, 313
Grilled Kielbasa and Cabbage, 352
Ham and Slaw Salad, 312
Harvest Sausage and Vegetable Casserole, 221
Zesty Autumn Pork Stew, **54**, 55

Carrots
Beef, Carrot and Noodle Bake, 173
Classic Beef Stew, 50
Creamy Bow-Ties with Ham and Vegetables, **108**, 109
Easy Seafood Risotto, 120, **121**
Hearty Turkey Dinner, 218
Honey-Barbecue-Glazed Pork Roast with Carrots and Corn, 236
Honey-Cumin Barbecue Pork Packets, 351
Italian Beef Stew, 201
Lamb and Lentil Casserole, 181
Lemon and Herb Salmon Packets, 353
Old-Fashioned Beef Stew, 202
Pork and Lentil Casserole, 181
Savory Pot Roast, **206**, 207
Smothered Buttermillk Chicken with Peas, 214
Steak and Potato Soup, 23
Swiss Steak Supper, 209
Tuna Primavera, 128
Turkey, Carrot and Noodle Bake, **172**, 173
Cashews
Chicken and Cashew Bake, 155
Glazed Turkey and Pea Pods, **68**, 101
Casseroles
Baked Chicken Gumbo, **166**, 167
Baked Ravioli and Meatballs, 153
Baked Salmon with Cilantro, **184**, 185
Baked Tuna and Noodles with Creamy Mushroom Sauce, 188
baking dishes for, 9, 10
Beef, Carrot and Noodle Bake, 173
Beef and Bulgur Casserole, 149
Beef and Potatoes au Gratin, 148
California Chicken Bake, 154
Cheddar Strata with Onions, 190
Cheesy Italian Sausage Casserole, 150
Cheesy Pizza Casserole, 150
Chicken and Cashew Bake, 155
Chicken and Rice Bake, 163
Chicken Drumstick Cacciatore Casserole, 165
Chicken Legs with Vegetables, 169
Chicken-Vegetable Strata, 162
Chicken with Cider Glaze, **156**, 157
Chicken with Italian Roasted Vegetables, 176
Country Chicken and Pasta Bake, 161
Curried Beef Casserole, 144
Deep-Dish Spaghetti Pie, 151
Easy Cheese Strata, 193
Easy Cheesy Manicotti, **196**, 197
Easy Turkey Lasagna, 175
flavor boosters for, 12
Garlic Shepherd's Pie, 146, **147**
Gremolata-Topped Sea Bass, 186
Ham and Brie Bake, 178
Harvest Sausage and Vegetable Casserole, 221
Hot Chicken Salad with Sage Biscuits, **138**, 158
Lamb and Lentil Casserole, 181
Lamb with Sweet Peppers and Garlic Sauce, 182, **183**
Layered Chicken–Black Bean Enchiladas, 164
Maple-Glazed Turkey and Rice Casserole, 170
Mashed Potato and Sausage Casserole, 180
Mozzarella and Pesto Strata, 191
Parmesan-Shrimp Pasta Bake, 187
Pork and Lentil Casserole, 181
Quick Lasagna, **142**, 143
Ranch Potatoes and Chicken Casserole, 160
reheating, 15
Sausage and Pizza Bake, 179
Spinach-Lasagna Casserole, 145
Stacked Enchilada Bake, **194**, 195
Texas Tater Casserole, 141
Three-Herb Chicken, 168
Tuna Twist Casserole, 189
Turkey, Carrot and Noodle Bake, **172**, 173
Turkey and Brie Bake, 178
Turkey and Corn Bread Stuffing Casserole, 174
Turkey and Tortilla Casserole, 177
Turkey Divan, 171
Turkey with Italian Roasted Vegetables, 176
unbaked, freezing, 14
Vegetable Strata, 192
Western Beef Casserole au Gratin, 152
Wild Rice and Beef Casserole, 140
Wild Rice and Chicken Cassserole, 159
Wild Rice and Ham Casserole, 159
Wild Rice and Turkey Casserole, 140
Cauliflower
Cream of Cauliflower Soup, 39

Curried Pork and Veggie Stew, 225
Italian Salami Toss, 319
Italian Tuna Toss, 319
yield from, 319
Cheddar cheese
Beer and Cheese Soup, 29
Cheddar Strata with Onions, 190
Cheddar-Stuffed Chicken Breasts, **340**, 341
Chicken, Artichoke and Red Onion Pizza, 260
Chicken-Vegetable Strata, 162
Deli Beef and Bean Tossed Salad, **282**, 283
Deli Ham and Bean Tossed Salad, 283
Double-Cheese, Spinach and Chicken Pizza, **256**, 257
Easy Cheese Strata, 193
Easy Taco Dinner, 73
Potato-Cheese Soup, 38
Spicy Chicken Chili, 66
Taco Pizza, 249
Vegetable Strata, 192
Western Beef Casserole au Gratin, 152
Wild Rice and Beef Casserole, 140
Wild Rice and Turkey Casserole, 140
Cheese. *See also* Cheddar cheese; Mozzarella cheese
Beef and Potatoes au Gratin, 148
Blue Cheese Tenders, 132, **133**
Blue Cheese Turkey Burgers, 347
Breakfast Pizza, 269
Buffalo-Chicken Chili, 64, **65**
California Chicken Bake, 154
Cheeseburger Pizza, 250
Chicken Gyro Pizza, **264**, 265
Chicken Pizza Mexicana, 261
Deli Beef and Bean Tossed Salad, **282**, 283
Deli Ham and Bean Tossed Salad, 283
Double-Cheese, Spinach and Chicken Pizza, **256**, 257
Double-Cheese Pepperoni Pizza, 268
Easy Cheesy Manicotti, **196**, 197
Easy Cheesy Vegetable Soup, **42**, 43
Easy Philly Cheesesteak Pizza, **252**, 253
Easy Taco Dinner, 73
Easy Turkey Lasagna, 175
fat-free or reduced-fat, for recipes, 13
feta, about, 328
feta, adding to salads, 12
Four-Cheese Pesto Pizza, 276
Greek Orzo Salad, 328, **329**
Greek Pita Pizzas, 275
Greek Pita Pizza with Chicken, 275
Grilled Texas Turkey Burgers, **348**, 349
Ham and Brie Bake, 178
Layered Chicken–Black Bean Enchiladas, 164
Mexicali Round Steak, 205
Parmesan-Shrimp Pasta Bake, 187
Pesto-Artichoke Pizza, 357
Quick Lasagna, **142**, 143
reducing amount, in recipes, 13
Roast Beef and Tomato Salad, 284
Salsa Pizza with Cheese Crust, 248
Salsa Pork Pizza with Cheese Crust, 248
Sausage and Pizza Bake, 179
shredding, tip for, 257
Sloppy Joe Pizza, 251
Southwest Cheese 'n Pasta, 129
Southwest Ham 'n Cheese Pasta, 129
Spicy Chicken Chili, 66
Spinach-Lasagna Casserole, 145
Spinach-Shrimp Salad with Hot Bacon Dressing, 316
Stacked Enchilada Bake, **194**, 195
Steak Caesar Salad, 280
Sun-Dried Tomato, Herb and Mushroom Pizza, 274
Swiss, garnishing soup with, 12
Swiss Potato and Cheese Skillet, 134
Tex-Mex Chicken Enchilada Packets, 350
Turkey and Brie Bake, 178
Turkey Burger Pizza, 250
Turkey Gyro Pizzas, 266
Cherries
Fettuccine and Chicken in Orange-Cherry Sauce, 86, **87**
Peach Cherry Chutney, **244**, 245
Pork Chops with Apple-Cherry Stuffing, 231
Turkey and Dried Cherry Salad, 310
Chicken. *See also* Chicken, cooked; Chicken breasts; Chicken thighs
Chicken and Rice Bake, 163
Chicken Drumstick Cacciatore Casserole, 165
Chicken Legs with Vegetables, 169
Chicken with Cider Glaze, **156**, 157
drumsticks, removing skin from, 165
Greek Pita Pizza with Chicken, 275
as ingredient substitution, 266

Chicken (*cont.*)
Three-Herb Chicken, 168
trimming excess fat from, 13
Chicken, cooked
Buffalo-Chicken Chili, 64, **65**
Caribbean Chicken and Black Bean Salad, **286**, 287
Chicken, Artichoke and Red Onion Pizza, 260
Chicken and Berries Salad, **278**, 304
Chicken and Cashew Bake, 155
Chicken and Vegetable Bow-Tie Soup, 25
Chicken-Curry-Couscous Salad, **288**, 289
Chicken French-Bread Pizza, **262**, 263
Chicken Gyro Pizza, **264**, 265
Chicken Paprika, 80, **81**
Chicken Pizza Mexicana, 261
Chicken-Vegetable Strata, 162
Chicken-Vegetable Stroganoff, 90
Chopped-Chicken Asian Salad, 290, **291**
Country Chicken and Pasta Bake, 161
Double-Cheese, Spinach and Chicken Pizza, **256**, 257
Fruited Taco Salad, **326**, 327
Garden Vegetables, Chicken and Pasta Salad, **300**, 301
Greek Chicken Salad, 294
Greek Orzo Salad, 328, **329**
Grilled Chicken Salad with Fruit, 309
Hawaiian Pizza, **258**, 259
Hot Chicken Salad with Sage Biscuits, **138**, 158
as ingredient substitution, 280
Layered Chicken–Black Bean Enchiladas, 164
Mediterranean Chicken Salad, **292**, 293
Mini White Pizzas, **246**, 277
Oriental Chicken Noodle Soup, 26
Quick Garden Chicken Salad, 295
Ranch Potatoes and Chicken Casserole, 160
Raspberry Chicken Salad, 298, **299**
Southwestern Chicken BLT Salad, 285
Spring Vegetable and Chicken Paella, 325
Tex-Mex Chicken Enchilada Packets, 350
Thai Chicken Pizzas, 254, **255**
Thai Chicken Salad, **296**, 297
Tuscan Bean and Chicken Salad, 331
Vegetable Chicken Paella, 135
White Chili, **66**, 67
Wild Rice and Chicken Cassserole, 159
Wild-Rice Chicken Salad with Raspberry Vinaigrette, **302**, 303
Chicken breasts
African Peanut-Chicken Soup, 24
Asparagus-Dijon-Chicken Fettuccine, 83
Blue Cheese Tenders, 132, **133**
Caesar Chicken with Orzo, **78**, 79
California Chicken Bake, 154
Cheddar-Stuffed Chicken Breasts, **340**, 341
Chicken and Julienne Potatoes, 112
Chicken-and-Pasta Stir-Fry, **88**, 89
Chicken Penne à la Marengo, 82
Chicken Stew with Potatoes, 53
Chicken with Italian Roasted Vegetables, 176
Citrus Ginger Chicken, **84**, 85
Dijon-Chicken Fettuccine with Green Peas, 83
Easy Chicken Alfredo, **92**, 93
Easy Mexican Chicken and Beans, 94, **95**
Fettuccine and Chicken in Orange-Cherry Sauce, 86, **87**
Italian Chicken Linguine, 127
Lemon Chicken with Fennel and Onions, 343
Mostaccioli with Vodka Sauce, **130**, 131
New England Baked Bean Stew, 52
Paella on the Grill, 342
Pesto Chicken Packets, **344**, 345
Spicy Chicken Chili, 66
Spicy Southwest Chicken Kabobs, 339
Szechuan Chicken and Pasta, **96**, 97
Teriyaki Chicken Stir-Fry, 91
Vegetable Chicken Stir-Fry, **98**, 99
Chicken thighs
Baked Chicken Gumbo, **166**, 167
Chicken Chili Verde, 215
Chicken Legs with Vegetables, 169
Chunky Chicken Chili, 213
Lime-Garlic Chicken with Rice, 212
Smothered Buttermillk Chicken with Peas, 214

Three-Herb Chicken, 168
Vegetable Chicken Stir-Fry, **98**, 99
Chickpeas. *See* Garbanzo beans
Chile peppers
Chicken Pizza Mexicana, 261
Easy Pork Chili, 237
Easy Steak Chili, 237
Grilled Texas Turkey Burgers, **348**, 349
Layered Chicken–Black Bean Enchiladas, 164
Tex-Mex Chicken Enchilada Packets, 350
Western Beef Casserole au Gratin, 152
Chili
Beef Steak Chili, 208
Buffalo-Chicken Chili, 64, **65**
Chicken Chili Verde, 215
Chunky Chicken Chili, 213
Cincinnati-Style Chili, **62**, 63
Classic Chili, **62**, 63
Easy Pork Chili, 237
Easy Steak Chili, 237
Hearty Beef Chili, 200
Turkey Chili Verde, 215
Vegetarian Chili, 61
White Chili, **66**, 67
Chowder
Chunky Vegetable Chowder, 47
Dill-Turkey Chowder, 217
Ham 'n Corn Chowder, 46
New England Clam Chowder, 58
Chutney
Peach Cherry Chutney, **244**, 245
Cilantro
Baked Salmon with Cilantro, **184**, 185
Black Bean and Salsa Noodle Soup, **32**, 33
California Chicken Bake, 154
Caribbean Chicken and Black Bean Salad, **286**, 287
Mexicali Round Steak, 205
storing, 33
Clams
New England Clam Chowder, 58
Coconut
Polynesian Pork Stir-Fry, **114**, 115
Thai Chicken Salad, **296**, 297
toasting, 297
Coleslaw mix
Asian Pork Salad, 313
buying, 313
Grilled Kielbasa and Cabbage, 352
Ham and Slaw Salad, 312
Cooking sprays, 13
Cookware, 8–11
Corn
Beef and Corn Kabobs, 335
Beef-Taco-Rice Skillet, 72
Black Bean and Salsa Noodle Soup, **32**, 33
Cajun Pot Roast with Maque Choux, 203
Chunky Vegetable Chowder, 47
Corn, Ham and Potato Scallop, 222
Corn, Roast Beef and Potato Scallop, 222
Deep-Dish Spaghetti Pie, 151
Dill-Turkey Chowder, 217
Easy Mexican Chicken and Beans, 94, **95**
Ham 'n Corn Chowder, 46
Honey-Barbecue-Glazed Pork Roast with Carrots and Corn, 236
Honey-Cumin Barbecue Pork Packets, 351
Mexicali Round Steak, 205
Southwest Cheese 'n Pasta, 129
Southwestern Pork Stew, 227
Southwest Ham 'n Cheese Pasta, 129
Spicy Southwest Chicken Kabobs, 339
Texas Tater Casserole, 141
Thai Chicken Salad, **296**, 297
Western Beef Casserole au Gratin, 152
White Chili, **66**, 67
Couscous
Chicken-Curry-Couscous Salad, **288**, 289
Crabmeat
Caesar Salad with Crabmeat, 323
Chopped Vegetable and Crabmeat Salad, **320**, 321
Easy Seafood Risotto, 120, **121**
Cranberries
Pork Chops with Apple-Cranberry Stuffing, 231
Turkey and Corn Bread Stuffing Casserole, 174
Turkey Breast with Wild Rice Stuffing, 216
Cucumbers
Caesar Salad with Crabmeat, 323
Caesar Salad with Lobster, 323
Chicken Gyro Pizza, **264**, 265
Greek Chicken Salad, 294
Greek Orzo Salad, 328, **329**
Italian Salami Toss, 319
Italian Tuna Toss, 319
Quick Garden Chicken Salad, 295
Ten-Minute Ham Salad, 311
Turkey Gyro Pizzas, 266
Curried recipes
Chicken-Curry-Couscous Salad, **288**, 289
Curried Beef Casserole, 144

Curried recipes (*cont.*)
Curried Pork and Veggie Stew, 225
Curry Dressing, 289
Moroccan Lamb and Rice, 239

D
Dutch ovens, 9

E
Eggplant
Ratatouille Soup, 40
Eggs
Breakfast Pizza, 269
lower-fat substitutes for, 13
Enchiladas
Layered Chicken–Black Bean Enchiladas, 164
Stacked Enchilada Bake, **194**, 195
Tex-Mex Chicken Enchilada Packets, 350
Escarole
about, 290
Chopped-Chicken Asian Salad, 290, **291**
Chopped Vegetable and Crabmeat Salad, **320**, 321

F
Fennel
Antipasto Vegetable Salad, 314
Lemon Chicken with Fennel and Onions, 343
Fish
Baked Salmon with Cilantro, **184**, 185
Baked Tuna and Noodles with Creamy Mushroom Sauce, 188
Fisherman's Grilled Packet, 354
Gremolata-Topped Sea Bass, 186
Halibut Asparagus Stir-Fry, **118**, 119
Italian Tuna Toss, 319
Lemon and Herb Salmon Packets, 353
Spicy Fish Stew, 57
Summer Salmon-Pasta Salad, 322
Summer Salmon Salad, 322
Three-Bean and Tuna Salad, 318
Tuna Primavera, 128
Tuna Twist Casserole, 189
Flavor boosters, 12
Freezing foods, 14
French-style dishes
Cheesy Broiled French Bread, 240
Country-French Turkey and Red Potatoes, 100
French Onion Soup, 240
Ratatouille Bean Stew, 241
Ratatouille Soup, 40
Fruit. *See also specific fruits*
Fruited Taco Salad, **326**, 327
Grilled Chicken Salad with Fruit, 309
Ham and Slaw Salad, 312
Pork Chops with Spiced Fruit Stuffing, 230
Turkey and Fruit Tossed Salad, 308
Turkey Salad with Fruit, 309
Wild-Rice Chicken Salad with Raspberry Vinaigrette, **302**, 303
Frying pans, 9

G
Garbanzo beans
Chicken-Curry-Couscous Salad, **288**, 289
Ratatouille Bean Stew, 241
Spring Vegetable Paella, 325
Turkey Tabbouleh Salad, 305
Vegetarian Chili, 61
Garlic
Garlic-Braised Beef and Potatoes, 204
garlic bread, preparing, 107
peeling, 141
Ginger
Citrus Ginger Chicken, **84**, 85
fresh, grating, 210
Ginger-Orange Beef Pita Sandwiches, 210, **211**
Ginger-Peanut-Shrimp Stir-Fry, 126
Honey Ginger Dressing, 297
Turkey-Ginger Tortellini Soup, 28
Grains. *See also* Rice
barley, protein in, 27
Beef and Bulgur Casserole, 149
Beef-Barley-Vegetable Stew, 48
bulgur, about, 149
Chicken-Curry-Couscous Salad, **288**, 289
Hearty Turkey-Barley Soup, 27
Turkey Tabbouleh Salad, 305
Green beans
Fettuccine and Chicken in Orange-Cherry Sauce, 86, **87**
as ingredient substitution, 53
Italian Beef Stew, 201
Potatoes, Green Beans and Tomatoes with Tofu, **136**, 137
Skillet Beef Stew, 70
Skillet Turkey Stew, 70
Steak and Potato Soup, 23
Three-Bean and Caper Salad, 318
Three-Bean and Tuna Salad, 318
Turkey and Sweet Potatoes, 220
Greens. *See also* Spinach
Caesar Salad with Crabmeat, 323

Caesar Salad with Lobster, 323
Caribbean Shrimp Salad, 317
Chicken and Berries Salad, **278**, 304
Chopped-Chicken Asian Salad, 290, **291**
Chopped Vegetable and Crabmeat Salad, **320**, 321
Deli Beef and Bean Tossed Salad, **282**, 283
Deli Ham and Bean Tossed Salad, 283
escarole, about, 290
Fajita Salad, 281
Fruited Taco Salad, **326**, 327
Greek Chicken Salad, 294
Grilled Chicken Salad with Fruit, 309
Italian Salami Toss, 319
Italian Tuna Toss, 319
Mediterranean Chicken Salad, **292**, 293
Raspberry Chicken Salad, 298, **299**
Roast Beef and Tomato Salad, 284
Southwestern Chicken BLT Salad, 285
Steak Caesar Salad, 280
Ten-Minute Ham Salad, 311
Thai Chicken Salad, **296**, 297
Turkey and Fruit Tossed Salad, 308
Turkey Salad with Fruit, 309
Turkey Taco Salad, **306**, 307
Tuscan Panzanella Salad, 324
Grilled dishes
Beef and Corn Kabobs, 335
Blue Cheese Turkey Burgers, 347
Cheddar-Stuffed Chicken Breasts, **340**, 341
Chicken Pizza Mexicana, 261
Fisherman's Grilled Packet, 354
Grilled Kielbasa and Cabbage, 352
Grilled Portabella and Bell-Pepper Sandwiches, **358**, 359
Grilled Teriyaki Burgers, 346
Grilled Texas Turkey Burgers, **348**, 349
Honey-Cumin Barbecue Pork Packets, 351
Lemon and Herb Salmon Packets, 353
Lemon Chicken with Fennel and Onions, 343
Mint-Smoked Lamb Chops, **332**, 338
Paella on the Grill, 342
Pesto-Artichoke Pizza, 357
Pesto Chicken Packets, **344**, 345
Pineapple-Lime Shrimp Kabobs, 355
Shrimp Kabobs, 356
Skewered Steak Dinner, 334
Spicy Southwest Chicken Kabobs, 339
Steak Caesar Salad, 280
Tex-Mex Chicken Enchilada Packets, 350
Vidalia-Topped Caesar Burgers, **336**, 337

H

Halibut
Halibut Asparagus Stir-Fry, **118**, 119
Ham
Classic Pizza, 271
Corn, Ham and Potato Scallop, 222
Creamy Bow-Ties with Ham and Vegetables, **108**, 109
Deli Ham and Bean Tossed Salad, 283
Ham and Brie Bake, 178
Ham and Slaw Salad, 312
Ham 'n Corn Chowder, 46
Honey-Dijon Ham, 223
Pork Tenderloin with Prosciutto, 116, **117**
prosciutto, about, 116
Southwest Ham 'n Cheese Pasta, 129
Ten-Minute Ham Salad, 311
Wild Rice and Ham Casserole, 159
Herbs. *See also* Basil; Cilantro
Lemon and Herb Salmon Packets, 353
Mint-Smoked Lamb Chops, **332**, 338
Mint Vinaigrette, 294
Sun-Dried Tomato, Herb and Mushroom Pizza, 274
Sun-Dried Tomato and Herb Pizza, 274
Three-Herb Chicken, 168
Hominy
Chunky Chicken Chili, 213

I

Italian-style dishes
Antipasto Vegetable Salad, 314
Baked Ravioli and Meatballs, 153
Caesar Chicken with Orzo, **78**, 79
Caesar Dressing, 280
Cheesy Italian Sausage Casserole, 150
Cheesy Lasagna Soup, 22
Cheesy Pizza Casserole, 150
Chicken Penne à la Marengo, 82
Classic Pizza, 271
Deep-Dish Spaghetti Pie, 151
Deep-Dish Turkey Pizza, 267

Italian-style dishes (*cont.*)
Double-Cheese Pepperoni Pizza, 268
Easy Cheesy Manicotti, **196**, 197
Easy Seafood Risotto, 120, **121**
Easy Turkey Lasagna, 175
Fettuccine Alfredo with Sausage, 107
Four-Cheese Pesto Pizza, 276
Italian Beef Stew, 201
Italian Chicken Linguine, 127
Italian Salami Toss, 319
Italian Sausage and Mostaccioli Soup, 34, **35**
Italian Shrimp Linguine, 127
Italian Tortellini Salad, 315
Italian Tuna Toss, 319
Italian Turkey-Rice Dinner, 219
Mostaccioli with Vodka Sauce, **130**, 131
Pesto-Artichoke Pizza, 357
Quick Lasagna, **142**, 143
Ravioli with Sausage and Peppers, **198**, 224
Sausage Pizza Pie, 270
Sausage with Fettuccine, 107
Shrimp Scampi Fettuccine, **122**, 123
Spinach-Lasagna Casserole, 145
Steak Caesar Salad, 280
Sun-Dried Tomato, Herb and Mushroom Pizza, 274
Sun-Dried Tomato and Herb Pizza, 274
Tuna Primavera, 128
Turkey-Pasta Primavera, 105
Tuscan Bean and Chicken Salad, 331
Tuscan Panzanella Salad, 324
Warm Tuscan Bean Salad, **330**, 331

J

Jicama
about, 327
Chopped-Chicken Asian Salad, 290, **291**
Chopped Vegetable and Crabmeat Salad, **320**, 321
Fruited Taco Salad, **326**, 327
Ginger-Orange Beef Pita Sandwiches, 210, **211**

L

Lamb
buying, 181
Lamb and Lentil Casserole, 181
Lamb with Sweet Peppers and Garlic Sauce, 182, **183**
Mint-Smoked Lamb Chops, **332**, 338
Moroccan Lamb and Rice, 239
trimming excess fat from, 13
Lasagna
Easy Turkey Lasagna, 175
Quick Lasagna, **142**, 143
Spinach-Lasagna Casserole, 145
Lemons
juicing, 295
Lemon and Herb Salmon Packets, 353
Lemon Chicken with Fennel and Onions, 343
Lemon Vinaigrette, 318
Lentils
Lamb and Lentil Casserole, 181
Pork and Lentil Casserole, 181
Limes
Honey-Lime Dressing, 317
Lime Cumin Vinaigrette, 327
Lime Dressing, 290, 321
Lime-Garlic Chicken with Rice, 212
Pineapple-Lime Marinade, 355
Spicy Lime Dressing, 287
Lobster
Caesar Salad with Lobster, 323

M

Mandolines, 148
Mangoes
cutting, 287
Fruited Taco Salad, **326**, 327
Marinades
Pineapple-Lime Marinade, 355
roasted-apple, about, 157
Saffron Marinade, 342
using nonmetal dish for, 335
Meat. *See also* Beef; Lamb; Pork
reducing amount, in recipes, 13
trimming excess fat from, 13
Meatballs
Baked Ravioli and Meatballs, 153
Mediterranean-style dishes
Chicken Gyro Pizza, **264**, 265
Greek Beef and Onion Stew, 51
Greek Chicken Salad, 294
Greek Orzo Salad, 328, **329**
Greek Pita Pizzas, 275
Greek Pita Pizza with Chicken, 275
Mediterranean Chicken Salad, **292**, 293
Paella on the Grill, 342
Spring Vegetable and Chicken Paella, 325
Spring Vegetable Paella, 325

Turkey Gyro Pizzas, 266
Vegetable Chicken Paella, 135
Vegetable Paella, 135
Microwave, reheating foods in, 15
Mint
Mint-Smoked Lamb Chops, **332**, 338
Mint Vinaigrette, 294
Mozzarella cheese
Antipasto Vegetable Salad, 314
Baked Ravioli and Meatballs, 153
Cheesy Broiled French Bread, 240
Cheesy Italian Sausage Casserole, 150
Cheesy Lasagna Soup, 22
Cheesy Pizza Casserole, 150
Chicken French-Bread Pizza, **262**, 263
Chicken Gyro Pizza, **264**, 265
Classic Pizza, 271
Deep-Dish Spaghetti Pie, 151
Deep-Dish Turkey Pizza, 267
Double-Cheese Pepperoni Pizza, 268
Easy Cheesy Manicotti, **196**, 197
Easy Turkey Lasagna, 175
Four-Cheese Pesto Pizza, 276
Hawaiian Pizza, **258**, 259
Mini White Pizzas, **246**, 277
Mozzarella and Pesto Strata, 191
Quick Lasagna, **142**, 143
Sausage Pizza Pie, 270
Spinach-Lasagna Casserole, 145
Sun-Dried Tomato and Herb Pizza, 274
Thai Chicken Pizzas, 254, **255**
Turkey and Tortilla Casserole, 177
Turkey Gyro Pizzas, 266
Mushrooms
Antipasto Vegetable Salad, 314
Baked Tuna and Noodles with Creamy Mushroom Sauce, 188
Beef-Barley-Vegetable Stew, 48
Beef Stroganoff, 71
Chicken-Vegetable Stroganoff, 90
Chicken with Italian Roasted Vegetables, 176
Classic Beef Stew, 50
cleaning, 359
Country-French Turkey and Red Potatoes, 100
Grilled Portabella and Bell-Pepper Sandwiches, **358**, 359
Halibut Asparagus Stir-Fry, **118**, 119
Mini White Pizzas, **246**, 277
Rich Cream of Mushroom Soup, 36
Savory Pot Roast, **206**, 207
Shrimp Kabobs, 356
Skewered Steak Dinner, 334
Spinach-Shrimp Salad with Hot Bacon Dressing, 316
Sun-Dried Tomato, Herb and Mushroom Pizza, 274
Turkey with Italian Roasted Vegetables, 176

N

Noodles
Baked Tuna and Noodles with Creamy Mushroom Sauce, 188
Beef, Carrot and Noodle Bake, 173
Beef Stroganoff, 71
Black Bean and Salsa Noodle Soup, **32**, 33
Chicken Paprika, 80, **81**
Chicken-Vegetable Stroganoff, 90
Easy Turkey Lasagna, 175
Oriental Chicken Noodle Soup, 26
Quick Lasagna, **142**, 143
Smoked Turkey Lo Mein, 102
Turkey, Carrot and Noodle Bake, **172**, 173
Nuts
almonds, toasting, 310
Chicken and Cashew Bake, 155
Fettuccine and Chicken in Orange-Cherry Sauce, 86, **87**
Glazed Turkey and Pea Pods, **68**, 101
reducing amount, in recipes, 13
walnuts, toasting, 86

O

Okra
about, 167
Baked Chicken Gumbo, **166**, 167
Shrimp Gumbo, 60
Olives
Antipasto Vegetable Salad, 314
Chicken French-Bread Pizza, **262**, 263
Chicken Gyro Pizza, **264**, 265
Chicken Penne à la Marengo, 82
Double-Cheese Pepperoni Pizza, 268
Easy Taco Dinner, 73
Fisherman's Grilled Packet, 354
Four-Cheese Pesto Pizza, 276
Greek Chicken Salad, 294
Greek Orzo Salad, 328, **329**
Greek Pita Pizzas, 275

Olives (*cont.*)
Greek Pita Pizza with Chicken, 275
Italian Chicken Linguine, 127
Italian Shrimp Linguine, 127
Mediterranean Chicken Salad, **292**, 293
Mostaccioli with Vodka Sauce, **130**, 131
Mozzarella and Pesto Strata, 191
Paella on the Grill, 342
Tuscan Panzanella Salad, 324
One-dish meals
brunch recipes, 16
casual gatherings recipes, 17
flavor boosters for, 12
freezing, 14
kid-friendly recipes, 16
making ahead, 14
packing, for potlucks or picnics, 18
potluck recipes, 17
pots and pans for, 8–11
reheating, 15
trimming fat and calories from, 13
Onions
Cheddar Strata with Onions, 190
French Onion Soup, 240
Greek Beef and Onion Stew, 51
Louisiana Oyster Gumbo, 37
Vidalia-Topped Caesar Burgers, **336**, 337
Oranges
Caesar Salad with Crabmeat, 323
Caesar Salad with Lobster, 323
Citrus Ginger Chicken, **84**, 85
Fettuccine and Chicken in Orange-Cherry Sauce, 86, **87**
Ginger-Orange Beef Pita Sandwiches, 210, **211**
Grilled Chicken Salad with Fruit, 309
Turkey Salad with Fruit, 309
Oysters
fresh, buying, 59
Louisiana Oyster Gumbo, 37
Oyster Stew, 59

P

Paprika, about, 163
Pasta. *See also* Noodles
Asparagus-Dijon-Chicken Fettuccine, 83
Baked Ravioli and Meatballs, 153
Blue Cheese Tenders, 132, **133**
Caesar Chicken with Orzo, **78**, 79
for casseroles, cooking, 161
Cheesy Italian Sausage Casserole, 150
Cheesy Lasagna Soup, 22
Cheesy Pizza Casserole, 150
Chicken-and-Pasta Stir-Fry, **88**, 89
Chicken and Vegetable Bow-Tie Soup, 25
Chicken-Curry-Couscous Salad, **288**, 289
Chicken Penne à la Marengo, 82
Cincinnati-Style Chili, **62**, 63
Country Chicken and Pasta Bake, 161
Creamy Bow-Ties with Ham and Vegetables, **108**, 109
Curried Beef Casserole, 144
Deep-Dish Spaghetti Pie, 151
Dijon-Chicken Fettuccine with Green Peas, 83
Easy Cheesy Manicotti, **196**, 197
Easy Turkey Lasagna, 175
Fettuccine Alfredo with Sausage, 107
Fettuccine and Chicken in Orange-Cherry Sauce, 86, **87**
Garden Vegetables, Chicken and Pasta Salad, **300**, 301
Ginger-Peanut-Shrimp Stir-Fry, 126
Greek Orzo Salad, 328, **329**
Honey-Garlic Shrimp and Linguine, 125
Italian Chicken Linguine, 127
Italian Sausage and Mostaccioli Soup, 34, **35**
Italian Shrimp Linguine, 127
Italian Tortellini Salad, 315
Mostaccioli with Vodka Sauce, **130**, 131
Parmesan-Shrimp Pasta Bake, 187
Penne with Beef and Sun-Dried Tomatoes, **74**, 75
Peppery Cajun Pork Pasta, 106
Quick Garden Chicken Salad, 295
Quick Lasagna, **142**, 143
Ravioli with Sausage and Peppers, **198**, 224
Sausage and Pizza Bake, 179
Sausage with Fettuccine, 107
Shrimp Scampi Fettuccine, **122**, 123
Southwest Cheese 'n Pasta, 129
Southwest Ham 'n Cheese Pasta, 129
Spinach-Lasagna Casserole, 145
Summer Salmon-Pasta Salad, 322
Szechuan Chicken and Pasta, **96**, 97

Tuna Primavera, 128
Tuna Twist Casserole, 189
Turkey and Dried Cherry Salad, 310
Turkey-Ginger Tortellini Soup, 28
Turkey-Pasta Primavera, 105
Peaches
Peach Cherry Chutney, **244**, 245
Peanut butter
African Peanut-Chicken Soup, 24
Ginger-Peanut-Shrimp Stir-Fry, 126
Thai Chicken Pizzas, 254, **255**
Peas
Caribbean Shrimp Salad, 317
Chicken and Cashew Bake, 155
Dijon-Chicken Fettuccine with Green Peas, 83
Ginger-Orange Beef Pita Sandwiches, 210, **211**
Ginger-Peanut-Shrimp Stir-Fry, 126
Glazed Turkey and Pea Pods, **68**, 101
Polynesian Pork Stir-Fry, **114**, 115
Smoked Turkey Lo Mein, 102
Smothered Buttermillk Chicken with Peas, 214
Spring Vegetable and Chicken Paella, 325
Spring Vegetable Paella, 325
Turkey and Corn Bread Stuffing Casserole, 174
Wild Rice and Chicken Cassserole, 159
Wild Rice and Ham Casserole, 159
Pepperoni
Double-Cheese Pepperoni Pizza, 268
Italian Tortellini Salad, 315
Peppers. *See* Bell peppers; Chile peppers
Pesto
Four-Cheese Pesto Pizza, 276
Mozzarella and Pesto Strata, 191
Pesto-Artichoke Pizza, 357
Pesto Chicken Packets, **344**, 345
Shrimp-Pesto Pizzas, **272**, 273
stirring into soup, 12
Pineapple
Caribbean Shrimp Salad, 317
Hawaiian Pizza, **258**, 259
Pineapple-Lime Marinade, 355
Pineapple-Lime Shrimp Kabobs, 355
Polynesian Pork Stir-Fry, **114**, 115
Pizza
Breakfast Pizza, 269
Cheeseburger Pizza, 250
Chicken, Artichoke and Red Onion Pizza, 260
Chicken French-Bread Pizza, **262**, 263
Chicken Gyro Pizza, **264**, 265
Chicken Pizza Mexicana, 261
Classic Pizza, 271
Deep-Dish Turkey Pizza, 267
Double-Cheese, Spinach and Chicken Pizza, **256**, 257
Double-Cheese Pepperoni Pizza, 268
Easy Philly Cheesesteak Pizza, **252**, 253
Four-Cheese Pesto Pizza, 276
Greek Pita Pizzas, 275
Greek Pita Pizza with Chicken, 275
Hawaiian Pizza, **258**, 259
Mini White Pizzas, **246**, 277
Pesto-Artichoke Pizza, 357
reheating, 15
Salsa Pizza with Cheese Crust, 248
Salsa Pork Pizza with Cheese Crust, 248
Sausage Pizza Pie, 270
Shrimp-Pesto Pizzas, **272**, 273
Sloppy Joe Pizza, 251
Sun-Dried Tomato, Herb and Mushroom Pizza, 274
Sun-Dried Tomato and Herb Pizza, 274
Taco Pizza, 249
Thai Chicken Pizzas, 254, **255**
Turkey Burger Pizza, 250
Turkey Gyro Pizzas, 266
Pork. *See also* Bacon; Ham; Pork sausages
Asian Pork Salad, 313
Barbecued Pork Chops, **228**, 229
Curried Pork and Veggie Stew, 225
Easy Pork Chili, 237
Honey-Barbecue-Glazed Pork Roast with Carrots and Corn, 236
Honey-Cumin Barbecue Pork Packets, 351
as ingredient substitution, 146
Peppery Cajun Pork Pasta, 106
Polynesian Pork Stir-Fry, **114**, 115
Pork and Julienne Potatoes, 112
Pork and Lentil Casserole, 181
Pork Chop Dinner wirh Rice and Veggies, 110, **111**
Pork Chops with Apple-Cherry Stuffing, 231
Pork Chops with Apple-Cranberry Stuffing, 231

Pork (*cont.*)
Pork Chops with Spiced Fruit Stuffing, 230
Porketta with Two Potatoes, 226
Pork Tenderloin with Prosciutto, 116, **117**
Pork with Squash and Onions, 113
raw, slicing, 55
Savory Barbecued Ribs, 232, **233**
Smoky-Flavored Barbecued Ribs, **234**, 235
Southwestern Pork Stew, 227
trimming excess fat from, 13
Zesty Autumn Pork Stew, **54**, 55
Pork sausages. *See also* Pepperoni
Breakfast Pizza, 269
Cheesy Italian Sausage Casserole, 150
chorizo, about, 342
Classic Pizza, 271
Easy Bean and Kielbasa Soup, 238
Fettuccine Alfredo with Sausage, 107
Grilled Kielbasa and Cabbage, 352
Italian Salami Toss, 319
Mashed Potato and Sausage Casserole, 180
New England Baked Bean Stew, 52
Paella on the Grill, 342
Ravioli with Sausage and Peppers, **198**, 224
Salsa Pork Pizza with Cheese Crust, 248
Sausage and Pizza Bake, 179
Sausage Pizza Pie, 270
Sausage with Fettuccine, 107
Potatoes. *See also* Sweet potatoes
Beef and Potatoes au Gratin, 148
Chicken and Julienne Potatoes, 112
Chicken Legs with Vegetables, 169
Chicken Stew with Potatoes, 53
Chicken with Italian Roasted Vegetables, 176
Chunky Vegetable Chowder, 47
Classic Beef Stew, 50
Corn, Ham and Potato Scallop, 222
Corn, Roast Beef and Potato Scallop, 222
Country-French Turkey and Red Potatoes, 100
Curried Pork and Veggie Stew, 225
Dill-Turkey Chowder, 217
Garlic-Braised Beef and Potatoes, 204
Garlic Shepherd's Pie, 146, **147**
Harvest Sausage and Vegetable Casserole, 221
Hearty Turkey Dinner, 218
Home-Style Potato Soup, **20**, 38
Honey-Cumin Barbecue Pork Packets, 351
Mashed Potato and Sausage Casserole, 180
Old-Fashioned Beef Stew, 202
Pork and Julienne Potatoes, 112
Porketta with Two Potatoes, 226
Potato-Cheese Soup, 38
Potatoes, Green Beans and Tomatoes with Tofu, **136**, 137
Ranch Potatoes and Chicken Casserole, 160
russet, about, 176
Savory Pot Roast, **206**, 207
Skewered Steak Dinner, 334
Skillet Beef Stew, 70
Skillet Turkey Stew, 70
Steak and Potato Soup, 23
Swiss Potato and Cheese Skillet, 134
Swiss Steak Supper, 209
Texas Tater Casserole, 141
Turkey with Italian Roasted Vegetables, 176
Vegetarian Chili, 61
Western Beef Casserole au Gratin, 152
Yukon gold, about, 169
Pots and pans, 8–11
Poultry. *See* Chicken; Turkey
Prosciutto
about, 116
Classic Pizza, 271
Pork Tenderloin with Prosciutto, 116, **117**

R

Raspberries
Chicken and Berries Salad, **278**, 304
Fruited Taco Salad, **326**, 327
Fruity Yogurt Dressing, 304
Raspberry Chicken Salad, 298, **299**
Raspberry Dressing, 298
Rice
Baked Chicken Gumbo, **166**, 167
Basil Rice Soup, 44, **45**
Beef-Taco-Rice Skillet, 72
brown, shelf life of, 110
California Chicken Bake, 154
Cheesy Turkey, Rice and Broccoli, 103
Chicken and Rice Bake, 163
Chicken Drumstick Cacciatore Casserole, 165
cooked, freezing, 43
Easy Cheesy Vegetable Soup, **42**, 43
Easy Seafood Risotto, 120, **121**

Italian Turkey-Rice Dinner, 219
Lemon and Herb Salmon Packets, 353
Lime-Garlic Chicken with Rice, 212
Maple-Glazed Turkey and Rice Casserole, 170
Moroccan Lamb and Rice, 239
Oriental Turkey and Rice, 104
Paella on the Grill, 342
Pork Chop Dinner wirh Rice and Veggies, 110, **111**
Shrimp Gumbo, 60
Spicy Fish Stew, 57
Spring Vegetable and Chicken Paella, 325
Spring Vegetable Paella, 325
Stir-Fried Beef and Broccoli, 76
Teriyaki Chicken Stir-Fry, 91
Turkey Breast with Wild Rice Stuffing, 216
Vegetable Chicken Paella, 135
Vegetable Paella, 135
Wild Rice and Beef Casserole, 140
Wild Rice and Chicken Cassserole, 159
Wild Rice and Ham Casserole, 159
Wild Rice and Turkey Casserole, 140
Wild-Rice Chicken Salad with Raspberry Vinaigrette, **302**, 303

S

Saffron
about, 325
Saffron Marinade, 342
Salad dressings
Caesar Dressing, 280
Curry Dressing, 289
Fruity Yogurt Dressing, 304
Honey Ginger Dressing, 297
Honey-Lime Dressing, 317
Lemon Vinaigrette, 318
Lime Cumin Vinaigrette, 327
Lime Dressing, 290, 321
Mint Vinaigrette, 294
Raspberry Dressing, 298
Salsa Bacon Dressing, 285
Sherry Vinaigrette, 284
Spicy Lime Dressing, 287
Toasted Sesame Dressing, 322
Salads
Antipasto Vegetable Salad, 314
Asian Pork Salad, 313
Caesar Salad with Crabmeat, 323
Caesar Salad with Lobster, 323
Caribbean Chicken and Black Bean Salad, **286**, 287
Caribbean Shrimp Salad, 317
Chicken and Berries Salad, **278**, 304
Chicken-Curry-Couscous Salad, **288**, 289
Chopped-Chicken Asian Salad, 290, **291**
Chopped Vegetable and Crabmeat Salad, **320**, 321
Deli Beef and Bean Tossed Salad, **282**, 283
Deli Ham and Bean Tossed Salad, 283
Fajita Salad, 281
flavor boosters for, 12
Fruited Taco Salad, **326**, 327
Garden Vegetables, Chicken and Pasta Salad, **300**, 301
Greek Chicken Salad, 294
Greek Orzo Salad, 328, **329**
Grilled Chicken Salad with Fruit, 309
Ham and Slaw Salad, 312
Italian Salami Toss, 319
Italian Tortellini Salad, 315
Italian Tuna Toss, 319
Mediterranean Chicken Salad, **292**, 293
Quick Garden Chicken Salad, 295
Raspberry Chicken Salad, 298, **299**
Roast Beef and Tomato Salad, 284
Southwestern Chicken BLT Salad, 285
Spinach-Shrimp Salad with Hot Bacon Dressing, 316
Spring Vegetable and Chicken Paella, 325
Spring Vegetable Paella, 325
Steak Caesar Salad, 280
Summer Salmon-Pasta Salad, 322
Summer Salmon Salad, 322
Ten-Minute Ham Salad, 311
Thai Chicken Salad, **296**, 297
Three-Bean and Caper Salad, 318
Three-Bean and Tuna Salad, 318
Turkey and Dried Cherry Salad, 310
Turkey and Fruit Tossed Salad, 308
Turkey Salad with Fruit, 309
Turkey Tabbouleh Salad, 305
Turkey Taco Salad, **306**, 307
Tuscan Bean and Chicken Salad, 331
Tuscan Panzanella Salad, 324
Warm Tuscan Bean Salad, **330**, 331
Wild-Rice Chicken Salad with Raspberry Vinaigrette, **302**, 303

Salami
Italian Salami Toss, 319
Salmon
Baked Salmon with Cilantro, **184**, 185
Lemon and Herb Salmon Packets, 353
Summer Salmon-Pasta Salad, 322
Summer Salmon Salad, 322
Sandwiches. *See also* Burgers
Ginger-Orange Beef Pita Sandwiches, 210, **211**
Grilled Kielbasa and Cabbage, 352
Grilled Portabella and Bell-Pepper Sandwiches, **358**, 359
Saucepans, 9
Sausages. *See* Pork sausages; Turkey sausages
Scallops
Shrimp and Scallops in Wine Sauce, 124
Sea bass
Gremolata-Topped Sea Bass, 186
Seafood. *See* Fish; Shellfish
Sesame seeds, toasting, 311
Shallots, about, 100
Shellfish. *See also* Shrimp
Caesar Salad with Crabmeat, 323
Caesar Salad with Lobster, 323
Chopped Vegetable and Crabmeat Salad, **320**, 321
Easy Seafood Risotto, 120, **121**
New England Clam Chowder, 58
oysters, fresh, buying, 59
Oyster Stew, 59
Shrimp and Scallops in Wine Sauce, 124
Shrimp
Caribbean Shrimp Salad, 317
deveining, 127
Ginger-Peanut-Shrimp Stir-Fry, 126
Honey-Garlic Shrimp and Linguine, 125
Italian Shrimp Linguine, 127
Paella on the Grill, 342
Parmesan-Shrimp Pasta Bake, 187
Pineapple-Lime Shrimp Kabobs, 355
Shrimp and Scallops in Wine Sauce, 124
Shrimp Gumbo, 60
Shrimp Kabobs, 356
Shrimp-Pesto Pizzas, **272**, 273
Shrimp Scampi Fettuccine, **122**, 123
Spinach-Shrimp Salad with Hot Bacon Dressing, 316
Skillet meals
Asparagus-Dijon-Chicken Fettuccine, 83
Beef Stroganoff, 71
Beef-Taco-Rice Skillet, 72
Blue Cheese Tenders, 132, **133**
Caesar Chicken with Orzo, **78**, 79
Cheesy Turkey, Rice and Broccoli, 103
Chicken and Julienne Potatoes, 112
Chicken Paprika, 80, **81**
Chicken Penne à la Marengo, 82
Chicken-Vegetable Stroganoff, 90
Citrus Ginger Chicken, **84**, 85
Country-French Turkey and Red Potatoes, 100
Creamy Bow-Ties with Ham and Vegetables, **108**, 109
Dijon-Chicken Fettuccine with Green Peas, 83
Easy Chicken Alfredo, **92**, 93
Easy Mexican Chicken and Beans, 94, **95**
Easy Seafood Risotto, 120, **121**
Easy Taco Dinner, 73
Easy Weeknight Beef-Veggie Mix, 77
Fettuccine Alfredo with Sausage, 107
Fettuccine and Chicken in Orange-Cherry Sauce, 86, **87**
flavor boosters for, 12
Honey-Garlic Shrimp and Linguine, 125
Italian Chicken Linguine, 127
Italian Shrimp Linguine, 127
Mostaccioli with Vodka Sauce, **130**, 131
Oriental Turkey and Rice, 104
pans for, 9, 10
Penne with Beef and Sun-Dried Tomatoes, **74**, 75
Peppery Cajun Pork Pasta, 106
Pork and Julienne Potatoes, 112
Pork Chop Dinner wirh Rice and Veggies, 110, **111**
Pork Tenderloin with Prosciutto, 116, **117**
Pork with Squash and Onions, 113
Potatoes, Green Beans and Tomatoes with Tofu, **136**, 137
Sausage with Fettuccine, 107
Shrimp and Scallops in Wine Sauce, 124
Shrimp Scampi Fettuccine, **122**, 123
Skillet Beef Stew, 70
Skillet Turkey Stew, 70
Southwest Cheese 'n Pasta, 129
Southwest Ham 'n Cheese Pasta, 129
Spicy Chicken Chili, 66
Swiss Potato and Cheese Skillet, 134
Szechuan Chicken and Pasta, **96**, 97

Tuna Primavera, 128
Turkey-Pasta Primavera, 105
Vegetable Chicken Paella, 135
Vegetable Paella, 135
Slow cooker meals
Barbecued Pork Chops, **228**, 229
Beef Steak Chili, 208
Cajun Pot Roast with Maque Choux, 203
Chicken Chili Verde, 215
Chunky Chicken Chili, 213
Corn, Ham and Potato Scallop, 222
Corn, Roast Beef and Potato Scallop, 222
Curried Pork and Veggie Stew, 225
Dill-Turkey Chowder, 217
Easy Bean and Kielbasa Soup, 238
Easy Pork Chili, 237
Easy Steak Chili, 237
French Onion Soup, 240
Garlic-Braised Beef and Potatoes, 204
Ginger-Orange Beef Pita Sandwiches, 210, **211**
Harvest Sausage and Vegetable Casserole, 221
Hearty Beef Chili, 200
Hearty Turkey Dinner, 218
Honey-Barbecue-Glazed Pork Roast with Carrots and Corn, 236
Honey-Dijon Ham, 223
Italian Beef Stew, 201
Italian Turkey-Rice Dinner, 219
Lime-Garlic Chicken with Rice, 212
Mexicali Round Steak, 205
Moroccan Lamb and Rice, 239
Old-Fashioned Beef Stew, 202
Peach Cherry Chutney, **244**, 245
Pork Chops with Apple-Cherry Stuffing, 231
Pork Chops with Apple-Cranberry Stuffing, 231
Pork Chops with Spiced Fruit Stuffing, 230
Porketta with Two Potatoes, 226
Ratatouille Bean Stew, 241
Ravioli with Sausage and Peppers, **198**, 224
Savory Barbecued Ribs, 232, **233**
Savory Pot Roast, **206**, 207
slow cookers for, 9
Smoky-Flavored Barbecued Ribs, **234**, 235
Smothered Buttermillk Chicken with Peas, 214
Southwestern Pork Stew, 227
Squash-and-Apple Bisque, 242, **243**
Swiss Steak Supper, 209
take-along tips, 18
Turkey and Sweet Potatoes, 220
Turkey Breast with Wild Rice Stuffing, 216
Turkey Chili Verde, 215
Soups. *See also* Chili; Stews
African Peanut-Chicken Soup, 24
Basil Rice Soup, 44, **45**
Beer and Cheese Soup, 29
Black Bean and Salsa Noodle Soup, **32**, 33
Black Bean Soup, **30**, 31
Cheesy Lasagna Soup, 22
Chicken and Vegetable Bow-Tie Soup, 25
Chunky Vegetable Chowder, 47
Cream of Broccoli Soup, 39
Cream of Cauliflower Soup, 39
Dill-Turkey Chowder, 217
Easy Bean and Kielbasa Soup, 238
Easy Cheesy Vegetable Soup, **42**, 43
flavor boosters for, 12
French Onion Soup, 240
Ham 'n Corn Chowder, 46
Hearty Tomato Soup, 41
Hearty Turkey-Barley Soup, 27
Home-Style Potato Soup, **20**, 38
Italian Sausage and Mostaccioli Soup, 34, **35**
Louisiana Oyster Gumbo, 37
Meatless Black Bean Soup, 31
New England Clam Chowder, 58
Oriental Chicken Noodle Soup, 26
Potato-Cheese Soup, 38
Ratatouille Soup, 40
Rich Cream of Mushroom Soup, 36
Shrimp Gumbo, 60
Squash-and-Apple Bisque, 242, **243**
Steak and Potato Soup, 23
Turkey-Ginger Tortellini Soup, 28
Southwestern-style dishes
Beef Steak Chili, 208
Beef-Taco-Rice Skillet, 72
Black Bean and Salsa Noodle Soup, **32**, 33
Black Bean Soup, **30**, 31
Buffalo-Chicken Chili, 64, **65**
California Chicken Bake, 154
Chicken Chili Verde, 215
Chicken Pizza Mexicana, 261
Chunky Chicken Chili, 213
Classic Chili, **62**, 63
Easy Mexican Chicken and Beans, 94, **95**
Easy Pork Chili, 237
Easy Steak Chili, 237
Easy Taco Dinner, 73

Southwestern-style dishes (*cont.*)
Fajita Salad, 281
Fruited Taco Salad, **326**, 327
Grilled Texas Turkey Burgers, **348**, 349
Hearty Beef Chili, 200
Layered Chicken–Black Bean Enchiladas, 164
Meatless Black Bean Soup, 31
Mexicali Round Steak, 205
Salsa Bacon Dressing, 285
Salsa Pizza with Cheese Crust, 248
Salsa Pork Pizza with Cheese Crust, 248
Southwest Cheese 'n Pasta, 129
Southwestern Chicken BLT Salad, 285
Southwestern Pork and Vegetable Stew, 56
Southwestern Pork Stew, 227
Southwest Ham 'n Cheese Pasta, 129
Spicy Chicken Chili, 66
Spicy Southwest Chicken Kabobs, 339
Stacked Enchilada Bake, **194**, 195
Taco Pizza, 249
Texas Tater Casserole, 141
Tex-Mex Chicken Enchilada Packets, 350
Turkey and Tortilla Casserole, 177
Turkey Chili Verde, 215
Turkey Taco Salad, **306**, 307
Vegetarian Chili, 61
Western Beef Casserole au Gratin, 152
White Chili, **66**, 67
Spinach
cooked, draining, 145
Deep-Dish Turkey Pizza, 267
Double-Cheese, Spinach and Chicken Pizza, **256**, 257
Easy Cheesy Manicotti, **196**, 197
Easy Seafood Risotto, 120, **121**
Greek Pita Pizzas, 275
Greek Pita Pizza with Chicken, 275
Spinach-Lasagna Casserole, 145
Spinach-Shrimp Salad with Hot Bacon Dressing, 316
Tuscan Bean and Chicken Salad, 331
Warm Tuscan Bean Salad, **330**, 331
Squash. *See also* Zucchini
Beef and Bulgur Casserole, 149
Caribbean Chicken and Black Bean Salad, **286**, 287
Italian Chicken Linguine, 127
Italian Shrimp Linguine, 127
Pork with Squash and Onions, 113
Skewered Steak Dinner, 334
Squash-and-Apple Bisque, 242, **243**
Summer Salmon-Pasta Salad, 322
Summer Salmon Salad, 322
Stews. *See also* Chili
Beef-Barley-Vegetable Stew, 48
Chicken Stew with Potatoes, 53
Classic Beef Stew, 50
Curried Pork and Veggie Stew, 225
Greek Beef and Onion Stew, 51
Italian Beef Stew, 201
Lamb with Sweet Peppers and Garlic Sauce, 182, **183**
New England Baked Bean Stew, 52
Old-Fashioned Beef Stew, 202
Oyster Stew, 59
Quick Beef and Vegetable Stew, 49
Ratatouille Bean Stew, 241
Shrimp Gumbo, 60
Skillet Beef Stew, 70
Skillet Turkey Stew, 70
Southwestern Pork and Vegetable Stew, 56
Southwestern Pork Stew, 227
Spicy Fish Stew, 57
Zesty Autumn Pork Stew, **54**, 55
Stir-fried meals
Chicken-and-Pasta Stir-Fry, **88**, 89
Ginger-Peanut-Shrimp Stir-Fry, 126
Glazed Turkey and Pea Pods, **68**, 101
Halibut Asparagus Stir-Fry, **118**, 119
Polynesian Pork Stir-Fry, **114**, 115
Smoked Turkey Lo Mein, 102
Stir-Fried Beef and Broccoli, 76
Teriyaki Chicken Stir-Fry, 91
Vegetable Chicken Stir-Fry, **98**, 99
woks for, 9
Stockpots, 9
Stratas
Cheddar Strata with Onions, 190
Chicken-Vegetable Strata, 162
Easy Cheese Strata, 193
Ham and Brie Bake, 178
Mozzarella and Pesto Strata, 191
Turkey and Brie Bake, 178
Vegetable Strata, 192
Strawberries
Chicken and Berries Salad, **278**, 304
Fruity Yogurt Dressing, 304

Sweet potatoes
African Peanut-Chicken Soup, 24
Polynesian Pork Stir-Fry, **114**, 115
Porketta with Two Potatoes, 226
Turkey and Sweet Potatoes, 220
Zesty Autumn Pork Stew, **54**, 55

T

Tofu
Potatoes, Green Beans and Tomatoes with Tofu, **136**, 137
Tomatoes
Beef Steak Chili, 208
Buffalo-Chicken Chili, 64, **65**
Cajun Pot Roast with Maque Choux, 203
Cheesy Lasagna Soup, 22
Chicken Drumstick Cacciatore Casserole, 165
Chicken Penne à la Marengo, 82
Chunky Chicken Chili, 213
Cincinnati-Style Chili, **62**, 63
Classic Chili, **62**, 63
Easy Pork Chili, 237
Easy Steak Chili, 237
Easy Weeknight Beef-Veggie Mix, 77
Fisherman's Grilled Packet, 354
Hearty Beef Chili, 200
Hearty Tomato Soup, 41
Penne with Beef and Sun-Dried Tomatoes, **74**, 75
Pesto-Artichoke Pizza, 357
Pesto Chicken Packets, **344**, 345
Potatoes, Green Beans and Tomatoes with Tofu, **136**, 137
Quick Garden Chicken Salad, 295
Ratatouille Bean Stew, 241
Ratatouille Soup, 40
Roast Beef and Tomato Salad, 284
seeding, 173
Shrimp Kabobs, 356
Southwestern Chicken BLT Salad, 285
Sun-Dried Tomato, Herb and Mushroom Pizza, 274
Sun-Dried Tomato and Herb Pizza, 274
Taco Pizza, 249
Turkey Tabbouleh Salad, 305
Tuscan Panzanella Salad, 324
Vegetarian Chili, 61
Tortillas
Chicken Chili Verde, 215
Easy Mexican Chicken and Beans, 94, **95**
Easy Taco Dinner, 73
Layered Chicken–Black Bean Enchiladas, 164
Stacked Enchilada Bake, **194**, 195
Tex-Mex Chicken Enchilada Packets, 350
Thai Chicken Pizzas, 254, **255**
Turkey and Tortilla Casserole, 177
Turkey Chili Verde, 215
warming, 215
Tuna
Baked Tuna and Noodles with Creamy Mushroom Sauce, 188
Italian Tuna Toss, 319
Three-Bean and Tuna Salad, 318
Tuna Primavera, 128
Tuna Twist Casserole, 189
Turkey
Blue Cheese Turkey Burgers, 347
Cheesy Turkey, Rice and Broccoli, 103
Country-French Turkey and Red Potatoes, 100
Deep-Dish Turkey Pizza, 267
Dill-Turkey Chowder, 217
Easy Turkey Lasagna, 175
Glazed Turkey and Pea Pods, **68**, 101
Grilled Texas Turkey Burgers, **348**, 349
Hearty Turkey-Barley Soup, 27
Hearty Turkey Dinner, 218
as ingredient substitution, 146
Italian Turkey-Rice Dinner, 219
Maple-Glazed Turkey and Rice Casserole, 170
Oriental Turkey and Rice, 104
Skillet Turkey Stew, 70
Smoked Turkey Lo Mein, 102
trimming excess fat from, 13
Turkey, Carrot and Noodle Bake, **172**, 173
Turkey and Brie Bake, 178
Turkey and Corn Bread Stuffing Casserole, 174
Turkey and Dried Cherry Salad, 310
Turkey and Fruit Tossed Salad, 308
Turkey and Sweet Potatoes, 220
Turkey and Tortilla Casserole, 177
Turkey Breast with Wild Rice Stuffing, 216
Turkey Burger Pizza, 250
Turkey Chili Verde, 215
Turkey Divan, 171
Turkey-Ginger Tortellini Soup, 28
Turkey Gyro Pizzas, 266
Turkey-Pasta Primavera, 105
Turkey Salad with Fruit, 309

Turkey (*cont.*)
Turkey Tabbouleh Salad, 305
Turkey Taco Salad, **306**, 307
Turkey with Italian Roasted Vegetables, 176
Wild Rice and Turkey Casserole, 140
Turkey sausages
Harvest Sausage and Vegetable Casserole, 221
Italian Sausage and Mostaccioli Soup, 34, **35**

V

Vegetables. *See also* specific vegetables
Antipasto Vegetable Salad, 314
Beef-Barley-Vegetable Stew, 48
Caesar Chicken with Orzo, **78**, 79
Chicken and Vegetable Bow-Tie Soup, 25
Chicken Legs with Vegetables, 169
Chicken-Vegetable Strata, 162
Chicken-Vegetable Stroganoff, 90
Chicken with Italian Roasted Vegetables, 176
Chopped Vegetable and Crabmeat Salad, **320**, 321
Chunky Vegetable Chowder, 47
Classic Beef Stew, 50
Country Chicken and Pasta Bake, 161
Creamy Bow-Ties with Ham and Vegetables, **108**, 109
Curried Beef Casserole, 144
Curried Pork and Veggie Stew, 225
Easy Cheesy Vegetable Soup, **42**, 43
Easy Weeknight Beef-Veggie Mix, 77
flavor boosters for, 12
frozen, thawing, 105
Garden Vegetables, Chicken and Pasta Salad, **300**, 301
Garlic Shepherd's Pie, 146, **147**
Harvest Sausage and Vegetable Casserole, 221
Hearty Turkey-Barley Soup, 27
Honey-Garlic Shrimp and Linguine, 125
Mashed Potato and Sausage Casserole, 180
Oriental Turkey and Rice, 104
Pork Chop Dinner wirh Rice and Veggies, 110, **111**
Quick Beef and Vegetable Stew, 49
Southwestern Pork and Vegetable Stew, 56
Spicy Fish Stew, 57
Spring Vegetable and Chicken Paella, 325
Spring Vegetable Paella, 325
Szechuan Chicken and Pasta, **96**, 97
Teriyaki Chicken Stir-Fry, 91
Thai Chicken Pizzas, 254, **255**
Tuna Twist Casserole, 189
Turkey-Pasta Primavera, 105
Turkey with Italian Roasted Vegetables, 176
Vegetable Chicken Paella, 135
Vegetable Chicken Stir-Fry, **98**, 99
Vegetable Paella, 135
Vegetable Strata, 192
Vinaigrettes
Lemon Vinaigrette, 318
Lime Cumin Vinaigrette, 327
Mint Vinaigrette, 294
Sherry Vinaigrette, 284

W

Walnuts
Fettuccine and Chicken in Orange-Cherry Sauce, 86, **87**
toasting, 86
Water chestnuts
Grilled Chicken Salad with Fruit, 309
Oriental Turkey and Rice, 104
Turkey Salad with Fruit, 309
Wild-Rice Chicken Salad with Raspberry Vinaigrette, **302**, 303
Wild rice
Turkey Breast with Wild Rice Stuffing, 216
Wild Rice and Beef Casserole, 140
Wild Rice and Chicken Cassserole, 159
Wild Rice and Ham Casserole, 159
Wild Rice and Turkey Casserole, 140
Wild-Rice Chicken Salad with Raspberry Vinaigrette, **302**, 303
Woks, 9
Wonton wrappers, toasting, 99

Y

Yogurt
fat-free or reduced-fat, for recipes, 13
Fruity Yogurt Dressing, 304
Grilled Chicken Salad with Fruit, 309

Raspberry Dressing, 298
Turkey Salad with Fruit, 309

Z

Zucchini
Breakfast Pizza, 269
Chicken Drumstick Cacciatore Casserole, 165
Easy Chicken Alfredo, **92**, 93
Easy Turkey Lasagna, 175
Peppery Cajun Pork Pasta, 106
Pesto Chicken Packets, **344**, 345
Ratatouille Bean Stew, 241
Ratatouille Soup, 40
Spring Vegetable and Chicken Paella, 325
Spring Vegetable Paella, 325
Summer Salmon-Pasta Salad, 322
Summer Salmon Salad, 322
Vegetarian Chili, 61